Bill DeWitt, Sr.

ALSO BY BURTON A. BOXERMAN
AND BENITA W. BOXERMAN
AND FROM MCFARLAND

George Weiss: Architect of the Golden Age Yankees (2016)

Jews and Baseball: Volume 1, Entering the American Mainstream, 1871–1948 (2007; paperback 2016)

Jews and Baseball: Volume 2, The Post-Greenberg Years, 1949–2008 (2010; paperback 2016)

Ebbets to Veeck to Busch: Eight Owners Who Shaped Baseball (2003)

Bill DeWitt, Sr.
Patriarch of a Baseball Family

BURTON A. BOXERMAN *and*
BENITA W. BOXERMAN

McFarland & Company, Inc., Publishers
Jefferson, North Carolina

Except where otherwise credited, all photos
are courtesy of the St. Louis Cardinals.

Library of Congress Cataloguing-in-Publication Data

Names: Boxerman, Burton Alan, 1933– author. | Boxerman, Benita W., author.
Title: Bill DeWitt, Sr. : patriarch of a baseball family / Burton A. Boxerman
and Benita W. Boxerman.
Description: Jefferson, North Carolina : McFarland & Company, Inc.,
Publishers, 2021. | Includes bibliographical references and index.
Identifiers: LCCN 2021033754 | ISBN 9781476672601 (paperback : acid free paper)♾
ISBN 9781476643373 (ebook)
Subjects: LCSH: DeWitt, William Orville., Sr., 1902–1982. | Baseball—
United States—History—20th century. | Major League Baseball (Organization)—
Biography. | Baseball team owners—United States—Biography. | Sports
executives—United States—Biography. | BISAC: SPORTS & RECREATION /
Baseball / History | BIOGRAPHY & AUTOBIOGRAPHY / Sports
Classification: LCC GV865.D456 B68 2021 | DDC 796.357092 [B]—dc23
LC record available at https://lccn.loc.gov/2021033754

British Library cataloguing data are available
ISBN (print) 978-1-4766-7260-1
ISBN (ebook) 978-1-4766-4337-3

© 2021 Burton A. Boxerman and Benita W. Boxerman. All rights reserved

*No part of this book may be reproduced or transmitted in any form
or by any means, electronic or mechanical, including photocopying
or recording, or by any information storage and retrieval system,
without permission in writing from the publisher.*

Front cover: Baseball executive Bill DeWitt, Sr.; team photograph
of the 1944 St. Louis Browns (both courtesy of the St. Louis Cardinals)

Printed in the United States of America

*McFarland & Company, Inc., Publishers
Box 611, Jefferson, North Carolina 28640
www.mcfarlandpub.com*

Table of Contents

Acknowledgments	vi
Foreword by Bill DeWitt III	1
Foreword by William O. DeWitt, Jr.	3
Preface	5
ONE—Growing Up in St. Louis	7
TWO—Branch Rickey's Protégé	12
THREE—Donald Barnes and the St. Louis Browns	25
FOUR—A World War and a World Series	47
FIVE—Richard Muckerman and the Post-War Years	67
SIX—An Owner at Last	89
SEVEN—A Three Ring Circus	107
EIGHT—Interregnum	116
NINE—A New Team, Another World Series	140
TEN—Elder Statesman	173
ELEVEN—The DeWitt Legacy	182
Chapter Notes	187
Bibliography	209
Index	217

Acknowledgments

We tried to make this book a true and in-depth study of a man who contributed 60 years of his life to baseball and who left a legacy of family who considered him their role model. We are grateful to many people who gave us their knowledge and time as we researched and wrote this book. Many of them are referenced in the notes and bibliography, but we would like to give special recognition to the following:

Not only did William O. DeWitt, Jr., and William O. DeWitt III endorse our proposed biography, they were generous in sharing their time as well as an extensive library of newspaper clips, pictures, and other memorabilia. They were also generous in developing a list of family and associates for us to interview, and in many cases, opened doors for us to speak with them.

Bill DeWitt, Sr.'s, daughters, Joan McKean and DeDe Lambert, provided many insights into family life in the DeWitt household. Joan was also able to share her memories about her father's final years.

Other members of the DeWitt extended family who were of great help included Bill Holekamp, Malcom (Mac) Holekamp, and Stark Holekamp.

Descendants of Browns' owners interviewed included Trent Phillips, Donald Barnes' granddaughter, and Richard Muckerman's granddaughter, Margo Muckerman Hields.

We were also able to talk with some of Bill DeWitt's notable baseball associates including Ed Stack, Whitey Herzog, and Bill Bartolomay.

We thank the librarians and archivists at the St. Louis County Library for their diligence and help. We also give Ed Wheatley, president of the St. Louis Browns Historical Society, a special thank you for his many kindnesses and we give another special thank you to Gary Kodner, who arranged the meeting that launched the creation of this book.

All of these individuals enriched this book, however, we take responsibility for any errors that remain.

Foreword
by Bill DeWitt III

My grandfather died in 1982 when I was in 8th grade. I was fortunate that I was able to spend enough time with him that I had a good sense of his personality and can recall many memories of times spent doing things with him. He was an optimistic, positive person who seemed to appreciate and truly enjoy his success in life, and he lit up when his grandkids came to visit. Whenever we left his company, he would take a $5 bill out of his pocket and say "here—take this, everybody needs a little walkin' around money" and of course we would be on our way with a smile and a warm memory of Granddaddy.

I used to snoop around his home office as a little kid and was in awe of the things he kept as mementos of his lifetime in baseball. There were the framed press pins on the wall, symbols of all the World Series and All-Star Games he attended from the early 1930s through the early 1980s. There were the old chairs made out of actual bats from golden era players on the Browns and Cardinals. And the signed pictures on the walls spoke to the connection he had to some of the most influential figures in the history of the game—Commissioner Landis, Rogers Hornsby, Branch Rickey, Stan Musial, Mickey Mantle, Pete Rose, and on and on.

I wasn't old enough to have the wisdom to push him to tell the great stories that he knew, but I did have one experience that gave me a feel for how interesting his life had been. It was probably 1980, towards the end of his time as chairman of the White Sox, and he brought me up to Comiskey Park in Chicago to catch a game as a 12-year-old. We sat up in the press box, where he made the rounds and spoke to dozens of people who passed through, all of them with something to discuss about the team, baseball in general, or an old baseball story from long ago. I remember Bill Veeck came up to me, chomping on a cigar, with his wooden leg causing a knocking sound when he walked, and rubbed my head and said something about being a chip off the old block. Then, to my utter amazement, he flicked open an ash tray that was imbedded in the side of his wooden leg and disposed of the ashes from the cigar, as if there was nothing unusual about it. On the other end of the press box during the seventh inning stretch, everybody stood, watched and smiled as Harry Caray sang the national anthem to the crowd and waved his fish net to the beat of the song, as the entire stadium sang along while looking up at him and smiling. The stadium was old and rickety, and full of dilapidated charm.

On that day in Chicago, I learned that the world of baseball was full of interesting characters who brought the history of the game to life just by being around each other and telling stories. I know my grandfather would be proud that I have made a career in baseball as he did, and maintained a love of the game while working behind the scenes and experiencing some things worthy of a few pretty good stories myself.

Bill DeWitt III, *the grandson of William O. DeWitt, Sr., grew up learning about baseball, thanks to his father and grandfather. He joined the St. Louis Cardinals in 1996 and has been president of the organization since 2008, overseeing all aspects of the business of the team and its affiliated entities.*

Foreword

by William O. DeWitt, Jr.

When Burton and Benita Boxerman approached us about their desire to write a book about my father's life in baseball, we embraced the idea wholeheartedly. My father had an extraordinary baseball career that was unusual in his era and would be difficult to replicate. He grew up in North St. Louis in a modest family and began selling peanuts and soda at the ballpark at age 14—and ended up running several MLB teams and owning two of them. How did this happen? When Browns general manager Branch Rickey needed an "office boy" to do odd jobs, he hired the young Bill DeWitt based on a great recommendation from the stadium concessionaire. They both moved over to the Cardinals soon thereafter, and my father worked his way up the organization quickly. He worked his way up to help build and oversee the Cardinals' groundbreaking farm system and became the team's treasurer. His career continued on a path that led to an association with five additional teams, serving as president and general manager for three of them. He was also the principal owner of the St. Louis Browns and the sole owner of the Cincinnati Reds. He was named Major League Baseball Executive of the Year in both the American and National Leagues—with the Browns in 1944 and the Reds in 1961. The teams he was with won eight Pennants and three World Series Championships.

Many of my earliest memories growing up revolved around baseball. I went to countless Browns games at Sportsman's Park (later named Busch Stadium) in the late '40s and early '50s, and my father's position led to some memorable moments for me. Each year when the Major League uniforms were ordered, I was included on the list. This was unusual, because back then official uniforms from the manufacturer were only available to on-field personnel. I became a batboy, but I wasn't old enough to become the primary one. But it enabled me to be on the field during batting practice, which was a lot of fun. I actually played pepper on occasion with some of the coaches and players and shagged fly balls. When Babe Ruth came to town on a tour of teams not long before he died, I had the good fortune of being the kid to meet him on the field in my Browns uniform, as he simulated a hitting tip to me in a pre-game ceremony. I was not quite seven years old, but I remember vividly meeting the great Yankee legend and treasure to this day the signed picture I have with him. Also, after Bill Veeck purchased the team from my father, my uniform was used for 3'7" Eddie Gaedel's famous pinch-hit appearance when he walked on four pitches due to his tiny strike zone. He had popped out of a giant cake between games of a doubleheader to introduce himself as the newest Brownie! As I got older, my father would bring me on scouting trips to see Yankees prospects in the '50s, and spring breaks from school were spent at Spring Training sites. Eventually, I ended up working for him in the Reds' front office in the summers, and full-time after graduating from business school in the mid–'60s. His knowledge of the game was incredible, and he included me in meetings and conversations with baseball people, both in the Reds organization and with other teams. My father's life revolved around baseball. He seemed to know everyone in the game on a first name basis; scouts and executives from other teams, minor league operators, umpires, college coaches, etc. He had experienced the game at every level of the front office, and I always felt that he appreciated the game as much as anybody, as it was truly his life's work.

My role as chairman and CEO of the Cardinals since 1996 has been a true labor of love, and my family and I—along with our investors, employees and fans—have enjoyed some amazing moments on and off the field. But for me the success comes with an added element of nostalgia because the Cardinals were the team that my father grew up with. Between his 20 years with the Cardinals and my 25 years in this role, our family has spent nearly half a century working for this great St. Louis institution.

I would like to thank Benita and Burton Boxerman for doing such a great job researching my father's life and baseball career. Although I experienced much of it firsthand, reading the book has given me additional insight and appreciation for the magnitude of his personal story and amazing baseball career.

William O. DeWitt, Jr., *the son of William O. DeWitt, Sr., grew up around baseball under his father's guidance. He has been principal owner, chairman and chief executive officer of the St. Louis Cardinals since 1996.*

Preface

While researching material for our book *George Weiss: Architect of the Golden Age Yankees,* we came across a very interesting press clipping noting that in 1954, one year after the St. Louis Browns had been sold to Baltimore, the New York Yankees hired former Browns executive and owner William O. DeWitt as assistant to general manager George Weiss. DeWitt, the paper stated, was considered an astute baseball man who would have a definite role to play with the Yankees.

The information intrigued us for two reasons. First, as lifelong residents of the St. Louis area, we had loved our city's hapless Browns but were not used to anyone associated with them being recognized as astute. Second, we hadn't realized that Bill DeWitt continued to be active in professional baseball long after he had left the Browns. Like many others, we had assumed that once the American League's "doormats" were no more, DeWitt would retire quietly from baseball, perhaps joining his brother Charlie in the insurance business.

We decided to do more research and soon discovered that although there had been a number of books written about the Browns, Bill DeWitt had not been the focus of any of them. When we further learned that his years with the Browns were only the beginning of a long and fascinating career in baseball, we decided that he definitely merited a biography.

We hope readers enjoy our biography of this man whose 60-year professional career was spent entirely in baseball. His six decades as a baseball executive contributed greatly to America's pastime.

ONE

Growing Up in St. Louis

In many ways, baseball is a game of generations. Its fan base developed as each age group passed down to the next its love and knowledge of the game. Parent and child often watched baseball together, discussing the intricacies of "America's game" and identifying the star players.

Baseball was also a generational sport on the field. Parents who had desired or achieved a career as a successful player taught their offspring how to play the game, and many sons equaled or surpassed their fathers' performance and ability. Noted father-son relations include Bobby Bonds and son Barry; Ray Boone and sons Bob, Aaron, and Bret; Ken Griffey, Sr., and son, Ken Griffey, Jr.; and George Sisler and sons Dave and Dick.

Other children grew up learning the business side of baseball. Often children of baseball's front-office management followed their fathers into high-level executive positions, although not necessarily with their parents' teams. At this time, the MacPhails (Larry, Lee, and Andy) and the DeWitts are the only three-generation families in major league baseball who have held the sports' highest executive positions.

The patriarch of the DeWitt family (and the subject of this book), William Orville (Bill) DeWitt, Sr., was an executive with many teams, including the St. Louis Cardinals, St. Louis Browns, New York Yankees, Detroit Tigers, Cincinnati Reds, and Chicago White Sox. His son, Bill DeWitt, Jr., was an owner of the Texas Rangers and is currently principal owner and managing partner of the St. Louis Cardinals; Bill Sr.'s grandson, Bill DeWitt III, is the Cardinals' president.

William O. DeWitt, Sr., was born in St. Louis just past the turn of the 20th century on August 3, 1902.[1] At that time in the city's history, St. Louis had greatly appealed to people living in the sparsely populated areas of Missouri and her neighbor states to the west. During the last quarter of the 19th century, St. Louis grew significantly in population and wealth, and by 1900 St. Louis was not only an agricultural and commercial hub, it was arguably fourth in population behind New York,

Chicago, and Philadelphia.² Four years later, in the summer of 1904, St. Louis hosted the Summer Olympic Games, giving the city the honor of being the first American city to be the site of an Olympic game.³

Possibly attracted by the opportunities a large city presented, Bill DeWitt's parents, William Joseph DeWitt, born in Kansas in 1871, and LuLu May Sowatch, born in 1878 in Conway, Iowa, were married in St. Louis on August 10, 1899.⁴ William Joseph and LuLu had two sons during the first three years of their marriage, Charles Wakefield De Witt, born on August 13, 1900, and William Orville DeWitt, born on August 3, 1902.⁵ Bill and his brother Charley, both baseball fans, grew up on the city's north side, not too far from the city's two professional ball parks, Robison Field and Sportsman's Park.⁶

The boys' father struggled to support the family, and for all but two of the 30 years he lived in St. Louis, the St. Louis City Directory listed his occupation as grocer or "meats." Records indicate that Joseph DeWitt's residence was almost always very close to his place of business, quite often upstairs from his grocery/meat market. In 1929 and 1930, the two years prior to his death, telephone listings and his death certificate listed his occupation as "Food Inspector Sanitary Section, Division of Health."⁷

Bill DeWitt was fortunate in having an older brother as a companion. They both enjoyed the usual childhood games of the era but most importantly, they were able to watch major league baseball together.⁸ When they were growing up, St. Louis was home to two major league baseball

Brothers four-year-old Charles W. DeWitt (left) and two-year-old William O. DeWitt (right) with Hero, their St. Bernard, in 1904.

teams, the American League Browns and the National League Cardinals. Although the teams played their home games in different stadiums, their fields were relatively close to each other; the Cardinals played in Robison Field, located at Vandeventer Avenue and Natural Bridge Road.[9]

St. Louis got its second major league team when the newly formed American League moved its Milwaukee team to St. Louis in 1902. The team, renamed the Browns, played their home games in Sportsman's Park, a minor league stadium located on the southeast corner of Grand and Dodier avenues. A few years later, Sportsman's Park was completely rebuilt, reopening on April 14, 1909. The Cardinals became tenants of the Browns in Sportsman's Park 11 years later.[10]

For the first two decades of the 20th century, the Cardinals finished no higher than third place, and they accomplished this feat only twice, in 1914 and again in 1917. In 1902, the new Browns team started well, finishing in second place in the eight-team league. During the following 15 years, they finished as high as fourth or fifth only three times, and most years they were at or near the bottom of the league. Some years they ended the season more than 25 games out of first place.[11]

St. Louis was also home briefly to the St. Louis Terriers, a member of the short-lived Federal League. The team was owned by two wealthy St. Louisans, brewer Otto Stifel and Phil Ball, a manufacturer of artificial ice. The Terriers existed for only two seasons, 1914 and 1915, but their home field was near enough for the DeWitt boys to also access this field via public transit.[12]

All these ball parks gave the DeWitt boys opportunities to bring home needed income for the family. In 1916, Bill DeWitt applied for and got a job in the concession department at Sportsman's Park. Not only would this allow him to bring in much-needed cash for the family, it would bring him closer to the game he really loved. Fourteen-year-old Bill was hired to sell peanuts and soda. Shortly afterwards Branch Rickey, who was both general manager and field manager, needed to replace his current assistant, who was leaving. He wanted a young man who could work the switchboard, answer the phone, and act as his secretary—in other words, he wanted a young man who could do far more than peddle peanuts.

Rickey received recommendations from three different people, all naming the same young man—Bill DeWitt. Browns groundskeeper Bill Stocksick replied that he was able to observe a number of young concessionaires from his office right across from the concession stand where the DeWitt brothers worked. Stocksick quickly endorsed Bill DeWitt, noting that despite his small stature and glasses, he seemed to be an especially hard worker.[13] Bill Nordeman, manager of the concessions department, heartily recommended DeWitt for the job. He told Rickey that DeWitt "packs the correct number of peanuts and keeps track of other things for me. Comes in after school and I know he wants to work all summer."[14]

Rickey also received a very positive recommendation from Roscoe Hillenkoetter, Rickey's current shorthand secretary who also helped Rickey with player problems. Hillenkoetter was leaving for the Naval Academy at Annapolis, but before his departure, he took time to predict that Rickey could depend on DeWitt, who was organized, enthusiastic, and a hard worker[15] Neither DeWitt nor Rickey could foresee the importance of a recommendation from Hillenkoetter, who graduated from the Naval Academy in 1919 and eventually reached the rank of Rear Admiral. In 1947, when Congress passed the National Security Act creating the Central Intelligence Agency, Hillenkoetter would serve as the agency's first director.[16]

An interview with Branch Rickey was considered an honor. Although only in his 30s, Rickey was earning a reputation as a savvy baseball executive. He had begun his baseball career as a player, but his lack of ability and refusal to play Sunday ball for religious reasons quickly ended his playing days. He was, however, achieving success and respect in the front office of the Browns.[17] For the interview, Rickey called the 14-year-old DeWitt into his office for an intensive Q&A session, subjecting the young prospect to a bombardment of questions about his family, his religious background, his schooling, and even his political preference. DeWitt thoughtfully answered all the questions and candidly told Rickey he came from a family of limited means. DeWitt impressed Rickey by his sincerity and openness, and Rickey quickly hired him. In 1916, shortly after his interview, William O. DeWitt began his front-office career in organized baseball at a salary of $3.50 a week.[18]

DeWitt worked under Branch Rickey for nearly two decades and thought of him as both a mentor and a friend. Rickey considered a formal education vital, and soon after he hired DeWitt, he insisted DeWitt better himself through education. Using his own life as an example, Rickey related that he had been a poor Ohio farm boy who had worked his way to a degree from Ohio Wesleyan by coaching the college baseball team. He also earned a law degree from the University of Michigan in similar fashion. Rickey frankly told DeWitt that he would keep his job with the Browns so long as he continued his formal education.[19]

In 1916, Philip De Catesby Ball, the former owner of the short-lived St. Louis Federal League Terriers, purchased the St. Louis Browns from its original owner, Robert Hedges.[20] One of Ball's first moves as new owner was to replace Branch Rickey as the team's manager with the experienced Fielder Jones, moving Rickey to the front office, where Ball could more easily control him. The two men's sense of morality was diametrically opposed—Ball considered Rickey sanctimonious, and Rickey could not tolerate Ball's crudeness.[21] Rickey confided to his friend and attorney George Williams that working for Ball was "the most trying and unpleasant relationship I have experienced."[22] Despite the conflict between Ball and Rickey, the 1916 season ended a string of seven consecutive losing seasons for the Browns, who completed the season with a record of 79–75. Unfortunately, it was only good enough for fifth place.[23]

The season may have ended, but the animosity between Ball and Rickey did not. Rickey began looking around for other possible baseball positions. He was disappointed after a potential spot with the Washington Senators fell through, but soon after, he was offered an even better opportunity.[24]

The ownership of St. Louis's National League team was in flux. Helene Robison Britton, who had inherited the Cardinals from her father and uncle in 1911, had had an active role in running the unprofitable team, but in early 1917, she gave up and decided to sell. A battle followed between a group led by Cardinals manager Millard Huggins and a group put together by Mrs. Britton's legal advisor, James Jones. The Jones group was made up of St. Louis' leading business owners, who had each bought stock in the team. While Huggins was out of town trying to raise capital, on March 15, 1917, Mrs. Britton sold the Cardinals and Robison Park to Jones's group for $350,000.[25]

The new owners now needed to hire an experienced baseball executive to run the team. For expert advice, Jones arranged a meeting of seven of St. Louis' leading sportswriters and asked them to recommend someone for the post. Secret ballots from all seven named Rickey as their choice. Acting on this strong recommendation, after the 1917 baseball season ended, James Jones and his associates signed Branch Rickey to a three-year contract as president of the team at $15,000 per year.[26]

Rickey accepted the Cardinals' offer and brought Bill DeWitt with him. He expanded the boy's role to personal secretary as well as general office boy.[27]

Two

Branch Rickey's Protégé

Branch Rickey's move from the St. Louis Browns to the St. Louis Cardinals in 1917 would have a profound effect not only on Rickey, but also on his protégé and personal secretary, Bill DeWitt. It would ultimately affect the future of baseball in St. Louis. Rickey would develop a farm system that turned the Cardinals into an outstanding professional baseball franchise. Bill DeWitt would remain in professional baseball for six decades and would be remembered as one of the game's shrewdest executives.[1]

On April 6, 1917, just as the 1917 baseball season was getting under way, Congress approved President Wilson's declaration of war against Germany, dragging the United States into World War I. The Cardinals did not feel the full impact of the conflict that year, going 82–70 and finishing in third place, 15 games out.[2] Rickey and DeWitt joined the Cardinals after the 1917 season was over, so they could only observe the action that year. The 1918 season, however, when many players were either drafted or enlisted, the Cardinals finished the war-shortened season in eighth place with a record of 51 wins and 78 loses.[3]

World War I personally affected Rickey greatly, however. His conservative and intensively political views impelled him to join the armed forces. Rickey's wife, Jane, objected to her husband's enlisting in the service, but to no avail. She argued that risking his life in the war with a wife and four children at home made no sense. "How could Branch consider taking the risk of leaving so large a family without a breadwinner?" she asked. But Rickey's mind was made up. With his trusted aide and personal secretary Bill DeWitt, and his chief scout Charley Barrett, he drove his wife and children back to Ohio, where they would live for the remainder of the war.[4]

The Cardinals' Board of Directors had mixed feelings about Rickey's enlistment for active duty, but they accepted his resignation, effective at the end of the 1918 season in August. It was understood that once the war ended, his contract would be renewed.[5]

Two. Branch Rickey's Protégé

Before leaving for his overseas duty, Rickey gave explicit instructions to DeWitt regarding his education. He was to study typing and shorthand at night and get a job during the day. DeWitt took Rickey's advice. During the day, he worked as an assistant cashier and stenographer at Case Threshing Machine Company. Because Rickey also persuaded DeWitt to study English, he took four years of English in one year, and when he was 17, Rickey made him the team secretary.[6]

Rickey spent four months and 16 days overseas with the 1st Gas Regiment of the Chemical Warfare Service. He was commissioned a major along with Percy Haughton, president of the Boston Braves. The Chemical Warfare Service dealt with the use of deadly gasses, a new idea in war put into use by the Germans and followed by the allies.[7] Also serving with Rickey, and commissioned Captains, were two of the major league's greatest players, Ty Cobb and Christy Mathewson.[8]

Bill DeWitt spent 1919–1936 with the St. Louis Cardinals under the supervision of his mentor, Branch Rickey.

Branch Rickey returned to baseball in November 1918, on the eve of what many historians have labeled "the Golden Age of Sports"—predicting a happy decade characterized by an increase in real income and a decrease in working hours. This decade, they claimed, would usher in prosperity for baseball.[9]

The 1919 financial conditions for the Cardinals, however, were worse than ever. The team's finances were so meager that the Cardinals were forced to hold spring training in St. Louis. They prepared for the upcoming season by working out at home, using the facilities of Washington University. In order to economize, Rickey assumed the duties of both team president and manager, saving the Cardinals $10,000 in salary.[10] Despite these economies (or maybe because of them), the 1919 season was another disaster for Rickey and the St. Louis Cardinals. In another war-shortened season, the Cardinals finished 54–83, seventh in a league with only eight teams.[11]

The Cardinals drew only 173,604 fans during the 1919 season, but Rickey was determined to develop a first-class team. Despite his lack of funds, Rickey was active at the winter meetings held in New York City that year, where he purchased third baseman Milton Stock and catcher Pickles Dillhoefer. Since Rickey refused to participate in Sunday baseball out of respect for his mother's teachings, he also acquired Johnny "Doc" Lavan, Burt Shotton, and Jimmy Austin to act as Cardinals manager on Sundays.[12]

Despite the setbacks encountered during Rickey's first two years with the Cardinals, he remained positive that he could "turn things around." Two of the Cardinals' larger investors, insurance man W. E. Bilheimer and team attorney James Jones, tried to help with a plan designed to increase attendance. The plan, eventually dubbed the St. Louis Cardinals' Knot Hole Gang, allowed anyone who bought a $25 share of stock in the Cardinals to give a season pass to a deserving underprivileged youngster. Unfortunately, those financially able to buy stock knew only boys who were able to purchase their own tickets, and they declined the offer. Rickey admitted, "We had no Knotholers at all the first half dozen games for the first season."[13]

Although Rickey liked the plan, he saw some obvious flaws. He applauded its intent, namely to allow youngsters who could not afford to attend Cardinals games the opportunity to do so at no cost, and he came up with a fix to make the Knot Hole Gang work. With the approval of the Cardinals' stockholders, the Cardinals gave the free admission tickets directly to local youth organizations to distribute to qualified boys between ten and 16. The Knothole Gang had two stipulations: (1) no boy could attend the games without parental consent; and (2) no boy could skip school to attend a game.[14]

The Knothole Gang proved to be a long-term success in unanticipated ways. By being a "Knot Holer," thousands of St. Louis youngsters who might never have attended a major league baseball game, including many who were St. Louis Browns fans, flocked to see the Cardinals play and became, over time, fans of the Cardinals instead.[15] Also, by close observation from his "insider position," many years later Bill DeWitt would know exactly how to create a similar troop known as the Brownie Brigade.

The Knothole Gang did help increase attendance, but in 1919, the St. Louis Cardinals were still suffering from lack of money. The Cardinals'

Board of Trustees turned to one of its own members, Sam Breadon, one of the group of St. Louis investors who had bought the Cardinals from Helene Britton. Like Rickey and DeWitt, Breadon began as a poor boy but in New York City, not the Midwest. With only a grade school education, Breadon took the advice of a friend to "go West," ending up in St. Louis and eventually becoming a successful automobile dealer. A huge Cardinals fan, Breadon first bought stock in the club in the mid–1910s, and when ownership began to struggle financially, he loaned the team $18,000. For the loan, Breadon received 72 percent of the team stock, with Rickey retaining the remainder. In the fall of 1919, Breadon took over from Rickey as president of the team, while Rickey became vice president and remained team manager. In return for Rickey stepping down as president, Breadon declared that the team would eagerly support Rickey's plan for a farm system, admitting that Rickey understood the mechanics of the game much better than Breadon.[16]

Before the team could fiscally support a farm system, however, Breadon first had to solve the Cardinals' financial problems. In a surprising move, the new team president sold the Cardinals' home field, League Park (formally Robison Field), for $275,000 and talked Browns owner Ball into leasing space in the Browns' Sportsman's Park, for Cardinals games to be played when the American League Browns were out of town. Ball was eager to accept Breadon's offer. At this time, the Browns were drawing more fans than the Cardinals, and confident his team was going to become a champion in the next year or so, Ball planned to use the rental fees to expand Sportsman's Park from 18,000 to 32,000 seats.[17]

Breadon used a large part of the money from the sale of League Park to pay off team debts to Mrs. Britton and to fund Rickey's farm system. "It was the most important move I ever made on the Cardinals," Breadon later said. "It gave us money to clean up our debts and something more to work with. Without it, we never could have purchased the minor-league clubs which were the beginning of our farm system."[18]

Branch Rickey conceived the idea of operating a farm system to be based on his own "Bible" of statistics and player notes, and on farm teams at several skill levels. The Cardinals would sign promising young players they would then assign to appropriate minor league clubs the Cardinals owned or to teams with which they had working agreements for first rights to draft or sell these players. Youngsters in the minors worked to grow skills, hoping for eventual positions with the Cardinals. Since the Cardinals owned the teams, they did not have to get into bidding wars with other and perhaps richer clubs.[19]

In addition to financing a farm system, Rickey and Breadon had to overcome one other obstacle—Commissioner Kenesaw Mountain Landis. Landis had always intensely opposed a farm system in baseball, disliking the concept of using the minor leagues merely to supply talent for the major leagues. The minor leagues, Landis argued, should act as independent businesses, and he insisted that minor league players not get stuck in the minor league systems of talent-rich organizations.[20] The Cardinals prevailed, however, allowing Breadon to use stadium sale proceeds to purchase the Cardinals' first farm teams—Fort Smith, Arkansas, Houston, and Syracuse.[21]

Charley Barrett remained the Cardinals' chief scout as Breadon was financially able to fund Rickey's farm system. Rickey, no longer having to carry out the duties of president of the team, had a free hand to concentrate fully on baseball operations. As the Cardinals' farm system quickly began to expand, Rickey named Bill DeWitt "de facto farm director," continuing to increase the responsibilities of his 19-year-old protégée.[22]

According to Barrett, Bill DeWitt was the young guy around the office, relied on to contribute and "do a lot of stuff." DeWitt never complained about his duties nor the requests, sometimes demands, from Branch Rickey. He would be thankful for what Rickey taught him and told anyone he encountered, "I think I knew more about Branch Rickey than anyone. I used to sleep at his house at night. I lunched there. I ate dinner at his house. And I knew him better than anybody during that twenty-year period."[23]

During the first half of the 1920s, neither St. Louis major league baseball team was outstanding. The Browns, without Branch Rickey, but with his star recruit George Sisler on the roster, posted losing records in 1920 and 1923. Even when Sisler became player-manager in 1924, the Browns' record was still below .500. In 1921, the team finished third with a winning mark of 81–73, but still 17½ games out of first place. In 1922, the Browns made a real run at the pennant, leading the league in July and the beginning of August, thanks in large part to Sisler's .402 batting average. But the Yankees overtook them, and the Browns were unable to catch up, finishing in second place, just one game out.[24]

Despite the stimulus of a new owner and a new method for building the team's roster, the Cardinals, too, posted a losing season in 1920, but finished third the next two years, with Rogers Hornsby winning the Triple Crown in 1922. The following two years, 1923 and 1924, were disappointing with the Cardinals having losing records and fifth- and sixth-place finishes, respectively.[25]

The years from 1925–1936 were among the most significant in the life and baseball career of the young Bill DeWitt. During the 1925 season, Sam Breadon fired Rickey as his field manager and replaced

Two. Branch Rickey's Protégé

him with Cardinals' star second baseman, Rogers Hornsby. He retained Rickey as vice president, asking him to concentrate on player development. A maturing Bill DeWitt, who was acquiring more and more executive experience, spent much time with his mentor Rickey, observing and learning about player development.[26]

Bill DeWitt continued to answer directly to Branch Rickey. Rickey was euphoric about DeWitt's work ethic and his willingness to increase his formal education. From 1925–1928, at Rickey's urging, DeWitt completed his undergraduate work at night, while carrying out his duties as one of the Cardinals' six-person administration. He attended St. Louis University's School of Finance & Commerce, finishing his undergraduate work at Washington University the following year. Following his mentor's example, in 1928 DeWitt enrolled in St. Louis University's law school for three years. DeWitt did not receive a law degree, but he passed the Missouri bar in 1931.[27]

Hall of Famer Rogers Hornsby spent 12 years with the Cardinals (1915–1926). He was a player-manager the final two years, but his on- and off-the-field antics were a distraction to the entire team.

Although several years older than most of his classmates, he seemed to be popular with them, as they elected him president of the Student Governing Body during his final year in law school. He was also respected by his professors. Even though DeWitt was not Catholic, the faculty selected him for Alpha Sigma Nu, a Jesuit honor group based on scholastic and school activity.[28]

Rickey was not the only Cardinals executive to recognize Bill DeWitt's capabilities. Before the baseball season opened in 1926, Sam Breadon appointed the 23-year-old DeWitt treasurer of the St. Louis Cardinals, increasing his responsibilities and his authority.[29] Because of his diligence and his ability to work well with people much older than he, DeWitt was slowly moving up the baseball executive ladder. From office boy, assistant team secretary, assistant farm director, and now team treasurer, DeWitt was gaining the respect and admiration of his superiors.

If 1926 was a good year for Bill DeWitt, it was a banner year for the St. Louis Cardinals. After more than 40 years, the team won its first pennant. The Cardinals had finished the 1925 season in fourth place due in large part to player-manager Hornsby, who won his second Triple Crown and was named the National League's MVP.[30] In 1926, Hornsby had an "off-year" offensively, hitting only .317 with 11 home runs, but the Cardinals finished the season with an 89–66 record, nosing out the second-place Cincinnati Reds by two games to face the New York Yankees in the 1926 World Series.[31] At the peak of its power, the Yankees' starting lineup was menacingly known as "Murderers' Row."

With no earlier model to guide him, the job of preparing all the physical details to host World Series games fell to the team's new treasurer. DeWitt had to plan for large crowds of Cardinals and Yankees fans, as well as additional local and national press and their specialized equipment, and he needed to engage experienced staffs to oversee concessions, ushering, security, and housekeeping.

DeWitt found that the most demanding part of the job involved the World Series tickets. He had to order them, oversee their distribution, and ensure that they reached the proper individuals and organizations. An insight into his personality is a letter written after the Series, thanking the firm who supplied the tickets and emphasizing that the tickets were "well-protected and obviated any successful attempt at counterfeiting."[32]

Despite their opponent's reputation for dominating offense, the Cardinals won the 1926 World Series, four games to three. The Yankees won the opening game of the World Series, 2–1, with Herb Pennock pitching a complete game. In Game Two, the Cardinals rebounded, defeating the Yankees, 6–2, as Grover Cleveland Alexander pitched a complete game. In Game Three, the Cardinals took the Series lead with Jesse Haines shutting out the Yankees, 4–0. The Yankees evened the Series by winning the fourth game, 10–5, with Babe Ruth hitting a home run and Waite Hoyt pitching a complete game. The Yankees took the lead in the Series by winning Game Five, 3–2, in a pitchers' duel between Cardinals hurler Bill Sherdel and the Yankees' Pennock.

Two. Branch Rickey's Protégé 19

The Series moved to Yankee Stadium for Game Six; the Yankees needed only one more win to capture the World Series. However, Grover Cleveland Alexander recorded a crucial victory in a rout over the Yanks, 10–2. In the deciding game, Hornsby called once more on Alexander. Although he had pitched a complete game the day before, he came to the mound in the seventh inning in relief of Jesse Haines to save the Cardinals' 3–2 lead. With the bases loaded, Alexander struck out Tony Lazzeri and then finished the game, holding the Yankees hitless for two and a third innings.[33] The game ended on a dramatic note when Babe Ruth, in the bottom of the ninth, walked with two away but was caught trying to steal second. On October 10, 1926, 38,093 unbelieving fans in Yankee Stadium watched the St. Louis Cardinals defeat the New York Yankees to win the World Series.[34]

Credit, of course, must be given to the Cardinals players who outperformed their opponents to win the Series, but the growing farm system contributed greatly to the victories on the field. Under Rickey's direction, and with counsel from scout Charlie Barrett, the Cardinals strategically acquired controlling interest in minor league teams. The first acquisition was a Class C team in Fort Smith, Texas. Other franchises at other levels soon followed—the Class D Austin Senators, the Class A Houston Buffaloes, and the Class AA Syracuse Stars. DeWitt, along with his other duties, became the de facto director[35] of the new and extensive Cardinals farm system.[36]

The Cardinals' farm system was successful because of Rickey's personal notebook, noting expansive lists of relationships and contacts, Charlie Barrett's scouting talent, and Bill DeWitt's ability to carry out Rickey's vision. The young stars developed by this system all played major roles in the Cardinals' success. Many participated in seasons from 1926 to 1934 that took the team to five World Series. The roster of outstanding young players included Jim Bottomley, George Toporcer, Lester Bell, Chick Hafey, Taylor Douthit, Ray Blades, Wattie Holm, Heine Mueller, Tommy Thevonow, Flint Rhem and Eddie Dyer. This farm system, originated by Rickey, DeWitt, and Barrett with modifications, would extend into the 21st century.

From 1926–1934, DeWitt capably handled his responsibilities as treasurer and his duties with the farm system. During these years, the Cardinals, under a variety of field managers, represented the National League in four more World Series: 1928, 1930, 1931 and 1934, losing to the Yankees and the Philadelphia Athletics in 1928 and 1930 and defeating Philadelphia and Detroit in 1931 and 1934, respectively.

The colorful Cardinals of 1934 quickly became known as the "Gas House Gang" and provided Bill DeWitt with a project that would allow him to use skills outside the usual duties of team treasurer. Although some claim that the team's argumentative shortstop, Leo "The Lip" Durocher, came up with the name, its actual origin remains controversial.[37] There was a New York street gang during the late-19th century that actually lived in the Gashouse District, an area with a foul smell, inhabited by drunks and "rowdies."

According to *New York World Telegraph* sportswriter Joe Williams, teams who came to New York to play the Yankees generally had no extra uniforms, and even when cleaned, they were spotted and looked unprofessional. Williams described the players as "slobs who acted like juveniles, used improper English when speaking to people, were never clean shaven and chewed tobacco and spit all over." Although Williams insisted that the Cardinals players were interlopers who crossed the railroad district for a game of baseball with the "nice kids," he admitted that the Cardinals had great ability, and he was fascinated with this "St. Louis Gas House Gang."[38]

One of the most prominent members of the Gas House Gang was Jay Hanna "Dizzy" Dean (also known as Jerome Herman Dean), who was a major factor in the Cardinals winning the 1934 World Series. Considered by many the leader of the Gas House Gang, Dean won 30 games while losing only seven, leading the National League in victories and becoming the last National League pitcher to accomplish that feat.[39]

Dean had joined the Cardinals in 1930. In the final game of that season, he pitched a three-hit game against Pittsburgh. However, he spent the entire 1931 season at Houston because of his undisciplined behavior. His brother Paul joined the club in 1934, brought up from the farm team in Columbus. The colorful Cardinals in the 1934 World Series included James "Ripper" Collins at first base, Frank Frisch, the playing manager at second base, Leo "Lippy" Durocher at shortstop, and Pepper Martin at third base. The outfield consisted of Ernie Orsatti and Chuck Fullis, alternating center fielders, Jack Rothrock in right field, and Joseph "Ducky" Medwick in left. The catching was handled by Bill DeLancey. In addition to the Dean brothers, the pitching staff consisted of three southpaws, Bill Hallahan, Bill Walker, and Jim Mooney, along with two right-handers, Jesse Haines and Tex Carleton.[40]

In the 1934 World Series, the Cardinals defeated the Detroit Tigers in seven games, the final game an 11–0 rout. Dizzy and Paul Dean combined for all four of the Cardinals' wins, and three Cardinals, Ripper Collins, Pepper Martin, and Joe Medwick, each had 11 hits in the seven games.[41]

Although Dizzy Dean played a major role in the Cardinals winning the National League pennant and the World Series in 1934, he caused

Two. Branch Rickey's Protégé

the Cardinals' front office many a sleepless night. He also made "good copy" for the press, as he was known to exaggerate, distort, and fabricate the news. Asked by J. Roy Stockton why his birthplace and birthdate seemed to change each time he talked to reporters, Dean responded in typical fashion:

> "They got good guys writin' for the papers over here [in Brooklyn]. I like Tommy Holmes and Bill McCullough and that McGowan. They says nice things about me and I'm nice to them.
>
> "I give 'em each a scoop last time we're here. It's funny, but their bosses all comes up with the same idea the same day. Told 'em to get a piece about old Diz. Well, Tommy come first and wanted to know where I was born, and I told him Lucas, Arkansas, January 16, 1911. Then it wasn't two minutes after he leaves that McCullough comes along, and doggone if he don't want the same piece. Now, I wasn't going to have their bosses bawl 'em out for both gettin' the same story, so I told Mack I was born at Bond, Mississippi that's where my wife comes from and I pick February 22, which is giving George Washington a break....
>
> "McGowan wanted the same story, but I give him a break, too, and says Holdenville, Oklahoma, August 22...."
>
> "But, Dizzy, which is your official birthday?"* I asked.
>
> "I'll swear I'm mixed up myself now," was the reply. "I always thought it was January 16 at Holdenville, but, do you know, my dad stood up in Branch

Jay Hanna "Dizzy" Dean pitched for the Cardinals from 1930 through 1937, and Rickey assigned DeWitt the unenviable task of keeping the colorful Dean in line.

Branch Rickey (left) gives some instructions to Johnny Leonard "Pepper" Martin, who, along with Dizzy Dean, went on to become one of the most outspoken members of the Cardinals' "Gashouse Gang."

> Rickey's office and said it was Lucas, Arkansas, August 22. Can you imagine that? I told him if anybody ought to know, it was me. I was the one bein' borned, for pity's sake. But I believe I'll keep 'em all. I got lots of friends at all three places and it kinda makes my wife feel good to say it's Bond, Mississippi; and maybe I'll add Bradenton, Florida, before I get through, especially if they changes the name to Deanville, like they said. Four birthdays shouldn't ought to be too many for me, do you think?"[42]

In 1932, the Cardinals hired Eugene Karst as major league baseball's first publicity man, whose original function was to supply the press with information about the team's expanding farm system. He was now given an additional job—clarify for the press Dizzy Dean's numerous conflicting declarations. In addition, Rickey assigned Bill DeWitt the task of handling Dean's many commercial off-field undertakings. Considered a celebrity, Dean's status resulted in many lucrative product endorsements.[43]

DeWitt served as Dizzy Dean's agent for three years while Dean was busy putting his name everywhere, on kites, pants, baseball uniforms, and sweatshirts. In addition, thanks to DeWitt, the Cardinals' pitching

Two. Branch Rickey's Protégé

Dizzy Dean and his brother "Daffy" were not only pitching aces for the Cardinals, they also could be seen in the movies. St. Louis Cardinals treasurer Bill DeWitt (far right) watches as Sam Sax of Warner Brothers prepares a picture of the Deans.

phenom endorsed a harmonica, cereal, and baseball hats. He did radio commercials, made appearances in vaudeville, and even appeared in a movie short.[44]

The relationship between Dean and DeWitt worked to the advantage of both, but it took a decision by Commissioner Landis and a concession by DeWitt to reach a final agreement. From 1934–1936, while Dean's salary as a pitcher came to a little more than $21,000, his non-baseball income was approximately $70,000. DeWitt understood that he was to receive one-third of the outside income earned through 1934, and then DeWitt's commission would be reduced to a more reasonable 10 percent. Dean believed that the agent's share of his income should be 10 percent throughout the entire length of the agreement and appealed to Landis. The Commissioner agreed with Dean and ordered DeWitt's percentage slashed to 10 percent for the entire length of the agreement. After giving the matter some thought, DeWitt sued Dean for $6,989, the exact amount he said Dizzy owed him for obtaining commercial contracts for Dean through 1935. The case was not officially decided until August 1939, when the two men reached a very friendly out-of-court cash settlement and DeWitt released Dean "from all obligations." Dean was traded to the Chicago Cubs after the 1936 season. Ironically, 1936 would also mark the departure of Bill DeWitt as an employee of the St. Louis Cardinals. DeWitt's move, however, would be much shorter than Dizzy's. In 1936, Bill DeWitt would be employed by the St. Louis Browns.[45]

THREE

Donald Barnes and the St. Louis Browns

The years 1936 and 1937 were among the most significant in Bill DeWitt's life to date, filled with both challenges and great opportunities. In his personal life, Bill DeWitt was in a serious relationship—serious enough that he purportedly had already bought a $1,500 engagement ring.[1] On March 21, 1936, Bill DeWitt married Margaret Holekamp, an acclaimed St. Louis horsewoman.[2] After their marriage, Margaret dropped her interest in horses, replacing it with an interest in baseball. She also traveled with her husband much of the time, including spring training.[3]

Margaret Holekamp was born into a very prominent St. Louis family who could trace their German roots at least as far back as the mid–19th century. The family's patriarch, Robert Augustus Holekamp, Margaret's paternal grandfather, was the son of a Lutheran minister who came to the United States in 1870 and settled in St. Louis. In 1879, he and James Gray established the firm Gray & Holekamp, a wholesale manufacturer and distributor of sashes and doors. The company ultimately became the largest dealer in St. Louis. In 1885, Holekamp bought Gray's ownership interest, and in December of that year he sold the company to Charles H. Huttig for $40,000.[4]

Holekamp became involved in numerous enterprises in St. Louis, and in 1908 he co-founded the Holekamp Lumber Company in Webster Groves with his four sons. In addition to the wholesale and retail sale of lumber and hardware, the firm was active in real estate development. Holekamp and his sons established many of the subdivisions and built many of the homes in Webster Groves, Kirkwood, and surrounding suburbs in southwestern St. Louis County. Eventually Holekamp Lumber expanded into an operation of six lumberyards; the company remained in business until the mid–1980s.[5] Holekamp died in 1922 after a brief illness and heart trouble.[6]

In addition to the lumber business, the Holekamp family was active with horses. Each of Robert August Holekamp's sons had his own stables, and Fred Holekamp, one of Robert August's sons and Margaret's father, owned one of the largest stables of saddle-bred horses west of the Mississippi River. Margaret, like her father and uncles, loved to ride and show the horses. She was a champion rider and belonged to several riding groups.[7] When the Great Depression hit the country, the breeding of horses became rare, and many horses were sold for dog food. Margaret's uncle Richard bought his niece her favorite horse in order to save it.[8]

Just a few weeks after his wedding, Bill DeWitt was back at work with Branch Rickey, touring the Cardinals' farm clubs. On April 1, Bill, his wife Margaret and Rickey left Bradenton, Florida, and headed to Columbus, Georgia, to look over a farm tryout camp. DeWitt was driving in a blinding rainstorm when, attempting to avoid a truck, he lost control of his car and hit the truck. Rickey was taken to a hospital in Columbus with severe lacerations about the head, neck, and face. He also had widespread bruises of his right shoulder and back. Fortunately, there were no fractures or internal injuries. DeWitt suffered superficial injuries which were addressed at the hospital, while Margaret escaped with scratches over both shins. Rickey remained hospitalized for several days under DeWitt's supervision. He recovered quickly, and there was no apparent long-term effect on Bill DeWitt or his job.[9] DeWitt,

On March 21, 1936, Bill DeWitt married Margaret Holecamp, a socially prominent St. Louis horsewoman whose best friend and closest riding companion was Anita Barnes, Donald Barnes's daughter.

Three. Donald Barnes and the St. Louis Browns

however, was about to experience even more dramatic changes in his professional life.

The chain of events had begun in 1933 with the death of Browns owner Philip Ball. After Ball died, no one came forward to buy the St. Louis Browns. The team reverted to Ball's estate and was directed by the three executors—Louis B. Van Weise, who became the president of the team, Lew C. McEvoy and Walter Fritsch. It was estimated that Ball had lost more than $300,000 during the 18 years he owned the team.[10]

Manager Rogers Hornsby informed his new bosses during spring training in 1934 that "If you gentlemen stick with me, and listen to me, we'll carry this club through to success. We've got to do this in respect to Mr. Ball's memory." But the team had little success that year.[11] The Browns continued falling steeply despite the estate's attempts to generate income by selling ball players, including star pitcher Bobo Newsom, who went to the Senators, and second baseman Oscar Melillo, dealt to the Red Sox.[12]

The 1935 season was another financial disaster for the St. Louis Browns. Team president Van Weise contacted Branch Rickey and asked him to help locate a buyer for the Browns. Rickey immediately delegated this task to his protégé, Bill DeWitt.[13] Fortunately for Van Weise (and for Rickey), DeWitt was just the person to handle the job.

One of Margaret DeWitt's closest friends was Anita Barnes, a former classmate at Nerinx Hall High School. The two had much in common, including a love of horses. Margaret attended Anita's wedding, and Anita, in turn, was invited to Margaret's and Bill's wedding. As a result of their friendship, the girls' parents also became close friends, and all often socialized together.[14]

Anita's father, Donald Barnes, was president of the American Investment Company, a small-loan firm listed on the New York Stock Exchange. Barnes' company was an innovative firm which specialized in financing installment payments on automobiles.[15] He began his business venture, the Auto Security Company, in Springfield, Illinois, in 1917. In 1927, Barnes incorporated, moving his base of operations to St. Louis. From an original business investment of $25,000, which he borrowed from a friend, his company became a $250 million enterprise.[16]

One evening when Bill and Margaret had dinner with the Barneses, the conversation turned to baseball. DeWitt mentioned the Browns' situation and Barnes interrupted him, indicating that he had always had a desire to "get into baseball." "It floored me," said DeWitt, "because I knew him only as a fan of the game. It had never occurred to me that he might want to get in."[17] DeWitt was surprised and delighted to hear of Barnes' interest in purchasing the Browns, especially since Barnes had never been a devoted fan or especially knowledgeable about baseball. When Barnes insisted that a major part of the agreement included DeWitt's joining the team as general manager, he was elated.[18]

The total price for the Browns, including their small farm system, was $325,000, and Barnes had a method for raising the money. He proposed that the public own the team, telling DeWitt, "That's the way to build up interest."[19] With DeWitt's agreement, Barnes applied for and received clearance from the Missouri Securities Commission to sell stock to St. Louisans at $5 a share. Barnes met with many executives of the city's brokerage houses, convincing them that purchasing the Browns stock was a "civic" act. These investment professionals raised $100,000. Barnes personally contributed $50,000; DeWitt put up $25,000; one of Barnes' friends invested $50,000; and International Shoe Company also made a large investment. The American League loaned the team $50,000. During most of 1936, Barnes and DeWitt worked diligently and managed to raise a total of $375,000, or $50,000 more than the price of the team, using the excess as working capital.[20] Nearly one-third of the total amount came from the sale of stock to the public.[21] In addition to the large donors who helped purchase the St. Louis Browns from the Ball Estate, 900 small investors, who paid $5.00 a share, were now part-owners of the team. The Browns would lease Sportsman's Park from the Ball estate, which retained ownership.[22]

In 1936, Donald L. Barnes, president of the American Investment Company, purchased the St. Louis Browns from the Phil Ball estate for $325,000. Barnes was the president of the team, and Bill DeWitt, Sr., became general manager.

The issue of night baseball still had to be settled before Donald Barnes and his syndicate would finalize ownership of the Browns. The first night game in the major leagues had been played in Cincinnati in 1935; it was a definite success financially, but the American League had banned night games. Barnes' syndicate required that this ban on night games be lifted, and in order not to negate the deal, the American League honored that request. The Cardinals, who were also using Sportsman's Park and would also benefit financially by increased attendance at Browns games, supported Barnes and agreed to work with the Browns to finance the installation of lights at Sportsman's Park.[23] Through this agreement, the Browns became the first American League team with the right to install lights in its ballpark. The two St. Louis major league teams began to work on a schedule which would include a limited number of night games and would work for both teams.[24] The Browns would not play their first night game at Sportsman's Park until the 1940 season.[25]

In November 1936, Donald Barnes became the president of the St. Louis Browns, and William O. DeWitt was named vice president and general manager. In his final year with the Cardinals, he was not only able to handle the day-to-day bill paying and gate receipts for his current team but also for the Browns, the team he was joining.[26] Nineteen thirty-six ended with another notable event for the DeWitts. On December 26, Bill and Margaret became parents of Joan Margaret DeWitt. Donald Barnes was her godfather.[27]

For his work in helping find a buyer for the St. Louis Browns, Branch Rickey received a commission of $25,000.[28] Branch Rickey received a prestigious award—*The Sporting News* named Rickey one of six outstanding figures in major and minor baseball during 1936, primarily because of the advancement of three of his executives to high positions: George Trautman to president of the American Association, Warren Giles to vice president and general manager of the Cincinnati Reds, and Bill DeWitt to vice president and general manager of the Browns.[29]

Even as the deal between Barnes and DeWitt was being finalized, DeWitt began to assess the problems that he and Barnes faced realistically. Two major problems were finding the best manager for the Browns and dealing with the current one, the man who had been fired as Cardinals manager for insubordination and gambling almost 10 years previously, Rogers Hornsby.

His history as manager of the St. Louis Browns was far from outstanding. Hornsby had been hired by the Browns in 1933, the year Ball died. He was the third Browns manager that year, and the team finished in the basement, 43½ games behind the pennant-winning Washington Senators.[30]

The Browns had little success under Hornsby in 1934, 1935, and

1936. He managed to finish the 1934 season in sixth place, but still 30 games out of first. In both 1935 and 1936, the Browns finished seventh. Attendance figures were horrendous. The Browns went 57–95 in 1936, 44½ games behind the pennant-winning New York Yankees. For the entire year, the Browns' attendance was only 93,000 fans, fewer than any other American League team.[31] Because spring training was coming up quickly, and despite his lack of success, Barnes and DeWitt retained Hornsby as field manager for 1937. Contract terms included a raise in salary in exchange for rights to 25 percent of profits based on stock Hornsby had purchased with gambling winnings.[32] The three of them began to make plans for the 1937 season.

Of course, finding the right manager was just one of DeWitt's challenges. Upgrading the player roster long-term was his primary mission, but his immediate problem was overhauling the roster for 1937. His objectives were sound: hiring scouts, building up the farm system, and acquiring some major league-quality players from other teams. Unfortunately, a lack of financial resources made the achievement of these goals almost impossible.[33]

DeWitt, like his mentor, Branch Rickey, began by developing a farm system for the Browns.[34] One of the first items on DeWitt's farm system agenda was dealing with the Texas League team, the San Antonio Missions, the only team the Browns actually owned at that time. He helped resolve the team management's struggles by sending the current business manager, who functioned as GM, to the minor league convention to broaden his understanding of the job. DeWitt next brought in the former head of the Florida State League, Ed Gilliland, as an executive assistant and vice president of the club.[35]

The current lack of a large farm system hampered DeWitt's ability to tender young players for trade or sale, but those who knew him expected DeWitt to "arrange working agreements" with other minor league teams, offering "reasonable" cash for players.[36] In less than ten days, DeWitt had taken "first steps" in building the farm system by hammering out such working agreements or "first call rights" with Class D Siloam Springs (AR), the Terre Haute club in the recently reorganized Three I League, and Des Moines of the Western League.[37]

Just as he had done for San Antonio, DeWitt continued building management for minor league clubs which had working agreements with the "big" club. At the same time DeWitt was scouting farm teams, he was adding professional scouts, including former top Cardinals scout Jack Fournier, who was hired as a possible manager and a scout.[38] J. Roy Stockton, sports editor for the *St. Louis Post-Dispatch*, wholeheartedly agreed with DeWitt's techniques. "What DeWitt is doing," wrote

Stockton, "is the only way the Browns can hope to reach their objective and it is encouraging to see the club building up its player-finding organization."[39]

DeWitt also tackled the issue of trying to increase fan interest and support with a little marketing. In St. Louis, the Browns sponsored a contest to see if fans wanted to change the team's name. Passes were offered to those who submitted the best letters arguing either for or against a name change. A panel of sportswriters and broadcasters selected several writers, choosing one to receive a pass for the 1937 season. The fans opposed changing the name by a 4-to-1 margin.[40]

Other schemes to increase attendance included a celebration on July 15, 1937, honoring the 1922 Browns, a team which finished only one game out of first place, fifteen years earlier. Barnes and DeWitt invited members of the 1922 Browns to come back to St. Louis, affording them opportunity not only to visit with the fans but to reminisce with each other. During the stay in St. Louis, players visited the graves of former Browns.[41]

DeWitt was very much aware that he was at a disadvantage financially in trading for players, although he still managed to snare a few good ones for the 1937 season via trades and independent signings.[42] For example, from the Seattle club he obtained Louis Koupal, the most effective pitcher in the Pacific Coast League. For the Browns, Koupal's record was 4–9 in 1937.[43] DeWitt also acquired pitcher Oral Hildebrand from the Cleveland Indians. He had pitched six years for the Tribe and wore a Brownie uniform in 1937 and 1938, then finished his major league career after winning 11 games for the New York Yankees in 1939 and 1940.[44]

The Browns hoped that their 1937 spring training site, San Antonio, a location chosen to save money, would encourage a "wealth of young player talent" to try out. They announced that the Browns would sign the "most promising" players for the Missions.[45]

Although DeWitt was doing his best to add strength to his roster, by mid–July it was obvious that the Browns were foundering and that Hornsby, their manager, was a major part of the problem. Despite his promises, Hornsby was again "playing the horses." Although he swore that he was no longer gambling, Pinkerton agents, who were tapping his telephone, presented wiretaps which proved he had been placing heavy bets on horses, even using clubhouse boys as runners while games were being played.[46] In July 1937, DeWitt confronted Hornsby on the gambling issue. The "Rajah" admitted that he had been playing the horses again, and DeWitt informed him that he "was through."[47]

Hornsby continued to claim that he still had two years remaining

Barnes (left) and DeWitt (right) inform Rogers Hornsby that he has been reappointed to a second two-year contract as Browns manager. Hornsby and DeWitt were certainly not strangers, as they had been together a decade earlier on the Cardinals.

on his contract. He eventually reached a settlement with the Browns, stating, "I am leaving my connection with the Browns without any hard feelings and with every good wish for their success. While my contract did not forbid my betting on horses, both Mr. Barnes and Mr. DeWitt have objected to my doing so, but these differences have not entered into the question of my playing ability."[48]

A year later, Hornsby destroyed his story about no hard feelings. Of course, Rogers Hornsby alleged that general managers "without playing experience were especially at fault for 'interference' with playing field pilots." He further maintained that DeWitt had interfered with his running the Browns and that the resultant feud with DeWitt was the real cause of his firing. "Although they said it was the old gambling stuff again.... As soon as I admitted that I had been betting on the races," said Hornsby, "they fired me."[49]

The Browns' record when Hornsby departed was 25 wins and 52 loses. His successor, another former Cardinals standout, Jim Bottomley, had an even worse record: 21–56.[50] For a few days near the end of the 1937 season, Bottomley was not with the club, supposedly a victim of the flu. Gabby Street took his place, losing all four games he managed.[51] The Browns finished the season trailing the first-place Yankees by 56 games.[52]

The Browns did not rehire Bottomley in 1938, but he did manage to find a job as manager with Syracuse in the International League.[53] Meanwhile, the Browns signed Gabby Street to manage the team in 1938.[54] The Browns were looking for their next manager to be a happy medium between Rogers Hornsby, who they felt had been too tough, and Jim Bottomley, who had been too gentle with his players. Street was the man they had been looking for.[55] He was excited about his selection and stated that managing the Browns was a great opportunity.[56]

At the winter meetings in December 1937, the Browns were delighted to obtain infielder/outfielder Red Kress, outfielder Buster Mills, and pitchers Bobo Newsom and Ed Linke.[57]

Manager Gabby Street had won two pennants and a World Series the first two years he managed the Cardinals in 1930 and 1931 and was eagerly looking forward to the 1938 season. He felt Barnes and DeWitt had made wise acquisitions through trades and purchases, as well as stocking his farm system with adequate prospects.[58] He was particularly pleased that his owner and general manager had acquired ten players and given up only four in recent trades. In addition to Newsom, Kress, and Mills, second baseman Oscar Mellilo, who could also coach, was purchased from the Red Sox, and Don Heffner acquired in a trade with the Yankees. In addition, the Browns' top brass had drafted first baseman George McQuinn from Newark. "I never saw McQuinn," said Street, "but from what I hear there need be no worry about that position."[59]

Spring training 1938 was held at Tech Field in San Antonio again. Both Bill DeWitt and his brother Charley, who was traveling secretary that year, found it impossible to persuade other major league clubs to schedule spring training games at the Browns' camp. As a result, the Browns were forced to play minor league and college opponents at their spring training site, but they were good for the team's morale.[60]

As the Browns began their spring training in 1938, DeWitt's efforts to build a farm system were showing success. Of the 22 teams in his farm system, the Browns owned and operated three—San Antonio; Springfield, Illinois, of the Three-Eye loop, and Johnstown, Pennsylvania, of the Mid–Atlantic League. They had working agreements with nine others teams in several leagues including the Arkansas-Missouri League; Kitty League; Ohio League; Evangeline League; East Texas League; Texas Valley League; Southeastern League; Northeast Arkansas League; and Western Association.[61] DeWitt's right-hand man in operating and overseeing these teams was Jack Fournier.⁶² Spring training raised hope for a better year for the Browns in 1938 as the team won nine straight games during spring training.⁶³

By mid-season, however, the Browns were once again struggling. Although the cry went up to fire Gabby Street, DeWitt immediately replied, "No, sir, Gabby Street will continue as our manager through the season. And I don't mean by that that we'll make a change next year. We'll cross that bridge when we come to it. But we're not making any change this season." DeWitt added that he was frustrated by the current Browns pitching but noted, "Gabby can't pitch for us."⁶⁴

By the middle of August, despite the Browns' horrible season, DeWitt continued to insist that Street's job as manager was secure. However, two weeks prior to the end of the season, DeWitt fired Street. Under Street, the Browns' record was 53–90, and the team was in seventh place; only Philadelphia had a worse record.⁶⁵ Despite his earlier denials that Street's job as manager was not in jeopardy, Street had been let go two weeks prior to the end of the 1938 season. For the remainder of the season, the manager of the Browns was one of their coaches, Oscar Melilo, who finished the season with a 2–7 record. For the entire 1938 season, the Browns managed to win only 55 games while losing 97, finishing in seventh place again.⁶⁶

For the third consecutive season, the Browns needed a new manager. One of the first persons DeWitt and Barnes contacted was Ray Schalk, generally recognized as the greatest catcher in Chicago White Sox history. He managed the Sox in 1927 and 1928.⁶⁷ Other aspirants included Harold "Muddy" Ruel, veteran catcher and coach. Many baseball pundits felt he had the best chance of landing the job because he had the qualities to be the new manager—he was a St. Louis native, had an American League background, and knew the proper techniques to work with young players. Other prospects included Burleigh Grimes, Frankie Frisch, and Jimmy Wilson, a former manager of the Philadelphia Phillies. While Frisch, Grimes, and Wilson were popular with the St. Louis fans, they were all associated with National League teams, and the consensus was that DeWitt and Barnes both preferred hiring someone who knew the American League and who would patiently show young players their mistakes and how to correct them. DeWitt stressed that the Browns were attempting to build up a young team that would endure.⁶⁸

While the Browns were involved with hiring a manager for the 1939 season, DeWitt didn't neglect looking for trades. In late fall, DeWitt make a trade with the New York Yankees, who sent the Browns catcher Joe Glenn and outfielder Myril Hoag in exchange for pitcher Oral Hildebrand and outfielder Buster Mills. Barnes stated that it was a straight player deal with no money involved. The Browns certainly needed a catcher, and Glenn, who hit .260 for the Yankees in 1938, got little playing time with Bill Dickey starting most games. The 30-year-old Hoag was considered one of the speediest men in baseball and a dependable outfielder. Hildebrand, the other acquisition and one of the league's outstanding pitchers when he was with the Cleveland Indians, never really helped the Browns. He had been handicapped by a sore arm and pitched infrequently. Buster Mills also failed to perform up to expectations either offensively or defensively.[69]

There was one managerial candidate neither DeWitt nor Barnes had solicited. Near the end of October 1938, Babe Ruth telephoned the Browns, wanting to manage the team in 1939. Surprised by the call, Barnes told him that the team would be glad to give him consideration along with others. Ruth had been mentioned several times as interested in a managerial job. He had been a coach with the Dodgers during part of the 1938 season, but once Leo Durocher was appointed to succeed Burleigh Grimes as Dodgers manager, Ruth was let go.[70]

J. Roy Stockton was not surprised that the Browns did not hire Babe Ruth as their manager. Stockton was sure that DeWitt did not consider Ruth "good managerial timber," or he would have been offered a job long ago. Stockton also felt that even when Ruth was playing for the Yankees, he never attracted crowds to Sportsman's Park. DeWitt also realized that even if Ruth were to turn out be a tremendous drawing card, he and Barnes felt he might be "a less than positive influence on young players."[71]

In early November 1938, Fred Haney, a former Cardinals and Tigers player, and for the past two years manager of the Toledo Mudhens, came to St. Louis to speak to Browns officials about the vacant managerial job.[72] The Browns were well aware that Haney had the support of Branch Rickey, who recommended that the Browns hire the 40-year-old. DeWitt had first offered the job to Oscar Melillo, but he declined, although he agreed to stay on as a coach.[73] Haney may have been Branch Rickey's first choice, but he was not the fans' favorite. They would have opted for either Ray Schalk or Muddy Ruel, and they let the Browns' management know it. The usually mild-mannered DeWitt was miffed at the fans' criticism of the new Browns pilot and defended the choice of Haney. He reminded the fans that under the new ownership of Don Barnes and his associates, the Browns had gained a reputation for changing managers. DeWitt believed that with Haney, this stigma would be erased. "It is our privilege to do what we think is best in trying a new man," DeWitt said.[74]

Although the Browns didn't own Sportsman's Park prior to the beginning of the 1939 season, De Witt oversaw a number of changes to the property. The "Babe Ruth" wall above the right field Pavilion was taken down. Originally erected to turn Ruth's home runs into balls in play, DeWitt explained that this barrier was now more of a hindrance to the Browns than to the visitors.[75] DeWitt also discussed how he and Barnes were working to assess fan interest and raise funds and attendance, especially for night baseball.[76]

Over the past winter, most of DeWitt's attention had been occupied with getting Bobo Newsom and other holdouts signed. The first player to agree to terms was pitcher Bill Cox, who inked his contract in January.[77] Their power-hitting third baseman, Harlond Clift, who was given a "fat increase" in salary, signed his contract February 2, 1939.[78] It seemed that for every player DeWitt signed, there were an equal number of holdouts. DeWitt had offered their first-string catcher, Billy Sullivan, a contract reducing his salary, hoping he could trade Sullivan for either a pitcher or outfielder. Two Californians, veterans Ralph Kress and Don Heffner, both demanded considerable raises, to which DeWitt replied, "They can stay in California until this time next year before we'll meet their terms. We have made our best offers to all the boys."[79] DeWitt was always confident that if he had to lose established players, he could find replacements who could step in and help the club. As he watched a workout of his club, he predicted that it would be greatly improved in 1939, particularly by the addition of the young second base-shortstop duo from San Antonio, Sig Gryska and John Berardino, who had been working regularly in infield practice during the spring.[80]

Newsom, however, was a special problem. He said flatly that he would not sign a contract for less than $20,000, arguing that he had won 20 games for a seventh-place club. Newsom also claimed it was solely due to his pitching that the Browns drew more than 130,000 fans in 1938, their highest attendance since 1931. DeWitt reassured Newsom that he would get a "substantial increase" over his 1938 salary, which was between $10,000 and $14,000, but he also reminded Newsom that along with his 20 wins, he lost 16 games and ended 1938 with a 5.07 ERA.[81]

DeWitt also refuted Newsom's argument regarding attendance, informing his pitcher that in 1938, the Browns' exciting new player, first baseman George McQuinn, had an exceptional season—posting a .324 batting average, 195 hits, 82 runs batted in, and 100 runs scored. DeWitt added that McQuinn was an outstanding fielder in addition to having had a 34-game hitting streak in July and August.[82] After demanding a face-to-face meeting with DeWitt, Newsom eventually signed his 1939 contract in early May for $15,000, only $1,000 more than the Browns had originally offered.[83]

Three. Donald Barnes and the St. Louis Browns

At the conclusion of spring training, Bill DeWitt and new manager Fred Haney felt confident they had a solid team. The infield, with Clift at third, Gryska at shortstop, Berardino at second, and McQuinn at first would compete competently. The peppy Harold Spindel, a catcher the Browns obtained from Seattle, was counted on to help the Browns improve not only in 1939 but in the future. DeWitt felt that a backup catcher, Sam Harshany, would also shore up the team. Two players new to the Browns, Myril Hoag and Joe Glenn, were also very eager to make it up to the Browns. According to observers of the team in Texas, these new players would also attract fans and help the Browns shed the distinction of having the lowest total attendance in the majors, as they did again in 1938.[84]

Despite his confidence in the 1939 Browns, DeWitt was still on the lookout for additional opportunities. In the middle of May, the Browns concluded a four-for-six player deal with the Detroit Tigers. The Browns shipped pitchers Bobo Newsom and Jim Walkup, outfielder Beau Bell, and shortstop Red Kress to the Tigers for outfielder Chet Laabs, infielder Mark Christman, and four pitchers: Vernon Kennedy, George Gill, Roxie Lawson, and Bob Harris. It was the biggest club-to-club trade in the American League for many years. Haney, DeWitt and Barnes all congratulated themselves on the deal.[85]

Their congratulations might have been a bit hasty. By June, Vernon Kennedy was pitching well for the Browns but had won only two games, compared with the four he had won with the Tigers. Chet Laabs, whose arm was injured the day prior to the trade, was inserted in center field and showed some promise despite the sore arm. Critics of the deal noted that the loss of Newsom and Red Kress had hurt the Browns. Since June 6, the Browns had lost 16 out of 20 games and won only two of 11 home games.[86]

Despite the losses, the ten members of the board of directors who represented the capital side of the ball club did all they could to help produce a winning team. When the board realized that since the Browns were incurring heavy losses while attempting to run a club and develop a farm system, each director put up $5,000 for the total of $50,000, and club owner Donald Barnes added $50,000 more as a loan to allow the team to operate for the remainder of the year. Barnes, an investment banker, was serving as president of the club without remuneration. He even paid his own expenses when traveling with the Browns.[87]

One of the few bright spots for Bill DeWitt during the 1939 season was the birth of his second daughter, Donna Dorothy (Dee Dee), on June 19. Again, the DeWitts asked Donald Barnes to be her godfather.[88]

By July, the Browns were nowhere near finishing the season in the upper division. They had the talent, but this talent was not reflected in the club's standing. Barnes and DeWitt confronted their manager about the obvious lack of "esprit de corps" and sagging team morale, but Haney took little responsibility for his team's poor performance. He blamed the players for being more interested in individual records than team results. He did, however, have an idea for a cure for the 1940 season. "Contracts should be awarded with a sliding pay based on team victories instead of personal records. ... I believe that by eliminating that 'me for myself' attitude from the squad, the Browns can go places next year."[89]

Haney claimed that management was behind him "100 percent," but the St. Louis evening dailies had different versions of Haney's managerial future. J. Roy Stockton stated that reappointing Fred Haney as Browns manager was a "wise move," while the Sports Editor of the *Star-Times*, Sid C. Keener, noted, "Haney has his work cut out for him."[90]

When professional sports teams continue to perform and draw fans poorly, there is often talk that the team should relocate. In the summer of 1939, there were rumors that the St. Louis Browns might be more successful in a different city. American League president William Harridge quickly quelled those rumors, denying that the Browns or any other team in the league was moving to another city. Harridge did leave the topic open by adding that it was certainly possible that relocation might occur in the future, but a move was not imminent.[91]

The Browns ended the 1939 season with a record of 43–111, finishing in the cellar, 64½ games out of first place. Having the home team advantage certainly did not apply to the Browns, who managed to win only 18 games at Sportsman's Park, while losing 59. Their pitching struggled, allowing 739 walks, 100 walks more than the next-wildest team. The Browns' pitchers had an earned run average of 6.01; no other major league team would have a higher average ERA until 1996, when the Detroit Tigers' staff average sank to 6.38.[92]

J. Roy Stockton brutally summed up the Browns' play in 1939 by calling it the worst he had ever witnessed for the Browns. Mincing no words, he said their last 1939 home stand was pathetic, careless, and stupid, and he chastised the team for lack of enthusiasm at bat. Stockton went on, "Infielders failed to cover second on potential double plays, opposing runners crossed home plate while Browns infielders were making throws to first base, and it appeared as if the only objective of all concerned was to get the game over as soon as possible."[93]

The Browns' Board of Directors obviously read Stockton's column, because the tenor of the team's investors had changed. Barnes and DeWitt endured a three-hour Board of Directors meeting where they managed to mollify, at least temporarily, an insurgent group who declared they would put no more money into the team. The Board also chastised DeWitt for not consulting them when he made trades. Two members of the Board resigned. One resignee, James R. Kearney, one of the original members of the syndicate which purchased the team in 1936, denounced the business policies of the club and was outspoken against the trade moves of both Barnes and DeWitt.[94] Despite the resignations, the remaining directors gave president Donald Barnes and business manager Bill DeWitt a vote of confidence.[95]

Bill DeWitt spent most of November 1939 concentrating on building a better roster for the new decade. *The Sporting News* dubbed DeWitt the "champion off-season optimist" as he declared that he didn't intend to seek any transactions at the upcoming owners' meeting. He maintained that he already had enough talent in his organization, including both the Browns and players in the farm system.[96]

As he scanned his 40-man roster for the 1940 season (18 pitchers, three catchers, nine infielders, and 10 outfielders,) DeWitt explained why he felt it was not necessary to look for trades, although he admitted he would not turn down any deal which would help fill a gap. DeWitt agreed that Johnny Lucadello would play for the Browns in 1940, but he highlighted Alan Strange, drafted from Seattle, who would be more than adequate at short. He also stated that Don Heffner, who played second so well in 1938, might challenge Berardino for that position in 1940. DeWitt made it clear that George McQuinn would remain at first base and star third baseman Harlond Clift would remain at the hot corner. When it came to the outfield, DeWitt mentioned Glenn McQuillen, Pete Kraus, Joe Grace, Joe Gallagher, Chet Laabs, and Myril Hoag as leading candidates. DeWitt then listed all the pitchers who would be fighting for a job with the Browns in 1940, and boasted about his three catchers— Joe Glenn, Sam Harshany, and Bill Swift, who had come up from San Antonio.[97]

In December, Bill DeWitt and Fred Haney led the Browns' delegation to the winter meetings in Cincinnati. The large group included president Don Barnes, scouts Ray Cahill, Pat Monahan, and Charley Stia, traveling secretary Charley DeWitt, and representatives of the club's minor league farm system, Ed Gilliland, Guy Airey, and Bill Osley.

True to his word, DeWitt was not active at the winter meetings, but when he returned he became involved in signing his players for the 1940 season. He understood that finances and player salaries were so low that most of his players, especially on the farm teams, were forced to take second jobs to make ends meet.[98] Others, including two of his Browns players, pitcher Ed Cole and infielder Johnny Berardino, were collecting unemployment insurance.[99] A third Browns player, Joe Glenn, a catcher the Browns had received from the Yankees in a trade, had applied for unemployment benefits in New York.[100]

Not all Browns players were hurting financially. Despite DeWitt's well-publicized plan to be economically conservative in issuing contracts, a few players were able to receive promised increases. For example, George McQuinn, who had an outstanding season in 1939, received a hefty increase in his salary, and DeWitt signed his star third baseman, Harlond Clift, at his 1939 salary despite Clift's lower batting average.[101]

Of course, the team's finances were hurting primarily because of sparse attendance. Other American League teams complained about going to St. Louis, where meager gate receipts didn't even cover expenses, much less make them profitable. American League president Will Harridge suggested that each owner sell one of his players to the Browns for $7,500. The other teams cooperated, but the Browns received only two players of any value—submarine pitcher Elden Auker and outfielder Walter Judnich. Judnich would play five seasons with the Browns before ending his major league career with the Pittsburgh Pirates after the 1949 season.[102] Auker had begun his major league career with the Detroit Tigers in 1933 and pitched for them through 1938. He spent the 1939 season with the Red Sox before going to the Browns, remaining with them until he finished his major league career after the 1942 season. His career record was 130 wins and 103 losses.[103]

In February 1940, the construction of lights at Sportsman's Park finally began. The Browns and Cardinals agreed to share the $150,000 cost for what both teams considered the most advanced lighting system available, using the latest scientific efficiency.[104] According to both Sam Breadon and Donald Barnes, the Sportsman's Park light system would contain all of the recent advancements in the field of lighting.[105] Although Barnes was instrumental in getting the American League to allow lights, he was disappointed that various delays and funding issues had held back the installation. St. Louis would become only the fourth American League team to play night games at home. Lights would prove very popular with the fans.[106]

On May 24, 1940, the Browns drew 24,827 fans at the club's inaugural night game. Elden Auker lost to the Cleveland Indians, 3–2. This was the third-largest crowd in Browns history and the first of 14 night games to be played that year.[107]

As another incentive for filling the park, DeWitt announced that

Three. Donald Barnes and the St. Louis Browns   41

membership cards were again available for the Browns' Boys and Girls Brigades for the coming season. As before, with the membership card, children ages 10 to 16 could attend all home games free except on special days and Sundays. Public and parochial schools once again would act as agents in distribution of the cards.[108]

While the lights were being erected in St. Louis, the Browns began their spring training in San Antonio with a large number of rookies at their camp. With so many rookies on the roster, manager Haney stressed "individualism," which he defined as personal initiative. "You might not like the way the players do certain things," said Haney, "but if it gets the best results for them individually, it must be the way to do it."[109]

By the end of June, DeWitt's trading had created the most effective pitching staff the Browns had had for several years. The infield was stable and working well. The press was calling for Haney and DeWitt to receive credit for both patience and confidence in their players. The two men kept a constant stream of players coming and going to Sportsman's Park. Bill DeWitt had traded for more than half of the team's starting pitchers when he acquired two more from Detroit—Vernon Kennedy and Bob Harris. The third starting pitcher, Elden Auker, was acquired from the Red Sox in Harridge's "mercy sale."[110]

When the Browns climbed to fifth place by July 5, Haney lauded the front office, especially Bill DeWitt, for how well he had been treating the players. For example, after a long road trip, DeWitt cancelled exhibition games to allow the players to attend the All-Star Game or see their families. "With that kind of co-operation," Haney said, "it's no wonder we have spirit."[111] Clearly, DeWitt was putting his players above the team's need for revenue. Although the Browns had to make up a $300,000 loss incurred during the past three years, Barnes and DeWitt even kept the players' salaries on a par with other major league clubs. According to the team manager, "Players were never treated better."[112]

Unfortunately, after the All-Star break, the Browns reverted to their "traditional" performance by losing 14 consecutive games in July. Coupled with earlier wins, however, the Browns still managed to finish in sixth place, with an improved, although still unenviable, record of 67–87, 11 games better than in 1939.[113]

At the meeting of the club's Board of Directors in September 1940, DeWitt was able to report more favorable news than at any time since he and Barnes took over the team in 1936. Some of the Browns' minor league teams, particularly the San Antonio Missions, had excellent gate receipts, and the installation of lights at Sportsman's Park helped boost attendance in St. Louis.[114]

DeWitt spent the remainder of 1940 discussing plans and making predictions about 1941. He was encouraged by the overall feeling of the investors who, in contrast to the previous year, were now hopeful of a first-division team in 1941. DeWitt encouraged this supportive feeling, stating that the Browns had "developed some of the most promising talent in the minor leagues."[115] He planned few roster changes, intending to stay with first-line players and to compensate them well. Somewhat surprisingly, given his trading reputation, DeWitt said he preferred to purchase players than trade for them. True to his word, DeWitt purchased two veteran pitchers from the Red Sox in a straight cash transaction—Dennis Galehouse and Fritz Ostermueller. Neither had had good years in 1940, but it was felt that both would strengthen the team in 1941.[116]

At the beginning of 1941, J. Roy Stockton assessed the 1941 Browns. He liked the infield, calling it "one of the best in the league." Also impressive was Vernon Stephens, a new acquisition, who Stockton felt would challenge Johnny Berardino for the shortstop job. George McQuinn, Don Heffner, and Harlond Clift seemed likely to fill the other three infield slots, with perhaps Johnny Lucadello challenging Heffner for the second base job. The Browns' outfield seemed set, and Stockton endorsed the talent behind the plate with young catchers Bob Swift and Joe Grace. It was the Browns' pitching that worried Stockton. Four of their starting pitchers, Johnny Allen, George Caster, Fritz Ostermueller, and Denny Galehouse, were no youngsters. "If they were to come through with good records in 1941," wrote Stockton, "the Browns could fly high. And that is the gamble Barnes and DeWitt are taking."[117]

Barnes and DeWitt were re-elected at the annual meeting of the Board of Directors. There was an air of optimism at the meeting, even though it was announced that the team finished in the "red" (again!) for the 1940 season. The consensus of the stockholders was, "We'll keep right on buying in an effort to give the Browns a winning team."[118]

Even though the Browns began 1941 by purchasing players, they did not neglect building up their farm system. Pueblo, Colorado, joined the Browns' system, and Denver also made an application. San Antonio continued its relationship with the Browns, and the new owner of the St. Joseph Saints renewed his team's agreement.[119] The existing farm system was beginning to pay dividends.[120]

DeWitt knew the value of good press and, to help create positive perceptions of the team, he added a new feature to the Browns' camp routine, a daily press conference making it easier for sports writers to get information on-site. DeWitt even set aside a suite of rooms for this conference, complete with daily refreshments.

During 1941 spring training, DeWitt, along with Barnes and

manager Haney, received some good news from the commissioner's office. Commissioner Landis would now allow a major league club to send players to the minors to protect them from the draft. DeWitt had called the old ruling the "bogey-man rule." He had long felt that it hurt clubs with young prospects on their roster, forcing the clubs to keep these prospects in the majors even if they were not ready to play there. DeWitt had three young prospects who needed further seasoning and would benefit from this new edict. One player he was especially concerned about was his star prospect, shortstop Vernon Stephens.[121] Marty McManus, former Browns second baseman and most recently field director of the San Antonio club, highly recommended Stephens to Bill DeWitt but felt he needed another year in the minors.[122]

Spring training is designed as the time for major league teams to prepare for the season ahead. On one occasion at least, this preparation set a new baseball record. Both the Browns and the Boston Bees (the 1941 name for the Boston Braves), conducted their spring training in Texas. Pleased to have another major league team in relatively close proximity, the Browns scheduled a three-game series with the Bees in Monterrey, Mexico. The games were the first ever played in Mexico by two major league clubs. Accompanying DeWitt on the trip to Monterrey was his wife, Margaret, along with his brother and traveling secretary, Charley DeWitt, and his wife.[123]

As spring training was coming to an end and the 1941 season was ready to begin, DeWitt noticed that his players had lost their defeatist mindset and that the spring training camp attitude was upbeat. This perspective was also shared by the front office as they attempted to find players who would help the Browns improve their record. They felt they had a good group of pitchers in Johnny Allen, Elden Auker, George Caster, Denny Galehouse, Vern Kennedy, Johnny Niggling, and Fritz Ostermueller; a good cadre of catchers in Rick Ferrell, Frank Grube and Bob Swift; established and promising infielders Johnny Berardino, Harlond Clift, Don Heffner, Johnny Lucadello, Georg McQuinn, Vern Stephens, and Chuck Stevens; and outfielders Roy Cullenbine, Joe Grace, Wally Judnich, Chet Laabs, and Bobby Estallela.[124]

Despite the new players and the positive outlook, six weeks into the 1941 season, the Browns were still having trouble winning baseball games. In fact, the team dropped 29 of its first 44 games, and the fans began blaming manager Haney for mismanaging the games and the players.[125] DeWitt and Barnes also felt that Haney was not the manager the Browns needed, and with few public details on the hunt for a replacement, on June 5, 1941, 20-year baseball veteran Luke Sewell became the Browns' seventh manager since 1929. Sewell was with the

Cleveland Indians in 1941 and was very happy with his job as a backup catcher and coach to manager Oscar Vitt. He intended to leave baseball after the 1941 season. DeWitt was especially enthusiastic about Sewell. "He knows the American League," DeWitt said. "He's not coming in cold, to experiment or to find out about the hitters in the league. He has considerable experience with pitchers and if our pitching can be helped, our ball club will be helped. He has no managerial experience, but he has been a coach and has been on successful clubs in the major leagues." Barnes had received permission to talk to Sewell about managing the Browns. Even Indians owner Alva Bradley urged Sewell to postpone his planned retirement to accept the offer.[126]

Haney was shocked to hear that he had been replaced as manager. "I did all I could," he said, "and the fellows did all they could, and there has been the finest feeling on the club." He admitted that his pride had been hurt but felt he had nothing against Barnes or DeWitt, since he had been in the baseball business long enough to realize that the manager gets it in the neck when things do not go right. Some felt that Haney had been the victim of high expectations, as this was supposed to be the year when the Browns moved up in the standings. These high hopes ultimately led to Haney's ouster.[127]

The Browns' record under Sewell's leadership was 55–55. They finished the season tied with the Washington Senators for sixth place at 70–84. While the Cardinals drew more than 600,000 fans, the Browns' attendance was barely 175,000. It was becoming obvious that St. Louis might not be able to support two major league franchises. The Browns were on track to lose $100,000 again in 1941. Even when night games were scheduled, the weather seemed to work against them, resulting in several rainouts. In addition, the team was sinking a large amount of money in the San Antonio franchise, and DeWitt still could not provide the farm club the support that other farm clubs had. As a result, the Browns' farm teams had a difficult time drawing 50,000 fans at home.[128] One of the few happy events during the 1941 season just ended was the birth of William O. DeWitt, Jr., on August 31. Like his older sisters, Bill Jr.'s godfather was Donald Barnes.[129]

By late 1941, the Browns' franchise, despite two sixth-place finishes, had reached rock bottom financially. The team continued to lose money, yet it was responsible for paying half the costs of operating Sportsman's Park, even though the Cardinals, with their larger crowds, were getting more of the benefits. As a result, the Browns had to reduce the number of farm teams and scouting staff. Stock in the club dropped in value, and the Browns were forced to ask the American League for loans to meet the club's expenses.[130]

Barnes and DeWitt realized it was no longer financially possible to maintain their baseball club in St. Louis. They began to think seriously about an idea years ahead of its time. Harry Arthur was an investor in the St. Louis Browns, and head of Fanchot and Marco Amusement Company, an entertainment enterprise in southern California. Arthur divided his time between St. Louis and Los Angeles and was well aware of the Browns' financial troubles. He had urged Barnes and DeWitt to move their franchise to Los Angeles in time for the 1942 season.[131]

After giving much thought to Arthur's proposal, Barnes and DeWitt decided to act on his advice. Los Angeles was eager to become a major league city, and Barnes and DeWitt were able to assemble a strong Los Angeles investment group to purchase the team's stock. In addition, Cardinals owner Sam Breadon was talked into giving the Browns $350,000 to leave so that he would have St. Louis baseball all to himself.[132]

Barnes and DeWitt were determined to move the St. Louis Browns to a new home in Los Angeles. Their team had been drained by financial losses because they were unable to draw fans in St. Louis, but they had a number of challenges to overcome first. Since 1903, when the Orioles left Baltimore for New York, no major league baseball franchise had moved, nor did any major league baseball team play west or south of St. Louis. Teams traveled by train and bus; cross country air travel was almost unheard of. In addition, professional baseball in Los Angeles was the domain of Philip K. Wrigley, owner of the Chicago Cubs. Would he sell his franchise rights and his ballpark in Los Angeles, where the Cubs operated a farm club in the Pacific Coast League? And finally, could a viable schedule be arranged for the convenience of all the teams in the American League?[133]

It was decided that Barnes and DeWitt would bring the Browns' move to Los Angeles up for a vote at the major leagues winter meeting to be held December 8 in Chicago. At first, the two Browns officials kept their plans to themselves until they could be assured that everything would fall in place. Things were moving favorably. Phil Wrigley agreed to relinquish not only his rights to Los Angeles, but also his minor league park there, and a reasonable travel schedule had been worked out. Barnes had completed arrangements for shifting the franchise to Los Angeles for the 1942 season.[134]

By this time, word of the Browns' planned move to Los Angeles was no longer a secret, and Barnes and DeWitt had received tacit approval from their fellow owners. Everything seemed on track for approval of the Browns' move to Los Angeles by the American League owners. The vote was scheduled for Monday, December 8, at the winter meetings in Chicago. Barnes and DeWitt arrived a day early and were attending a Chicago Cardinals football game on Sunday, December 7, when they and the rest of the world heard that the Japanese had attacked Pearl Harbor and that an invasion of the West Coast was possible. At the major league meeting the next day, following Congress' formal declaration of war against Japan, Barnes officially withdrew his proposal to move the St. Louis Browns to Los Angeles. The motion to shelve the request to relocate the Browns was unanimously approved.[135]

Four

A World War and a World Series

Despite the United States being at war in 1942, the inability of the Browns to move to a more lucrative market, and the increased pressure on their finances, the 1942 season would turn out to be one of the team's best. One concern that was answered early in the year was the status of baseball during the world conflict. In 1917, when the U.S. entered World War I, minor leagues were shut down and major league baseball shortened its 1918 season to end on Labor Day.[1]

In 1942, the concern was even greater, but major league baseball had formidable allies, not the least of whom was the president of the United States, Franklin D. Roosevelt. Although Roosevelt was a baseball fan, DeWitt gave credit to Washington Senators owner Clark Griffith for influencing the president to act to sustain baseball during the war. DeWitt also gave a lot of credit to Robert Hannegan, FDR's close political advisor. Both DeWitt and Barnes were close with Hannegan, a St. Louisan and DeWitt's high school classmate. Hannegan was the one who persuaded FDR to write the famous Green Light letter to Baseball Commissioner Landis. In the letter, FDR not only expressed compelling reasons for continuing the game, but also made the case for more night games to allow workers to attend.[2] Despite FDR's endorsement of night games, DeWitt had to spend the first part of 1942 waiting for the number of night games to be determined and hopefully increased.[3]

While waiting to hear from the Commissioner's office about the status of night games in 1942, Barnes and DeWitt made some player acquisitions. The Browns purchased infielder Don Gutteridge, a fleet-footed infielder and former St. Louis Cardinal, on a conditional basis. They also announced the purchase of pitcher Albert "Boots" Hollingsworth from Sacramento of the Pacific Coast League. "We simply got a chance to look at two good players in Gutteridge and Hollingsworth, and we'd be foolish if we didn't give them a chance," said DeWitt.[4]

Despite his acquisitions, however, DeWitt still had to figure out how to operate a club with more debts than assets. Some of the team's smaller investors had dropped out, refusing to buy more stock, which had plunged from its original price of $5 to $2 per share. The financial situation brightened considerably when St. Louisan Richard Muckerman invested $300,000 in the team, buying 150,000 of 180,000 newly issued shares. Muckerman's family had emigrated to St. Louis in the mid–19th century and founded Polar Wave Ice and Fuel Co, which sold its products in 28 states and Mexico. Muckerman was heir to the firm, now called St. Louis City Ice and Fuel, and served as its vice president. Born April 9, 1897, Muckerman was only five years older than DeWitt but declared he had been a Browns fan for decades. Muckerman, an avid sports enthusiast, had made a small investment in the Browns in 1939, and at the team's January 1942 meeting, he was named to the Board of Directors. In March he was elevated to vice president.[5] Margo Hields, Muckerman's granddaughter, told the authors that her grandfather's money allowed Barnes, DeWitt, and the team's manager, Luke Sewell, to maintain their policy of keeping the Browns' most prominent players and trying to acquire others on the cheap.[6]

Because it took time to work out the details to acquire the new funds, DeWitt waited until the league deadline of March 15 to send out contracts to his returning players. Salary cuts were not as drastic as anticipated, and many players accepted without extended bargaining. Outfielder Walter Judnich signed his contract and received permission to start for Florida early.[7] Another early signer was veteran third baseman Harlond Clift, who inked his contract and departed for the Browns' camp in DeLand, Florida. Despite the absence of nine members of the squad, Bill DeWitt stated that he wasn't worried about contract difficulties.[8]

In addition to the need to draft players for military service, the war also caused some unexpected events. Just as the 1942 season was starting, DeWitt and Barnes not only lined up their player roster, but also began replacing the scouts let go the previous year in a money-saving effort. They hired former Cleveland general manager C. C. Slapnicka as chief scout and supervisor of farm teams. Barnes felt that as Bill DeWitt's assistant, Slapnicka would identify and tenaciously obtain young players for the farms, allowing DeWitt to concentrate on the Browns.[9] However, Slapnicka resigned in August because he had to return home to Cedar Rapids, Iowa, to supervise building a new house that was begun before the government restricted materials needed to complete the house.[10]

DeWitt, nonetheless, working closely with manager Luke Sewell, was able to spend more attention improving the Browns' roster. The improved financial situation not only paid off the club's loans from Barnes and the American League, it allowed DeWitt to retain minor leaguers such as Vern Stephens instead of selling them for cash to a rival team. In fact, the Browns soon put Stephens in the regular lineup to replace John Berardino, who was going into the military. The Browns also began to add good players from outside the farms.[11]

The Browns did unusually well during spring training, winning 16 exhibition games and losing only five, raising hopes for a better finish than in previous years.[12] Surprisingly, the Browns continued their good play into the 1942 regular season. Elden Auker, under Sewell's tutelage, had won five out of seven games by mid–May, and lefty Al Hollingsworth officially signed with the Browns.[13] The Browns also obtained Mike Chartak to fill in at Berardino's infield spot. By September, the press began to notice Vernon Stephens' outstanding play and tabbed him the likely American League Rookie of the Year. The boost provided by Muckerman's money and the Browns' improved play under Luke Sewell helped propel the team to a third-place finish, the club's best since 1928. Auker and Denny Galehouse provided the pitching, Chet Laabs, with his .275 batting average, 27 home runs and 99 RBIs, and Stephens' .294 batting average, 14 homers, and 92 RBIs provided the offense.[14]

There was more good news on the financial side. Enthusiastic defense workers flocked to the Browns' night games, and the team increased attendance by 45 percent because of having more night games and improvement in the team's play. However, the Browns still were among the lowest drawing franchise in the American League.[15]

As the 1942 season wound down, DeWitt and other GMs had to begin planning for 1943 spring training even though it was not entirely certain that the government had given a qualified go-ahead for major league baseball to play in the upcoming year. Planning had to deal with both minor and major difficulties. The war effort had confiscated many Florida hotels used by teams, and the draft was taking men even from the Browns' front office.[16] DeWitt announced to the Deland Chamber of Commerce that gasoline rationing and other uncertainties had influenced his decision not to return to Florida in 1943. "Under normal conditions, we probably would have returned without question," he wrote.[17]

At first, DeWitt thought the Browns might have to train close to home and, like other clubs, perhaps would be forced to curtail their spring activities. However, Barnes agreed to a training site in Anaheim, California, used by the Athletics the past three years.[18] Earlier the Browns had announced that they were purchasing 11 players from their farms and other clubs. Pitcher Frank Sanford, infielders Mark Christman and Bob Dillinger, and outfielder Milton Byrnes were four of the players coming from the Browns' Toledo farm club. Frank Mancusco, a catcher and brother of Gus Mancuso, was brought in from the San Antonio farm.[19] The Browns also announced that the team had rehired Luke Sewell for the 1943 season: "We are well pleased with his job of bringing the Browns up to its third place."[20]

The Browns quietly waited until their St. Louis rivals triumphed over the Yankees, four games to one, in the 1942 World Series before they made their roster announcements. *The Sporting News* noticed that a significant number of the Browns were fathers of dependent children. The paper commented that Bill DeWitt, with three children of his own, might have strategically chosen the family men, not only for their skill but also for their likelihood of deferral from the draft.[21]

Major League Baseball had to cope with one more abrupt change of plans before the year ended. The national Defense Transportation Coordinator urged all teams to stay close to their home field for spring training. The Browns, Cubs, White Sox, and Pirates had all arranged training at various California locations, and now had to redo those plans. Bill DeWitt, with the fallback option of going to San Antonio again, also began searching for new training facilities for the Browns. DeWitt was both appreciative and amused by some of the offers which came his way, including keys to cities and ball parks. DeWitt tried to explain that he didn't expect a full indoor field or even one where outfielders could chase flies. He needed indoor space for infield practice and space for his team to conduct races. He even made a blueprint design of what he was looking for.[22]

Sedalia, Missouri, had an indoor facility with a ground floor that could be made to resemble the diamond at Sportsman's Park. The University of Missouri at Columbia offered its facilities to the Browns. The Browns also received invitations from Caruthersville, Cape Girardeau, Hannibal, and Poplar Bluff, which DeWitt toured with Sewell to inspect possible training camp sites.[23]

In 1942, Bill DeWitt assembled a good war team, and Luke Sewell managed it superbly, resulting in the team's third-place finish with a percentage of .536. This marked the first time since 1929 that the Browns finished the season above .500.[24] While the Browns were exciting their fans in St. Louis, it was rumored that Branch Rickey, general manager of the Cardinals, was considering leaving that post at the end of 1942. It was no secret that Rickey always considered St. Louis his home. Since his protégé, William DeWitt, was the Browns' general manager, and the team had just finished a strong third in 1942, he might return to the St.

Four. A World War and a World Series

Louis Browns. J. Roy Stockton wrote that the deal had already been consummated and that Rickey's coming to the Browns was a " done deal."

A second rumor had Rickey heading to the Detroit Tigers to help the team build a farm system. A third rumor turned out to be the correct one. Shortly after Rickey's Cardinals beat the Yankees in the World Series, it was announced that the Brooklyn Dodgers had asked Rickey to succeed Larry MacPhail as president and general manager of the Dodgers. He admitted that as a country boy from Ohio, he felt more at home in St. Louis than in the big city. However, he admitted that a compelling factor for choosing Brooklyn was that it gave him the opportunity to build another team alongside his son, Branch Rickey, Jr., who had become frustrated working for the Larry MacPhail regime.[25]

As the war progressed, major league owners and general managers found it more difficult to field a stable lineup. Players were drafted or were working in defense plants or jobs vital to the war effort. Many managers had to rely on the team's minor league system as the season continued. The Browns were not immune from the war's effects on professional baseball. Walter Judnich, who had hit .313 in 1942, and promising outfielder Glenn McQuillen were both drafted into the U.S. Army Air Force.[26] Elden Auker, one of the best pitchers on the staff, went into the defense industry, and his loss was not filled immediately. As players departed, DeWitt's skills at finding talent in the minor leagues began to pay off.

DeWitt also began to scout for players let go by other clubs. In December 1942, the Philadelphia Athletics released outfielder Mike Kreevich, and he immediately received an "attractive" offer from the Browns. Kreevich had played with the Chicago White Sox for seven years before going to Philadelphia. "We are trying to land him," said DeWitt. "Manager Sewell likes him. His home at Mount Olive, Illinois, is in the St. Louis territory and he would like to play here. He'd be good insurance for us at any rate."[27] Kreevich played three years for the Browns before he ended his major league career with the Washington Senators in 1945.[28] The Browns also got a break when two of their better players, George McQuinn and Vernon Stephens, failed physicals and were rejected from the draft.[29]

A player DeWitt purchased from the Washington Senators in a straight cash deal had a familiar name: pitcher Paul Dean, younger brother of Dizzy Dean. Although a lame arm had seemingly ended Paul's major league career after the 1941 season, he came back in the Texas League in 1943 and impressed the Browns, winning 19 and losing only eight games with Houston.[30]

The Browns began their 1943 spring training in March in Cape

Girardeau, Missouri. Bill DeWitt announced the additional signings of Mike Chartak and catcher Rick Ferrell.[31] DeWitt also announced that third baseman Harlond Clift had agreed to terms.[32]

The Browns did get one more break when the 1943 season began. Outfielder Chet Laabs, who had hit 44 home runs for the Browns over the two previous seasons, received a notice from his draft board to report for induction into the Army on April 15, just as the season was starting. He received a reprieve on April 9 when the draft regulations were changed to exempt any man who was 27 or older, married, and working in a defense plant. Bill DeWitt helped Laabs get a defense job, qualifying him on all counts. In fact, his draft board told Laabs that working in a defense plant was a good idea should he be called again. During the 1943 season, Laabs commuted to the Browns from Detroit on weekends. "I'd catch the midnight train to St. Louis," said Laabs. "Priorities went to servicemen, which was absolutely right. But it meant I either sat in a chair or had to sleep on the floor or stand." DeWitt was also able to find a job in a defense plant for one of his starting pitchers, Denny Galehouse.[33]

As the 1943 season progressed, the Browns continued making additions and subtractions in personnel, both on and off the field. President Donald Barnes announced in June that Jimmy Conzelman, who had resigned as coach of the Chicago Cardinals in the National Football League, would head public relations for the Browns. In making the announcement, Barnes said, "Bill DeWitt and I believe that Conzelman's background in athletics and business and his national reputation ... will make him an excellent addition to the Browns organization."[34]

The 1943 team was more noted for roster moves than for actual play on the field. In June, DeWitt announced a straight cash transaction when Don Heffner, former reserve Browns infielder, became the property of the Philadelphia Athletics. Heffner, who had come to the Browns from the Yankees in 1938, was traded with two reserve infielders. The number of infielders would drop to one soon because shortstop Vernon Stephens was nearing his army induction.[35] Just a few days later, the Browns lost Paul Dean, who retired after pitching 13⅓ innings. He decided to run a barrel factory in lieu of baseball. He won 50 games in his career and lost 30.[36]

DeWitt finally heard some good news when the Browns' Toledo farm club sent the parent team hard-hitting outfielder Al Zarilla. DeWitt was thankful for the addition to the team's roster, but he admitted that with the Eastern teams all coming to Sportsman's Park in the near future, the Browns could use all the available help.[37]

In the middle of the 1943 season, the Browns signed Luke Sewell to

During World War II, major league teams were limited in their travel, forcing them to train closer to home. The Browns went to Cape Girardeau, Missouri, where the temperatures were cold but fortunately fan enthusiasm to see major leaguers play ball was high.

a new two-year contract as manager, extending his job through the 1945 season. Barnes and DeWitt expressed satisfaction with Sewell's work and wanted to demonstrate their confidence in the future of baseball. Sewell had been described as a manager and handler of players. Both Barnes and DeWitt described Sewell as quiet, capable, hard-working, good with players, and studious, but a man who "has fire in him, too, when aroused."[38]

Although the 1943 season still had more than a month remaining, the Browns realized it would be difficult to catch the first-place New York Yankees. Instead, they looked forward to 1944 and attempted to improve their roster by making trades to start rebuilding the club with younger players. The Browns sent pitcher Johnny Niggling and veteran third baseman Harlond Clift to Washington in return for third baseman Ellis Clary and pitcher John Miller. The Browns also received some cash in the deal.

In making the trade, DeWitt said, "Naturally we are disappointed in the showing of our club and what we are now trying to do is to get some youths in the lineup." Obviously, DeWitt was intimating that more deals might follow. In the trade with the Senators, the Browns acquired a 25-year-old and 27-year-old and traded players who were 31 and 38.[39]

Later that month, in another trade with the Senators, the Browns sold pitcher Bobo Newsom for cash. Newsom came to the Browns from the Brooklyn Dodgers in a trade for southpaws Archie McKain and Fritz Ostermueller. Newsom had pitched for nine major league teams and had been on the Browns in 1934, 1935, 1938, 1939, and 1943. The Browns picked him up again in 1943, hoping he would help the team's pennant push, but he started only nine games and was knocked out each time. His one victory was against the eighth-place Phillies. This trade sent Newsom to the Senators for the third time.[40]

Another indication that the Browns were already looking forward to the 1944 season was DeWitt's trips to watch their minor league teams' games. After a trip with Luke Sewell to Toledo, where their team played the Cardinals' Columbus Red Birds, both men were pleased. "We saw some pretty good-looking players who are likely to help us next year," said DeWitt. "I don't want to mention names, as Toledo is in the American Association playoffs and anything I say might affect the showing of Jack Fournier's players." DeWitt did say, however, that both he and Sewell were impressed with Jack Sanford and Jack Kramer, players the Browns had sent to Toledo. Another player who must have made an impression was outfielder Harold Epps. DeWitt signed him in late September.

DeWitt obviously was satisfied with the Browns' spring training site in Cape Girardeau, for he invited the Pittsburgh Pirates president, Bill Benswanger, to share the Cape training location with the Browns in 1944. Benswanger agreed, but the move required the approval of Commissioner Landis. The general order on spring training camps was that they must be east of the Mississippi River and north of the Ohio. This rule did not apply to the Browns, since they were given permission to train in their home state.[41]

During the annual winter meetings in 1943, the major league owners discussed racial integration and issued a formal policy stating that "each club is entirely free to employ Negro players to any and all extent as it desires. It is a matter solely for each club's decision without any restriction whatsoever." This declaration was the result of a plea from Paul Robeson, the well-known singer, representing Negro newspapers.[42] It would take four years for any team to act on this ruling, and the Browns, under Bill DeWitt, would be the third team to racially integrate.

At the meeting, Don Barnes led the fight for more night games in St. Louis. The next task for DeWitt would be to provide enough fans to patronize the team's night games. DeWitt's efforts to make deals to improve his team were unsuccessful, and he had to admit, "We soon found out the only players on our club in whom any one was interested were our key men."[43]

The Browns left the winter meetings feeling despondent. After 42 years of competition for local patronage, St. Louis Cardinals owner Sam Breadon and St. Louis Browns owner Donald Barnes, agreed on one major point—St. Louis was simply not a two-team major league city. Don Barnes stated, "St. Louis simply can't support two major league teams and there isn't any use kidding yourself otherwise. The increased night games should help us, but will not entirely solve our situation."[44]

Bill DeWitt even had to deny rumors that the Browns gobbled up a lot of National Defense List players from disbanded leagues and placed them on the roster of their Toledo farm club. "That isn't so," said DeWitt. "It is true that we have some 200 players on the National Defense List of the Toledo club, but they are all men who played for our Toledo, San Antonio and Springfield, Illinois, clubs."[45]

There was no question that the War was causing havoc on major league baseball. Neither St. Louis professional baseball team was able to negotiate salaries with its players because they had no idea which players would be available for the coming season. DeWitt admitted that he would not send out contracts until just prior to the February 15 deadline. "Maybe by that time we will have some idea to whom we are to send contracts," said DeWitt.[46]

As the Browns looked at their likely roster for the 1944 season, there was a ray of optimism in the 1943 batting figures. Three players—Vern Stephens, Chet Laabs and George McQuinn—were among the 15 league leaders in the runs-batted-in department for 1943. Stephens drove in 91 tallies, Laabs 85, and McQuinn 74, and McQuinn played in 12 fewer games than Stephens and 26 fewer than Laabs. Only two other clubs—the American League champions New York Yankees and the Detroit Tigers—had as many as three players among the 1943 RBI leaders. Both Barnes and DeWitt were delighted by these statistics, but they wondered when the entire team might improve. They were forced to admit that "there are no deals on the fire."[47]

In 1944 the Browns once again trained at Southeast Missouri State University in Cape Girardeau, 100 miles south of St. Louis. DeWitt and his staff arranged to have dirt put on the floor of the school's field house, then installed one of the first pitching machines and a batting cage. The Browns also were fortunate that their farm club in the American Association, the Toledo Mudhens, also conducted their spring training at the Browns' camp, giving the Browns greater familiarity with their players.[48]

Team Picture of the 1944 pennant-winning St. Louis Browns.

If the weather was too cold or snowy, Sewell could always move his team indoors. DeWitt surmised that having the ability to practice indoors allowed the Browns to start the season "at least a week" ahead of the other seven American League teams in both their conditioning and practice.[49]

The Browns may not have been the most talented team in the American League in 1944, but they led both leagues in a major area—18 men classified as 4-F. The Browns did not have the luxury of having all 18 for the entire season, but they were able to play in enough games to give the team a distinct advantage in the pennant race. Chet Laabs was classified 4-F because of severe headaches, the result of a brain concussion caused by a beaning in 1938. Fred Holekamp, Bill DeWitt's father-in-law, gave Laabs a job at a St. Louis war plant. He managed to play in 66 games for the Browns in 1944.[50]

Pitcher Denny Galehouse worked at a Goodyear aircraft plant in Akron, Ohio. When the season opened, he was a Sunday pitcher, taking an overnight train to wherever the Browns happened to be playing that weekend, pitching the first game of the doubleheader, then returning to his job. When he was informed by his draft board that if he left his war job, he would not be inducted immediately, Galehouse joined the Browns as a full-time hurler in late summer. He wound up with a record of 9–10.[51]

Four. A World War and a World Series

One of the Browns' best hitters was outfielder Al Zarilla. Not a 4-F, Zarilla got his draft notice too, but DeWitt came to the rescue once again when he convinced the army brass at Jefferson Barracks to wait until the end of the season before inducting his player. Fortunately for Zarilla and DeWitt, the Browns' 1944 season lasted six games longer than the other seven teams in the American League.[52]

Other players on the Browns roster who were rejected by the draft board included first baseman George McQuinn, star shortstop Vern Stephens, center fielder Mark Kreevich, and pitcher Bob Muncrief. Pitchers Jack Kramer and Frank Mancuso had been in the military but had been discharged. Infielder Mark Christman got a job in a defense plant and played baseball when possible.[53]

Morale in professional baseball was at an all-time low. Because so many of the game's outstanding players were being drafted, talk was widespread of perhaps curtailing major league baseball while the country was at war. Alva Bradley, owner of the Cleveland Indians, advocated this action. He felt that closing down baseball for the duration of the war was the proper alternative to offering fans a substandard game. Branch Rickey agreed, warning that baseball was in danger of losing its place in the hearts of Americans. "Baseball must take heed or football will become our national sport," he warned.[54]

Rickey was also worried about the future of baseball because of the deterioration of the minor leagues. In 1940, at the peak of the minor league system, there were 43 leagues in 314 cities. Three years later, the draft had so dried up the supply of players that only nine minor leagues with a total of 62 teams were able to function.[55]

Attempting to negate such talk, the Elmira baseball club of the Eastern League held a "fans banquet" featuring as one keynote speaker the 81-year-old manager of the Philadelphia Athletics, Connie Mack. "Baseball will continue to be played for the duration," said Mack, "because it is necessary to maintain the morale of our fighting forces. Despite the handicap of the manpower shortage, teams will go ahead and do the best they can to provide baseball, if only for that purpose."[56] Bill DeWitt added, "pennant races in all the leagues will be interesting for the duration of the war because of the continual change of the roster which might make it possible for a team to go from last to first place in a week or 10 days."[57]

At least one positive resulted from all the discussions about the plight of major league baseball during the war. Prior to 1944, Sportsman's Park in St. Louis was segregated. Black fans were required to sit in the right field pavilion, where they had to watch the game through a screen that stretched from the outfield wall to the roof above. This segregation of fans ended after the 1944 season, when Sportsman's Park became the last professional ballpark to end the practice.[58]

The war was having an unusual effect on both St. Louis teams. Both had delayed the start of spring training to give their players additional time at their war jobs. DeWitt declared that spring training would be held regardless of the delay, and "even if we should have a small squad, we will start work on March 20 as we have to put teams on the field for the opening of the season, April 18."[59]

Meanwhile, as DeWitt had observed, his team's roster changed almost daily. Barney Lutz, an outfielder the Browns had obtained in a deal with the Athletics, was re-classified from 3-A to 1-A. Southpaw pitcher Al Milner passed his pre-induction exam in Cleveland and expected to be called to duty around the time the Browns started training. Pitcher Paul Dean, still carried on the Browns' retired list, passed his physical on February 25 and was also awaiting a call from the Army.[60]

All the remaining Browns were in camp and had signed their contracts by the first week in April. Luke Sewell refused to discuss his analysis of the team and its chances. His only comment was, "We arrive in Detroit in time to play the opening game with the Tigers and I'll have five fellows ready to start. After that I don't know about the other 150."[61]

The Browns won the first nine games of the 1944 season and proceeded to lose ten of their next 15 games, dropping to third place

After spending his first two years in the major leagues pitching for the Philadelphia Athletics, Tex Shirley spent the 1943 season in the New York Giants' minor league system. Traded to the Browns in 1944, Shirley appeared in one game in relief, pitching two scoreless innings.

behind the New York Yankees and the Washington Senators. St. Louis fought back and enjoyed a ten-game winning streak; by August they had a 6½-game lead over the Yankees, thanks mainly to shortstop Vern Stephens. Stephens was considered the brightest product of DeWitt's farm system. Willis Butler, a scout for the Browns, spotted his talent and brought him to DeWitt's attention. The Browns signed Stephens for a bonus of $500 and sent him to Springfield, Illinois, at the age of 17. In 1941 he was promoted to Toledo and later that same year he was called up to the Browns, where he appeared in three games. Stephens became the regular Browns shortstop until 1947, when he was traded to the Boston Red Sox.[62]

By mid–August, pennant fever was becoming evident in St. Louis. Both the Browns and Cardinals were receiving 100 applications each day for World Series seats. Jim Bassford, advertising manager for the Cardinals, announced he was returning all requests for reservations, explaining that none would be accepted until the National League pennant was "mathematically secure." Only then would seats go on sale. Bill DeWitt also returned the applications as soon as they arrived and indicated he would wait until the Browns' chances were more secure or until Commissioner Landis determined prices.

Despite the caution voiced by the city's two major league teams, hotels continued to report that an amazing number of people had decided to visit St. Louis in early October—so many that reservations had to be turned down. One hotel employer said things looked so bad he thought the Office of Defense Transportation might have to have a requirement limiting travel and housing to those who had a certificate of necessity—and necessity would not mean a choice seat behind third base.[63]

While the Browns were fighting in 1944 to win their first pennant, Donald Barnes' presence, with few exceptions, was low-key. He allowed Luke Sewell and Bill DeWitt to run the club and tended, if possible, to avoid interference. However, he could not avoid the realization that for a team in the midst of a pennant race, the Browns should be drawing more fans to the games. Checking his attendance figures, he discovered that despite being a first-place team, the Browns had drawn only 25,000 more fans than last year, when they finished sixth. Barnes' first reaction was to surmise that the St. Louis fans were perhaps given "too much baseball."[64] Browns fans were displeased with Barnes' comments and began booing the Browns at their home games.[65]

As the 1944 season neared its end, DeWitt stated that it should give the Browns a psychological boost to know that it was possible for them to finish in front. He also felt it would be easier in the future to persuade young players to cast their lot with the Browns.[66]

The final series in 1944 pitted the Browns against the Yankees and the Tigers against the last-place Senators. The Browns trailed the Tigers by one game, and the third-place Yankees still had a mathematical chance of winning the pennant. The Browns had to sweep the Yankees while receiving help from the Senators. In a twilight doubleheader with the Yankees on Friday, September 29, the Browns did sweep the Yankees, winning the first game, 4–1, and the second, 1–0. On the same day, Washington held the Tigers to a split. On Saturday, both the Tigers and the Browns won. On Sunday, October 1, the last day of the season, before a crowd of 34,625 fans, the largest in Browns history, the Browns defeated the Yankees, 5–2. If the Tigers had won their game, there would have been a playoff game in Detroit the following day. No playoff game was needed, as Dutch Leonard and the Washington Senators defeated the Tigers, 4–1, with the help of a home run by Stan Spence. The Browns had won their only American League championship by one game over the Tigers.[67] In 1944, the club outdrew the Cardinals for the first time in 20 years.[68]

The Cardinals, on the other hand, had won their third straight pennant in a cakewalk, coming in 14½ games ahead of the second-place Pittsburgh Pirates.[69] The Cardinals entered the World Series as clear favorites against the Browns. But the Browns won the opener, 2–1, when Denny Galehouse outdueled Mort Cooper. A two-run homer by George McQuinn was all the offense the Browns needed.[70]

In the second game, Browns pitcher Nels Potter committed two errors, a mishandling of the ball and a wild throw on a bunt in the third inning. Mark Christman's bobble the following inning allowed the Cardinals to score another unearned run. After the Browns tied the game in the seventh, the Cardinals singled the winning run home in the bottom of the 11th. Bob Muncrief took the loss, while Blix Donnelly was the winning pitcher for the Cardinals.[71]

In Game Three, the Browns, now the home team, chose Jack Kramer to oppose Ted Wilks. The Browns scored four runs on five hits in the third inning after two men had been retired. Kramer, who pitched a complete game, struck out 10 Cardinals in a 6–2 victory.[72]

With the Cardinals trailing the Browns two games to one, more than 35,000 fans jammed Sportsman's Park for Game Four. The Cardinals tied the series when Harry "The Cat" Brecheen pitched a complete game as the Cardinals defeated Sig Jakucki and the Browns, 6–1. Stan Musial clouted a two-run homer, the only World Series homer of his long career. The Series was now tied at two games each.

In a rematch between Cooper and Galehouse in Game Five, both hurlers pitched complete games, but home runs by Cardinals Ray

Four. A World War and a World Series

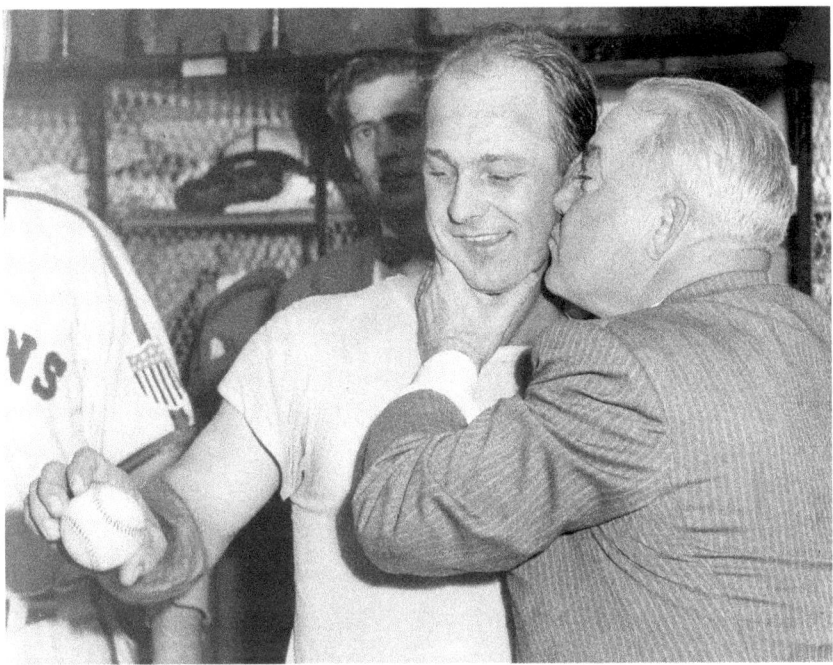

Browns owner Don Barnes (right) gives a congratulatory kiss to outfielder Chet Laabs, the hero of the final game in 1944. His power hitting helped defeat the New York Yankees, giving the Browns their only pennant in the team's history.

Sanders and Danny Litwhiler were all the runs Cooper needed. The fifth game was played before 36,569 fans, the largest crowd ever to watch the Browns play in St. Louis.[73]

Game Six, the final game of the "trolley series," was played on Monday, October 9, and was won by the Cardinals, 3–1. The Browns managed only three hits off Max Lanier and Ted Wilks. Two of the Cardinals runs were unearned, as Vern Stephens' throwing error helped the Cardinals win their fifth world championship and second in three years.[74]

Once the World Series is over, it is customary for the two participating teams to receive a share of financial receipts. As one of his last official acts, Commissioner Landis decreed that half of the 1944 World Series receipts were to be donated to war-relief agencies and that 10 percent of the players' shares were to be placed in war bonds. Sadly, Bill DeWitt commented, "Landis's decision really was a jolt to us financially because we really needed that money."[75]

The Sporting News selection of "No. 1 men in baseball" for the 1944 season honored three St. Louisans. Marty Marion, the Cardinals'

The Browns' pitching staff for the 1944 World Series. Back row, left to right: George Caster, Willis Hudlin, Weldon West, Sigmund "Jack" Jakucki, Bob Muncrief, and Jack Kramer. Front row, left to right: Tex Shirley, Denny Galehouse, Sam Zoldak, Al Hollingsworth, and Nelson Potter.

shortstop, was voted No. 1 among all players; Luke Sewell, Browns manager, was named the No. 1 manager; and William O. DeWitt, Browns general manager, was chosen the top baseball executive of 1944.[76]

Frederick G. Lieb, noted sportswriter and author, stated that DeWitt could be justly proud of this honor. "This distinction," said Lieb, "as well as all others that have marked Bill's career, were gained the hard way, for no one ever handed William Orville anything on a silver platter. He has climbed solely on his own work and ability."[77] Lieb could have given one more accolade. In 1942, two years before the Browns won their pennant, every one of their 14 farm team affiliates won a pennant or finished in the first division.[78]

In January 1945, baseball and other professional sports received the latest order from selective service announcing that deferred men classified 2-A and 2-B who had quit essential war jobs without approval were liable for induction into the armed forces. President Roosevelt also requested that Congress make 4-Fs available in "whatever capacity is best for the war effort."[79] Reacting to the president's order, DeWitt

Four. A World War and a World Series

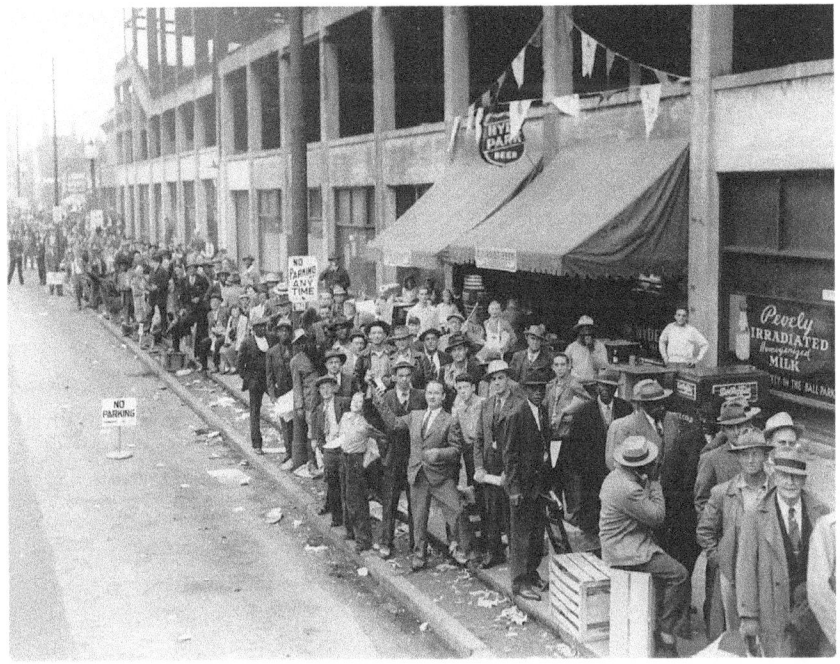

The Browns were not accustomed to drawing such large crowds, but they enjoyed both the size and the enthusiasm of the fans when the team participated in their one and only World Series in 1944.

stated, "You can't tell a thing about it as yet. We're going to do what the government says."[80] Cardinals executive Sam Breadon and DeWitt were very much in the dark regarding the manpower situation but they agreed that baseball would continue unless told to stop.[81]

Two weeks before the usual opening of spring training, no definite date had been set. DeWitt announced that he favored March 12 although he had no idea how many of the 34 players on the Browns' reserve list would be available when he officially opened camp in Cape Girardeau. The Browns' roster included 17 pitchers, four catchers, six infielders, and seven outfielders.[82]

Even though the Browns had won the American League pennant in 1944, Donald Barnes still needed to find a way to compete with the city's other baseball franchise, the Cardinals. DeWitt stated that the Browns were in better condition regarding contracts than a year earlier at this time. Ever the pre-season optimist, he believed that the Browns were justified in looking for another pennant. They had returning veterans such as catcher Frank Mancuso and pitcher Jack Kramer, who had been discharged for physical reasons. "Pete Gray, the one-armed outfielder," said DeWitt, "is almost sure to be on hand when practice gets started, because there is little likelihood of him being taken into service or into a war plant." In an uncharacteristic move, Barnes signed the one-armed player, in part to bring fans to the Browns' games. He felt that Gray could be an attraction if he could play. Barnes denied that signing Gray was in any way a publicity stunt, insisting that baseball observers felt that Gray was one of the best prospects in the minors.[83]

DeWitt's goal was to get the Browns ready to finish in first place in 1945. When the team began spring training on March 12, a dozen players had signed their contracts and shown up in Cape Girardeau. At the last minute, one of the team's brightest rookie prospects was off the roster. Pitcher Ellis Kinder notified DeWitt that he had been accepted for military duty. The Browns had counted on Kinder, who won 19 games and lost only six the previous year for Memphis of the Southern Association. He became the Browns' fourth player to enter the armed forces in 1945.[84]

On May 1, 1945, the Browns received their first and only World Series rings.

De Witt indicated that of the 16 players he classified as hold outs, only three— pitcher Jack Kramer, catcher Myron Hayworth, and outfielder Gene Moore—had not reported to Cape Girardeau. DeWitt was particularly concerned with the failure of Jack Kramer to sign. Kramer was asking for an increase of $5,000 over what he had earned in 1944. DeWitt, however, only indicated that the club had made him what it thought was a generous offer, but the pitcher refused to sign.[85]

The 1945 major league schedule

Four. A World War and a World Series 65

announced in mid–March listed the Browns for 43 home night games. In addition, one of the Browns' holiday dates was a twilight-night combo in Washington on Memorial Day; the Browns were also scheduled for a twilight-night doubleheader in Detroit on June 12.[86]

DeWitt informed the press that the Browns might have discovered three "finds of the season." He listed Pete Gray first; the second "find" was "Babe" Martin, who could play both the outfield and catch and had a very unusual family background. Of Yugoslavian descent, Boris Michael Martinovich was the son of a one-ime professional wrestler and member of the King's Guard in Belgrade. DeWitt's third "find" was Leonard Schulte, whose bad knee could qualify him for the Browns' 4-F infield.[87] None of the three had a major league career lasting more than two years.[88]

Pete Gray, the one-armed outfielder, continued to attract much attention from onlookers who were amazed at his ability to hit, field and throw, despite his handicap. Browns coach Freddy Hofmann talked of little else. "Why, he whacked several balls which would have been against the right field screen in Sportsman's Park," declared Hofmann. "I believe he will hit the screen regularly."[89] Bill DeWitt assured the baseball writers that Gray was going to have to qualify on his own merits. "Take my word, Pete Gray is going to make the major league grade on ability—not on sympathy, or as some sort of a front window showpiece. And if he can't make the grade, he'll be the first one to ask to be sent away."[90]

Luke Sewell also made it clear that he was not giving Gray any special treatment, telling the press Gray would have to "stand or fall" on what he showed. "We can't play him if he weakens the team." Gray had an excellent attitude; he was courteous to the press, he displayed a pleasant, winning smile, and for the most part he was accepted by his teammates. However, as the season progressed and the Browns fell to seventh place, some of his mates began to blame Gray for their dismal season and were openly critical of him. They resented what they felt was the Browns' decision to risk a pennant for good public relations. Gray spent only the 1945 season in the major leagues.[91]

There was also disagreement in the Browns' front office between Barnes and Richard Muckerman, the largest minority stockholder, over policy. Finally, DeWitt suggested to Barnes that since he and Dick Muckerman were unable to agree on how to run the ball club, Barnes should buy out Muckerman's interest. Barnes replied that he really didn't want to invest any more money or time on what he considered a bad investment. DeWitt made the same suggestion to Muckerman, who took him up on the it. On August 10, 1945, as World War II was ending, Donald

In 1945, the St. Louis Browns purchased Pete Gray, a one-armed outfielder, from the Memphis Chicks. He played 77 games for the Browns and hit .218. Most of his teammates resented his being in the lineup, claiming he cost his team a first-place finish. The Browns released him prior to the 1946 season.

Barnes disposed of his American League championship team, selling out to Richard Muckerman, announcing: "Now that the Browns have won their first American League pennant and the company is in favorable financial position, I feel the purpose for which I entered baseball is accomplished."[92]

The sale of his holdings to Muckerman netted Barnes $200,000. Barnes claimed that he had accomplished "my three big ambitions; I finally saw a St. Louis American League pennant go up; I saw Sportsman's Park jammed on the last day of the '44 season; and I am leaving the Browns in sound financial condition." He did not state, however, that he had left the Browns mired in seventh place in the American League.[93]

Five

Richard Muckerman and the Post-War Years

Richard D. Muckerman, a Browns rooter since the George Sisler era, was the executive vice president of City Ice and Fuel Company in St. Louis, and the newest owner of the St. Louis Browns.[1] Unlike Barnes, he had been an avid Browns fan his entire life and for years had been buying stock in the Browns. Muckerman owned a private box at Sportsman's Park. In 1922, he attended the three games when the Browns played the New York Yankees and nearly won the pennant. He added that when the Browns got to the World Series in 1944, he "was the happiest man in St. Louis."[2]

Muckerman made it evident that DeWitt was going to run the team. "I told Bill DeWitt just to keep me informed as to what he is doing, but that his judgment is mine so far as running the ball club is concerned. What takes place on the field is up to Sewell," Muckerman continued. "I certainly am not going to try to tell him what to do and I am with Sewell and DeWitt 100 percent."[3]

Muckerman's team was entrenched in seventh place when the sale was finalized, but the Browns had a resurgence beginning with a mid–August homestand. The Browns divided a six-game series with the Indians and then took three of four games from the Athletics, three of five from the Senators, four straight from the Yankees, four of seven from the Red Sox, and five straight from the White Sox. It was the Browns' pitching that helped the team move up in the standings. During one homestand, the Browns' rotation of Hollingsworth, Jakucki, Muncreif, and Potter restored the Browns' hope of winning a second consecutive pennant.[4]

The Browns played .657 ball in August, thanks to Hollingsworth's amazing pitching, the team's outstanding defense from Don Gutteridge and Mark Christman, and the timely hitting of Vern Stephens, George McQuinn, and Chet Laabs. Their remarkable homestand helped lift the

Browns from seventh place, 10½ games out of first, to third place, only four games behind the league-leading Detroit Tigers and three games behind the second-place Washington Senators.[5] It would mark the last St. Louis Browns finish in the first division.

Not only did Muckerman retain DeWitt and Sewell, Jimmy Conzelman was kept as the team's public relations agent. Muckerman also retained control of the club's minor league teams, which included San Antonio in the Texas League, Toledo in the American Association, Springfield Illinois in the 3-I League, and Youngstown in the Ohio State League. In addition, he maintained working agreements with several other minor league organizations. Muckerman also approved Luke Sewell's recent trade sending outfielder Mike Kreevich to Washington and losing relief pitcher George Caster to Detroit on waivers.[6]

In September, DeWitt revealed that in 1946, the Browns would return to Anaheim for their spring training after three springs in Cape Girardeau. It would mark the first time government regulations removed the restrictions that a major league baseball team had to train close to home. DeWitt expected the Browns would be playing their exhibition games with the two Chicago teams and Coast league clubs.[7]

Bill DeWitt made his first trade since Muckerman replaced Barnes as owner of the Browns. In a straight swap, with no money involved, the Browns sent first baseman George McQuinn to the Philadelphia Athletics for first baseman Dick Siebert. Athletics manager Connie Mack said, "Both DeWitt and I thought a change would do our clubs a lot of good, and these players too. Both have been with us for many years. That was the only thought we had in mind making the trade." In St. Louis, DeWitt said the trade was the first of several planned to strengthen the club for the 1946 season.[8]

Later that month, DeWitt announced that Johnny Berardino, who had been in the navy since early in the 1942 season, had received his discharge and would be available for the Browns' 1946 season.[9] But to the probable relief of many of his teammates, DeWitt sent Pete Gray to the Toledo club of the American Association. When Gray heard the news over the radio, he admitted, "I figured I had a bad year, and I knew deep down I was going to be sent somewhere else. But I really didn't care. Even the salary didn't mean anything, as long as I was playing baseball and it was every day."[10]

In December, baseball's Major League owners held their 1945 winter meeting in Chicago. It was baseball's first conference since WWII and the first convention since "Happy" Chandler had been elected commissioner. DeWitt attended the meeting for many reasons. Many important issues were on the table and, of course, it would give DeWitt an opportunity to see his old friend, Branch Rickey, now an executive with the Brooklyn Dodgers. It was also the first major baseball gathering since Rickey had signed Jackie Robinson.[11]

As the executives were about to leave the meeting, Rickey, who was sitting near DeWitt, felt ill and whispered to his friend, "William, please help me, the room is spinning. If I get up, I'll make a fool of myself." DeWitt was concerned about his friend's health, for Rickey had been keeping his usual hectic pace. He described his condition to DeWitt: "My balance is off; I can't stand up straight; and the pain in my ear is overwhelming." DeWitt managed to get Rickey back to his hotel room and called Branch Rickey, Jr. Father and son took the next available train back to Brooklyn, where Rickey checked into a hospital. Tests determined he was suffering from a very painful and relatively rare condition, Meniere's disease. It was caused by an imbalance in the inner ear, resulting in vertigo, nausea, and lack of balance. Rickey was back in form in ample time to plan the Dodgers' spring training.[12]

At the conclusion of the 1945 season, Browns general manager William O. DeWitt and Manager Luke Sewell each won a Sporting News Award for their accomplishments in 1944. Luke Sewell won for leading the Browns to a pennant and making the team a worthy foe for the Cardinals in the World Series. The Cardinals had been expected to make the World Series a runaway, and it was agreed that Sewell's managing in 1944 was due to the knowledge he assimilated during his days as a catcher, coach, and military pilot.[13]

DeWitt's award for Executive of the Year was the result of his rare accomplishments in giving St. Louis its first American League pennant winner and making the Browns a success at the gate in one year. DeWitt was praised for converting the Browns from a second-division outfit into a championship team through his judicious acquisition of talent. He was recognized for taking chances in disposing of veterans who previously had been the mainstays of the team, giving the Browns enough strength to "tip the scales."[14]

DeWitt hoped that his team could improve its third-place finish in 1945 by getting off to a good start in 1946. Their spring training starting date was earlier than previous years because DeWitt had to trim his oversized squad down to the maximum for Opening Day. DeWitt also pointed out that he certainly didn't lack for outfielders, as five outfielders—Walt Judnich, Joe Grace, Al Zarilla, Glen "Red" McQuillen, and Albert "Fuzz" White—all ex-servicemen, had already signed their 1946 contracts. DeWitt was counting on these returning veterans to add a much-needed punch to the team's offense. DeWitt also added six more outfielders—Milt Byrnes, Lou Finney, Chet Laabs, Gene

Moore, George Bradley, and Boris Martin—to his spring training roster as insurance.[15]

The 1946 spring training differed from previous ones in one important way. DeWitt discovered that the housing shortage at Anaheim, California, was acute, and he notified the 65 players expected to report that they would be quartered in three hotels and several private homes, asking them not to bring their wives.[16] DeWitt did not expect that this suggestion would be very popular, and he was correct. Fred Sanford, a recently released GI and one of the most highly regarded of the new pitchers said, "I didn't see my wife and kids for two years while I was serving in the Pacific theater, and I intend seeing something of them now. They'll be at Anaheim."[17]

The first holdout of 1946 was pitcher Jack Kramer, who said he would not sign his contract since it proposed a pay cut of $2,000.[18] Another player who refused to sign was Vern Stephens. Salary was not the issue; Stephens objected to clauses regarding his conduct. He had received several disciplinary fines in the 1945 season.[19]

One of the veterans on the Browns' roster, Don Gutteridge, who played five seasons for the Cardinals and four for the Browns, was given the job as player-manager of the Browns' No. 1 farm club—Toledo of Class AAA American Association. DeWitt said, "Don gave loyal service to the club. He was a hustler and will be an asset to our organization."[20] Gutteridge's going to Toledo created the opportunity to insert Bob Dillinger, a highly-touted Army infielder, into Sewell's 1946 postwar Browns inner defense. Dillinger, who was called "Player of the Pacific," could play any infield position, although he was considered best at third base. However, with Mark Christman claiming that position, it was unlikely he would be dislodged. Sewell, pleased with the versatility he had on his team, said that every position on the team, with the exception of shortstop, was wide open.[21] After the signing of four more players, outfielders Lou Finney and Bernard Lutz and pitchers Sam Zoldak and Fred Sanford, Jack Kramer remained the only important holdout. DeWitt said, "My contract negotiations with all the other players are proceeding favorably."[22]

The Browns soon realized that they had a serious holdout on their hands, and it was not Jack Kramer. It was their star, Vern Stephens. At the end of February, DeWitt announced that he was going to Anaheim to discuss the problem. At the same time, Luke Sewell talked with Stephens for two hours without reaching an agreement.[23] Stephens maintained that the Browns continued to tell him he had had a bad year and continued to offer the same contract he had been turning down. "I led the league in fielding, led the league in home runs, and batted .290. And who else on the club drove in 89 runs? All that doesn't add up to a bad year," countered Stephens.[24] DeWitt said he was sending a new contract to Stephens, adding that the disgruntled shortstop was not for sale. "He will play with the Browns or remain idle in so far as organized baseball is concerned."[25] By the end of March, Stephens had yet to sign a contract with the Browns, and there were rumors that he would sign with the Washington Senators. "We resent any suggestion like that," said DeWitt. "We are not offering any trades."[26]

There were also rumors that Stephens was heading for Mexico to play in the Mexican League. The Pasquel brothers, who were trying to establish a big Mexico baseball league, spoke with Stephens to finalize a deal with the Browns shortstop. Luke Sewell called that a serious move on Stephens' part. "If Stephens signs the contract with the Pasquels and is not on hand with the Browns for the opening of the season on April 16, he automatically will face a five-year suspension from organized baseball under Commissioner Chandler's recent edict."[27] DeWitt offered Stephens $13,000, but Stephens said he had been offered more and that he was prepared to enter a five-year contract with the Pasquel Brothers. He added, "I won't have anything to do with the Browns unless they call me."[28]

When DeWitt arrived in California, he first heard that Stephens had already won a game for Vera Cruz. After listening to the story, DeWitt responded, "Well, what do you want me to do? Break down and cry? It's fine for Stephens and there's nothing we are going to do about it. The Browns are not worrying. We've got two men for shortstop—Mark Christman and Leonard Schulte. Christman will not hit the long ball, but he'll outhit Stephens for an average. We are not worried."[29]

Five days later, Stephens rejoined the St. Louis Browns and quickly signed a one-year contract. Neither the Browns nor league officials penalized him. American League president William Harridge said the league wouldn't penalize Stephens because he had not signed a previous contract with the Browns. None of the Browns officials would disclose the terms of his new contract.[30] Commissioner Chandler, who also refused to penalize him, urged other major leaguers who had signed with Mexican League clubs to return before the opening of the season and avoid facing a five-year suspension.[31]

The major league schedules had been announced early in March, and the Browns were pleased that they were slated to play 42 night games at home, more than any other American League team. The Cardinals had 38 home night games, giving St. Louis baseball fans the opportunity to see more than half the home games at Sportsman's Park under the lights.[32]

The increase in night games brought a change to two popular youth programs offered by the St. Louis MLB clubs. For years, both the Cardinals and Browns had allowed children 16 years and under to be admitted free—the Cardinals' Knothole Gang and the Browns' Brownie Brigade. DeWitt announced a substitute plan beginning with the 1946 season. Children under the age of 16 would still be admitted free to games, but only in chaperoned groups upon application by various organizations. This change was designed to prevent possible juvenile delinquency from unchaperoned children at night games. "We are trying to avoid destruction of property, injury to other children and theft of property belonging to other children. The children will continue to be seated in their usual place in the grandstand along the left field foul line."[33]

DeWitt felt that once he had solved his dispute with Vern Stephens, his personnel problems were over. Unfortunately, that was not the case, for he had to resolve an issue with Connie Mack. DeWitt had traded first baseman George McQuinn to Mack's Philadelphia Athletics even up for first baseman Norman Siebert. After four days in Anaheim, Siebert informed DeWitt that he had a radio job in St. Paul, Minnesota, his hometown, and that he intended to retire as a player. After one short meeting with DeWitt, Siebert left training camp.[34] DeWitt told Mack that if Seibert was serious about quitting baseball, the Browns expected another player or a cash settlement from the Athletics. The Philadelphia president and manager expressed indignation. "He wanted to give me an argument," said DeWitt, "but I reminded him that my action was protected and governed by baseball laws."[35] DeWitt reminded Mack that the Browns were not going to "hold the bag" while Siebert made up his mind. "I explained to Mr. Mack that if he desired to protest my recall of McQuinn or a settlement, we should carry the case to Commissioner Chandler."[36]

DeWitt was quite disappointed by the Commissioner's ruling. According to Chandler, McQuinn would remain the property of the Philadelphia Athletics. Since Siebert quit baseball after failing to come to terms with the Browns, Chandler's ruling meant the Browns would have to stand the loss.[37]

While DeWitt was waiting for Chandler's ruling, he continued to make roster moves. He traded a minor league outfielder along with some cash to the New York Yankees for catcher Kenny Sears, a slugging backstop. DeWitt felt that the acquisition of Sears gave the Browns greater catching strength than it had had in years.[38] He purchased right-handed pitcher Ellis Kinder, the most recent arrival from military ranks, from the minor league Memphis squad. He also optioned catcher Babe Martin to Oakland of the Pacific Coast League, subject to 24-hour recall.[39]

Five. Richard Muckerman and the Post-War Years

Even after the season began, DeWitt continued adjusting the Browns' roster. Before the club embarked on a long road trip, he sold outfielder Lou Finney and pitcher Al Minar to the Phillies on inter-league waivers, and outfielder George Bradley was optioned to Toledo. DeWitt was especially sorry to release Sundra, one of the club's best prewar pitchers. However, Sundra returned from the army with two damaged knees, and he was unable to pivot or get his old stuff back on the ball.[40]

DeWitt obtained outfielder Jeff Heath, a former GI who had been in the navy for four years, for Joe Grace and pitcher Al LaMacchia, a former St. Louis American Legion star who at one time was highly regarded as a pitching prospect. It seemed redundant that DeWitt acquired outfielder Heath when he already had Grace, but at the time DeWitt made the deal, Heath's batting average was .283 compared to Grace's average of .227. Both DeWitt and Sewell were aware that Heath could be a "troublemaker" at times, but when Sewell was a coach for the Indians, he got to know Heath and was sure he knew how to handle him. "I'm not concerned with what Heath used to do or the things they said he did," said Sewell. "If he can hit that ball for me, I'm sure we'll get along."[41]

The Browns were also concerned about their pitching. It had been weeks since Nels Potter, one of the team's starting pitchers, pitched a complete game. He had been taking x-ray treatments in his right arm and shoulder. "It never fails," said DeWitt. "Just as Kramer now is pitching well for us, and Galehouse shows signs of regaining his form, we have Potter laid up with a lame arm."[42]

The club still had players who were performing well but who were overlooked. Bill DeWitt was outspoken when second baseman Johnny Berardino was omitted from the American League's 25-man All-Star squad. In a telegram to American League president Will Harridge, DeWitt called the omission a gross injustice, unfair to the player, the entire club, and the fans of St. Louis. He recommended returning the player selection to a vote of fans in the future.[43]

Sewell's record as Browns manager in 1946 was 53–77.[44] Although Sewell had won a pennant for the Browns in 1944, few people remembered that the team won the pennant primarily because the best players for the New York Yankees and Boston Red Sox were still in the service. Even Muckerman failed to realize that once the war ended, it would be difficult for the Browns to compete with teams whose star players like DiMaggio, Williams, Feller, and Greenberg were returning from the service.[45]

Although Sewell had won a pennant for the Browns with the best players DeWitt could provide, Muckerman decided the team needed a new manager. It came as no surprise that he wanted to make the change

Johnny Berardino had an 11-year career in the major leagues, including seven with the St. Louis Browns, but he is equally recognizable for his numerous movie roles and his three-decade portrayal of Dr. Steve Hardy on the TV soap opera, *General Hospital*.

before the end of the season.[46] On August 31, 1946, and under pressure, Luke Sewell resigned as manager of the St. Louis Browns, effective immediately "for the good of the club." Muckerman accepted Sewell's resignation and appointed former catcher Zack Taylor to replace him.[47] Taylor, who played for the Browns organization in San Antonio and Toledo, was well-liked by the players. However, it was obvious that Taylor would not be managing the team in 1947. Muckerman said, "I have two or three men in mind."[48] The club said it had made a satisfactory salary settlement with Sewell, who was to be paid in full for 1946 and also receive the greater part of his salary for 1947.[49] Herold D. "Muddy" Ruel, a native St. Louisan, signed a two-year contract to manage the Browns, the club with which he made his professional debut as a catcher in 1915.[50]

The Browns finished the 1946 season in seventh place, with a record of 66–88, 38 games behind the pennant-winning Boston Red Sox.[51] In addition to naming Muddy Ruel their new manager, Muckerman made a few other appointments: Robert Finch, nine-year veteran of baseball's

Muddy Ruel, new manager of the Browns, meets with owner Richard Muckerman and general manager Bill DeWitt, Sr.

front offices, joined the Browns as farm club director and assistant to Bill DeWitt. Former chief scout Jack Fournier, who had been with the Brooklyn Dodgers since leaving the Browns, was appointed director of scouting, and Bill's brother, Charley DeWitt, was appointed traveling secretary. Most importantly, Muckerman emphasized that Bill DeWitt, vice president and general manager, would continue to have complete charge of the operations of the entire Browns organization.[52]

During the 1946 season, Muckerman spent half a million dollars to purchase Sportsman's Park from the Phil Ball estate. At the end of 1946, he spent close to $750,000 more to completely refurbish Sportsman's Park.[53] He repaired leaky roofs and broken chairs, constructed new ramps, upgraded the elevators and powder rooms, and installed new concession stands and a VIP lounge. Muckerman also authorized more than $700,000 to construct a new field for the San Antonio Missions, their number one farm team. When all the repairs were completed, the team's traveling secretary, Charley DeWitt, estimated that Sportsman's Park was valued in the neighborhood of $1.25 million.[54]

Bill DeWitt began preparing for 1947 spring training and working on players' contracts for the 1947 season. Although DeWitt agreed that the Browns had set a record attendance figure for 1946, he felt that none of the players deserved pay raises. "I only wish that more of our players had done something to justify increases," said DeWitt, "but I've scanned the official records of our players, and they're not all complimentary."[55]

Surprisingly, once players received their contracts, many signed and returned them quickly. Jeff Heath, a frequent holdout when he played for the Cleveland Indians, was the first player to sign and return his 1947 contract. As expected, terms of the contract were not disclosed. Bill DeWitt anticipated no difficulties in signing other members of the club, saying, "I just started the job the first of the year and it probably will be another week or 10 days before all of them have been placed in the mail."[56]

Home with a bad cold, DeWitt was delighted to receive premier shortstop Vern Stephens' signed contract. Stephens' refusal to sign a year ago had led to a confrontation with Mexican baseball. The GM was also very pleased with signing Johnny Berardino, a player who had given him headaches previously. DeWitt received more good news when Fred Sanford, who was looked upon as the rookie most likely to succeed, signed his 1947 contract. The 27-year-old pitcher came to the Browns from Toledo late in the year and pitched two consecutive shutouts for the Browns. In fact, the elated DeWitt was happy to get all his key men signed and have his new manager prepared to take over the club when spring training was scheduled to begin in Miami, Florida.[57] DeWitt also signed two rookies, native St. Louisan Jerry Witte and Lester Moss, of whom much was expected. Witte hit .314 for Toledo and led the American Association in home runs with 46. Moss, a catcher, also played in Toledo in 1946, when he hit .297. Both men were called up to the Browns in the late fall.[58] By the middle of February, only six of the squad's 40 players had not signed a contract. DeWitt said none of the unsigned players could be regarded as holdouts and that he expected them all to be in the fold prior to the opening of spring training.

One of the reasons given for the Browns' poor performance in 1946 was the large number of holdouts which interfered with spring training. Muckerman wanted to avoid many holdouts impacting spring training; he ordered DeWitt to sign all players without haggling over salaries. "We'll have none of that this season," he told DeWitt. "Sign the players without bickering." DeWitt followed Muckerman's instructions.[59]

DeWitt was not only involved with the signing of the Browns' players, he was working the team's radio broadcast. Harry Caray and Gabby Street were going to air the Cardinals' games. DeWitt announced that Johnny O'Hara and Dizzy Dean would broadcast both the Browns' home

Five. Richard Muckerman and the Post-War Years

and road games. Although Dean said he was "still going to pull for the Cardinal players because they're a great bunch," he was "happy to be out of the Cardinal chain," adding "the office part, anyway." DeWitt said that radio surveys for 1946 showed that Dean had the largest baseball following in St. Louis, and "the Browns are happy to offer Dean the opportunity to continue his contracts with his large local following." DeWitt said that some of the Browns' games would be televised over KSD-TV on an experimental basis.[60]

The Browns began their spring training with an optimistic outlook. Expectations were high for a successful 1947. Much of this sanguinity came from *The Sporting News*' pick of the Browns to finish fifth. Heavy emphasis was placed on Ruel's appointment. "The Browns are envisioned as rising from the muck."[61]

Bill DeWitt had been elated when he first learned that the Browns' 1947 spring headquarters would be Miami, Florida. He felt that locale was not only ideal from a weather perspective but also that it would be a financial boon for the organization. He was completely wrong on this latter assumption, realizing quickly that the Florida training base did not meet his expectations. Costs were much too high, and the club would have to pay out about $30,000 more than it took in. DeWitt wondered if it was worth while financially for the Browns to train at what he called "this playground of the wealthy."[62]

Furthermore, attendance at exhibition games was poor. A Sunday exhibition game with Brooklyn drew only 2,000 spectators. He quickly discovered that people continued to stay away from the ballpark while the horse and dog tracks were running; the jai alai games also did a thriving business. Even though the cost of a ball game was much cheaper than a clubhouse admission to either Gulfstream or Hialeah, the Browns never played before a capacity crowd of 3,000 fans. DeWitt could never understand why players such as Hank Greenberg, Ralph Kiner, Mort Cooper, or Johnny Hopp could not draw fans to the ballpark.[63]

Two other teams were training in the Miami area: the Pittsburgh Pirates, just across the causeway at Miami Beach, and the Boston Braves, 24 miles away at Fort Lauderdale. DeWitt learned that the Pirates were having the same problem in drawing fans to the ballpark.[64] Two months later, DeWitt made it official. He stated that in 1948 the Browns would visit San Bernardino, California, for their spring training. He said the Browns had decided not to return to Miami because there would be "inadequate playing facilities next year." Miami officials planned to enlarge the Orange Bowl at the expense of the adjacent ballpark.[65] DeWitt added that San Bernardino, the former training headquarters of the Pirates, offered excellent climate in addition to outstanding facilities. He also emphasized that it is "a city of 50,000, located only 60 miles east of Los Angeles." DeWitt announced that the Pirates were also moving their spring training headquarters somewhere in the Los Angeles area in 1948.[66]

Much of the baseball news during 1947 was routine: preparing for spring training, holdouts and their eventual signings, the discovery of rookies who might have an impact on a team's final standing, and comments on the season when it ended. The most important story of the 1947 baseball season involved the racial integration of major league players.

In 1947, three major league clubs integrated—the Brooklyn Dodgers, the Cleveland Indians, and the St. Louis Browns. The story of Robinson's signing a contract to play in Montreal and his promotion to the Dodgers is well known. Robinson hoped that he had led the way for other teams to sign players based on their ability to play baseball and not the color of their skin. He was especially pleased when two teams in the American League also added black players to their rosters. On July 4, 1947, the Cleveland Indians signed 22-year-old Larry Doby, an infielder-outfielder for the Newark Eagles of the Negro National League. Branch Rickey, who had signed Robinson, was well aware of Doby's abilities and would have been delighted to have him on the Dodgers, but he already had a number of outfield candidates, and the last thing he wanted was to corner the market on black players.[67]

Unlike Robinson, Larry Doby had leapfrogged the minor leagues to become the first black player in the American League. Robinson wrote of Doby, "I am glad to know that another Negro player is in the majors. I'm no longer in there by myself."[68]

By the end of June 1947, the Browns were in last place in the American League and playing ball in a nearly empty stadium. Both Bill DeWitt and Richard Muckerman were aware that Jackie Robinson was drawing large crowds at whichever ballpark he played. At that time, St. Louis was the most southerly city in major league baseball, and Muckerman and DeWitt hoped possible black fan interest in an African American baseball player might help fill up their desolate park. In July 1947, Rickey's former protégé, Bill DeWitt, general manager of the St. Louis Browns, became the third major league official to join the integration program. Owner Richard Muckerman gave DeWitt permission to sign not one, but two black outfielders, Willard Brown and Hank Thompson, to join his struggling team. Both outfielders came from the Kansas City Monarchs, the most prominent team to play in the Negro Leagues.[69] DeWitt was chiefly interested in 36-year-old Willard Brown, a powerful hitter,

Five. Richard Muckerman and the Post-War Years 79

Branch Rickey often met with the DeWitt brothers when he was in St. Louis.

but also signed 21-year-old Thompson in order for the two players to help support each other.[70]

Unfortunately, the Browns' efforts to attract more people to the ballpark simply did not work. In their haste, Muckerman and DeWitt ended up with an outfielder who had seen better days and a youngster who was simply inexperienced. Both players were released prior to the end of the 1947 season. Thompson resurfaced with the New York Giants in 1949 and would play on two pennant winners in 1951 and 1954. Willard Brown's major league career consisted of 21 games and 67 at-bats with the Browns.[71]

DeWitt and the Browns have been criticized unfairly for insincerity in integrating their club. When DeWitt obtained both Brown and Thompson, he stated, "It seems that this large Negro population should have some representation on their city's ball team." St. Louis did have one of the highest non-white populations among major league cities. DeWitt really wanted to see a black player succeed in St. Louis, and not merely for financial reasons. The Browns made an honest attempt to recruit black players, and they made inroads in this area before most of their contemporaries.[72]

In 1947, the Browns became the third major league organization to integrate when they signed Henry Thompson (left) and Willard Brown (right).

In addition to the two black players the Browns obtained from the Monarchs, they negotiated an option on Negro Leagues star Piper Davis of the Birmingham Black Barons at the same they acquired the rights to Brown and Thompson. The 30-year-old Davis was considered by many a better player than either Brown or Thompson. Davis was the player-manager of the Barons, however, and he preferred to lead them to the Negro American League pennant. Unfortunately, the Browns let his option lapse.[73]

In late July–early August, both local fans and the American League began to worry about the viability of the St. Louis Browns. The plight began to attract potential buyers as they witnessed the team's stock dropping below $3.62 per share, the lowest it had been since Muckerman purchased the franchise. Emory C. Perry of Chicago was rumored to have made an offer for purchasing the Browns on behalf of a syndicate. Muckerman said he didn't know the man, had never even heard of him, and had received no offer. If he should receive an offer to sell the club, Muckerman replied, "Well, you always look at an offer, even if it's for a race horse."[74]

Perry, a consulting engineer, was a friend of Babe Ruth and claimed to be a representative of a Chicago baseball syndicate interested in the Browns franchise. If the club was purchased, with Ruth in the front

Five. Richard Muckerman and the Post-War Years

office, the team would move the franchise to California, probably Los Angeles.[75]

Over the next few weeks, Perry made an offer of $1 million for the team. In addition to the team, Perry wanted five minor-league clubs and Sportsman's Park. When he discovered that the Browns had had no scouts during the war and were therefore far behind in competing for young talent, his enthusiasm dwindled. He ran into further obstacles when he learned that if he moved the team to Los Angeles, he would discover that conditions had changed since Barnes had made his aborted attempt to move the Browns in 1941. Any outside team now attempting to infringe on the territory of an existing Pacific Coast League team had to pay a penalty.[76] When Muckerman challenged Perry to make a solid bid, Perry disappeared from the scene.[77]

In the final month of a miserable season, with the Browns deeply mired in the cellar, DeWitt discovered another way to draw fans into the ballpark. Throughout most of the 1947 season, Dizzy Dean, while broadcasting the team's home games, constantly berated the pitching staff of the Browns, wondering how they had the gall to pick up their paychecks. He boasted that despite his age and his absence from the mound, he was still better than any pitcher on the Browns' roster.

DeWitt sensed an opportunity to draw some fans into the ballpark on the team's final 1947 game; he started the game with Dean on the mound. Dean lasted several innings before leaving the game with a pulled leg muscle. He received a standing ovation from 16,000 fans, the second-highest attendance for a game that year. St. Louis lost, marking 95 defeats, the most the Browns had lost since 1939.[78] Attendance dropped by more than 200,000 from the previous year.

The Browns ended the 1947 season in the cellar with a record of 59–95, 38 games behind the New York Yankees.[79] Kramer was the only pitcher with double-digit wins (11–16). Potter slumped to 4–10 and knew he would not be back with the Browns in 1948. Ellis Kinder, who broke in with the Browns in 1946, appeared in 34 games and went 8–15. Fred Sanford lost 16 games, Bob Muncrief lost 14, and Sam Zoldak lost 10, making six pitchers with losses in double figures.[80]

Weeks after the end of the season, rumors arose that Muddy Ruel's two-year contract would be bought out. It was also rumored that Ruel did not see eye to eye with general manager Bill DeWitt and his brother Charley on club policy. Muckerman voiced his disappointment with both Ruel's and the team's performance. Ruel shared his disappointment with the Browns but took exception to Muckerman's evaluation of his work. "I fell heir to a seventh-place team, and I feel certain the material was not on hand to improve the Browns position," he argued.[81]

On November 5, Bill DeWitt announced that Zack Taylor would return as Browns manager, the post he held temporarily between the firings of two of his predecessors. Coach Fred Hoffman was rehired for the tenth consecutive season, and Ralph Winegarner, manager of the Browns' Elmira club of the Eastern League, was brought in to replace coach Earle Combs. Combs, a former Yankees outfielder, left on his own, supposedly to try for a coaching job with his old skipper, Joe McCarthy, now managing the Boston Red Sox.[82]

Zack Taylor made one promise when he took over the reins of the Browns. "I can't say much about the team because I haven't seen the Browns in action since last spring. But I don't think we've got an old ball club and I expect to have a better spirit among the players than before. Spirit is as important on a baseball team as it is on any other job."[83] One of Bill DeWitt's first comments to the press was that every man on the team was subject to trade if such a deal would strengthen the team.[84] It was a statement sure to deflate morale, but DeWitt kept his word.

In reality, DeWitt's objective may have been less about strengthening the team than about improving the Browns' immediate financial position. After spending approximately $2,000,000 on the purchase and renovation of Sportsman's Park and the construction of a new park for their affiliate in San Antonio, Muckerman faced a mountain of debt. Looking back in 1951, Sid Keener, writing in *The Sporting News*, described a dire situation: "Action was necessary. Immediate action. Creditors were pressing claims for collection.... There was only one avenue of escape—the sale of assets in the form of players."[85]

On November 17, DeWitt, as he promised, made his first megadeal. He sent Vern Stephens and Jack Kramer to the Boston Red Sox in exchange for pitchers Jim Wilson, Al Widmar, and Joe Ostrowski; catcher Roy Partee; infielder Eddie Pellagrini; and outfielder Pete Layden—along with $310,000 in cash.[86] After he completed the trade, DeWitt declared, "I'll bet that before winter is over, the Browns will have made more deals than any other team in baseball."[87]

While the Browns were busy unloading their players, another bid to purchase the team materialized. This interest originated in Los Angeles, but the bid came from Baltimore. Rob Rodenberg, president of the Baltimore Colts of the All-American Professional Football Conference, was interested in acquiring a major league baseball franchise for Baltimore to replace the minor league team in the International League already in Baltimore.[88] Rodenberg's bid had to clear two roadblocks. First, it depended on the Cardinals buying the St. Louis ballpark and then leasing it back to him for $35,000 per year. The second problem,

Five. Richard Muckerman and the Post-War Years

which killed the deal, involved Frank Shaughnessy, International League president. He made it clear to Rodenberg that the International League had no intention of allowing any one to transfer one of his franchises around.[89] There were other offers for the Browns franchise in the next few months, but none of them involved a serious offer.

The player trade with the Boston Red Sox opened the proverbial flood gates. DeWitt did a thriving business over the next 13 months in a succession of trades that generated much-needed money for the Browns. On November 18, the day after the Stephens-Kramer trade, DeWitt sent pitcher Ellis Kinder and infielder Billy Hitchcock to the Red Sox in exchange for infielders Sam Dente and Bill Sommers, pitcher Clem Dreisewerd, and $65,000; two days later, he traded Muncrief and Judnich to the Indians for pinch hitter and outfielder Joe Frazier, outfielder Dick Kokos, pitcher Bryan Stephens, and $25,000; on December 4, he sold slugging outfielder Jeff Heath to the Braves for $25,000; and on December 9, he landed infielder John Berardino with the Indians, who gave up outfielder–first baseman George Metkovich and $50,000. (After Metkovich was returned to Cleveland a few months later, the Indians sent an additional $15,000.)

Other revenue-generating moves followed in 1948. On June 5, DeWitt shipped outfielder Ray Coleman to the Athletics for outfielder–first baseman George Binks and $20,000; on June 15, DeWitt moved pitcher Sam Zoldak to the Indians for another hurler, Bill Kennedy, and $100,000; a month later, on July 18, he sent catcher Les Moss to the Red Sox for pitcher Jim Suchecki, catcher Matt Batts, and a player to be named later (pitcher Jim McDonald), along with $100,000; on October 4, he traded Dente to the Senators for pitcher Tom Ferrick, infielder John Sullivan, and $25,000; and on December 13, he exchanged Fred Sanford and Roy Partee for Sherm Lollar, Red Embree, Dick Starr and, again, $100,000, all courtesy of the Yankees.[90] In addition, DeWitt sold the Browns' rundown AAA farm club in Toledo to the Detroit Tigers, who purchased the Mud Hens for $200,000 in December 1948, realizing a profit of some $150,000.[91]

It is not surprising that the majority of DeWitt's sales and trades were received negatively. DeWitt insisted that by cleaning out the dugout, the Browns would build a fast, young, hustling ball club for summer 1948. He also pointed out that his new team could not possibly do worse than the recently sold "stars" who finished in the cellar last year.[92]

During 1948, the Browns continued to unload their players all around the major leagues. And they continued to monopolize the headlines both on the field and off. Early in the year, Bill DeWitt was in Barnes Hospital with a severe gall bladder attack, but his brother, Charley, pinch-hit for him, trying to mollify the New York Yankees, who were criticizing the Browns for their deal with the Boston Red Sox, which they felt gave the Sox an advantage in the 1948 pennant race.[93]

Bill DeWitt spent three weeks in the hospital and was scheduled for surgery in February. During his stay, new manager Zack Taylor came to visit, and the two men spent some time discussing the coming year.[94] DeWitt also received a letter from Jerry Priddy, sold by Washington to the Browns. He wrote DeWitt that he was elated to play with a young, hustling team, and in a park better suited to his hitting. He wrote, "I expect to have the kind of year I honestly feel I am capable of having with the bat." He predicted the team would surprise some critics.[95]

The Browns' spring training for the 1948 season was scheduled to begin March 1 in San Bernardino, California, for one season. The training site would then revert to the Pirates, who had trained there for the past seven years. Since Bill DeWitt had had his gall bladder attack and his appendix removed on February 16, he would have to miss the first few weeks of spring training. Charley was in charge.[96]

Only three players on the champion 1944 Browns team remained on the 1948 roster. Replacing those who had left were mostly younger players, the majority of them making their first real bid for a place on the big league roster. Many of these players were strangers to both Taylor and the fans, and it would be weeks after training camp opened before DeWitt could assess their capabilities.[97] Browns management found itself in a very stressful situation. They would be required to justify to the fans that the players obtained from the Red Sox and Indians would strengthen the Browns and were necessary apart from financial considerations.[98]

On March 25, Bill DeWitt announced that the Browns had closed an agreement for the use of the Burbank (California) municipally owned baseball park as a training site for the next two seasons. The new field was approximately 10 miles from downtown Los Angeles. The Browns' agreement with Burbank city officials covered the next two years with an option for renewal.[99]

Months earlier, the Browns had severed their relations with the Toledo Mudhens, their AAA affiliate. Bill DeWitt, who arrived at the Browns' training camp for the first time since his surgery, announced that the Browns expected to acquire another Triple-A club. Since an acquisition had yet to be completed, DeWitt declined to elaborate further except to stress that Triple-A connections were vital to an expanding farm system. Triple-A teams covered the long jump from the AA Texas League to the majors. In addition, a AAA club could keep 37 players on its reserve list.[100]

Five. Richard Muckerman and the Post-War Years

Bob Dillinger, who broke in with the Browns in 1946, was the team's regular third baseman the following three years. He led the American League in stolen bases all three years before being traded to the Philadelphia Athletics.

After a week of observing his players working out, DeWitt was delighted. "I don't see the tenseness in this squad that has been apparent in other seasons. This is a bunch of ambitious young kids who are getting a lot of fun out of hard work. The whole picture here has been cheering to me, and I'm not a bit afraid of what's going to happen in the American League race." DeWitt felt that the inspiration he had obtained from the squad had been a tonic to him, both mentally and physically.[101]

Despite DeWitt's optimism for the 1948 season, the Browns were again not attracting fans to their games. DeWitt argued that the home team ought to determine if a game should be played during the day or at night. He promised that when the major leagues met in St. Louis in July, he would put the unlimited night game proposal on the agenda. "Three clubs in the American League," explained DeWitt, "have refused to play as many night games in St. Louis as we would like. The Tigers have granted us only two games, the Red Sox have agreed to five games, and the Yankees will play only three. We'd like to play them seven more games which would be a difference of about $35,000 in gate receipts for the Browns. We could buy a pretty good ball player for that amount."[102]

Whether DeWitt's theory that the sparse attendance at Browns games was due to a lack of night games, there was no denying that the Browns were not drawing fans into Sportsman's Park. For a night game with the Philadelphia Athletics, only 2,288 fans turned out, and the entire four-game series drew less than 12,000. The Browns were averaging 4,700 per game, and DeWitt said an average of 7,500 was needed to break even financially.[103]

In late June of 1948, with the Browns in seventh place, Muckerman said on a radio interview that he had been frequently asked if he would move the Browns out of town. He answered, "As long as the people of St. Louis want the Browns here, I will not move them." He added that it was up to the fans of St. Louis whether they wanted the team to remain in the city.[104]

Both newspapers and many fans criticized Muckerman for his comments. Sid Keener, a longtime St. Louis sportswriter, blamed Muckerman for the Browns' worst record and their poor attendance. He emphasized that when the Browns won the pennant in 1944, they averaged more than 6,600 per game, but in 1938, when the team was deep in the second division, they averaged 2,500 plus. "It was not a matter of loyalty," argued Keener. "It is a matter of placing a contending team on the field."[105]

Finally, sportswriter J. Roy Stockton urged Browns fans to be patient, noting that the team had done better than most experienced observers expected. He praised Zack Taylor for the way he had handled a young team which had much to learn. "There is promising material in Brownie uniforms," wrote Stockton. "The fans must be patient. It ought not to be necessary to suggest to Muckerman that he be patient and considerate. You can't cry people into your shop, no matter what you're selling."[106]

For most of 1948, Bill DeWitt and the Browns continued to make more headlines and news for activities off the field rather than on. Muckerman's blast against the fans for their failure to patronize the Browns was explained by Bill DeWitt. "Mr. Muckerman wasn't concerned about the Browns' financial affairs because the club is now in good shape. He was simply disturbed because the fans in St. Louis have not shown enough to support our ball club."[107]

Stockton commented on the number of letters he had received concerning the plight of the Browns. He noted that most of the writers preferred to remain anonymous and directed their letters to Muckerman rather than Bill DeWitt. They questioned whether Muckerman, neither a baseball man nor a public relations man, should be running a baseball team. These letter writers, for the most part, complimented the DeWitt brothers and praised manager Zack Taylor for the club spirit and hustle despite its many one-sided defeats.[108]

By the beginning of August, the Browns were still making little progress on the field, and Bill DeWitt began to deny emphatically a press report out of the East that the Browns were going to fire Taylor as manager at the end of the season. "Zack has done a good job of developing young ball players," maintained DeWitt, "and we feel that he's going to be even a better manager for us. So why should eastern writers tell us that we're going to drop Zack when we know we're not?"[109] In fact, in the middle of September, the Browns re-signed Taylor as their manager with a "substantial raise in pay." Bill DeWitt announced, "We feel the club will make further progress under his leadership next season."[110]

On June 19, 1948, Babe Ruth visited St. Louis to attend an American Legion event. Always eager to help youngsters improve their hitting skills, he demonstrated to Bill DeWitt, Jr., son of Bill DeWitt, Sr., the proper way to grasp a major league baseball bat.

Stockton praised DeWitt's confidence in Zack Taylor by renewing Taylor's managerial contract for another year, and he liked Taylor's positive outlook for the 1949 season. Taylor told Stockton that he admired DeWitt for "establishing as many young ball players as big leaguers as we have done this year. We have boys we know can be stars in the majors."[111]

The Browns ended the 1948 season with a record of 59–94, finishing in sixth place, 37 games behind the pennant-winning Cleveland Indians. They could thank the ineptitude of the White Sox and Senators that they were able to move up to sixth place.[112]

Ever since the conclusion of the 1948 season, there were rumors that the Browns would be sold. During the winter meetings, Harold

Pauley and his brother Edwin, California real estate operators, had been mentioned as possible purchasers. Although rumors that the Pauley brothers would buy the Browns persisted, Bill DeWitt finally declared, "There's nothing in it. Nobody has made an offer."[113]

Rumors that the Browns and the Yankees were about to make a trade, however, became a reality when the Yankees landed their much sought-after pitcher, Fred Sanford, from the Browns. The Browns also sent the Yankees catcher Roy Partee. In return, the Yankees sent the Browns three players, catcher Sherman Lollar and pitchers Red Embree and Dick Star, along with $100,000. After the trade concluded, DeWitt announced that the Browns would make no further deals, ending a long-standing rumor that the Browns would dispose of Bob Dillinger, Cliff Fannin, and other stars.[114] It was also reliably reported that Bill DeWitt and his brother, Charley, had a verbal agreement with Muckerman that they would be permitted to match any offer made for the club by any outside interest.[115]

Six

An Owner at Last

By the winter of 1948, Richard Muckerman made it known that he intended to sell his major league franchise and was looking for a buyer. With the war no longer an issue, many cities that had no major league baseball team and were enjoying a post-war economic boom were anxious to make a bid for the Browns. Muckerman, however, felt that if it were at all possible, he preferred to keep the team in St. Louis. He knew that Bill DeWitt was in a much better position financially to buy the team since he had made a profit selling so many of his players following the 1948 season, and he decided to give DeWitt the first opportunity to bid on the team.[1]

On February 2, 1949, William and Charles DeWitt announced that they had purchased the 56 percent of the stock which Richard C. Muckerman owned to supplement the two percent they already held themselves. With the purchase, the DeWitt brothers became the sixth group to hold controlling interest in the team since St. Louis became a member of the American League in 1902. No price was disclosed, but seasoned baseball observers believed that they had paid nearly $1,000,000 for the stock. Bill DeWitt maintained his position as general manager and announced that Zack Taylor would continue as manager. No personnel changes were contemplated except that Charley DeWitt would be the team vice president.[2]

Muckerman sold to the DeWitts because he knew they would keep the team in St. Louis. He had had numerous offers for the Browns from individuals who offered him more money for the team, but he stated, "Those persons did not have the best interests of the city at heart."[3]

Charley was quite familiar with the front office operations of the Browns, having served as traveling secretary many years before he and his brother purchased the club.[4] Charley owned a number of businesses, including the DeWitt Insurance Agency, which he founded in 1925 and which provided one of his main sources of income.[5]

After he sold the Browns, Muckerman continued his involvement

Charlie (left) and Bill DeWitt had reason to smile. In February 1949, they purchased the Browns, and they owned the team until they sold it to Bill Veeck in 1951.

with the City Ice and Fuel Company as well as supporting the Catholic Archdiocese of St. Louis and serving Democratic Party interests. His infusion of cash had enabled the team to thrive during World War II and win its only pennant. Muckerman's ownership of the Browns lasted a little over three seasons. While dressing for mass on March 15, 1959, he suffered a fatal heart attack at his home at the age of 62.[6]

One of the DeWitt Brothers' first acquisitions in early 1949 was not a player but a coach. John Tobin, one of the most proficient bunters in the history of baseball, was signed to teach the team the art of bunting. Tobin, who hit .331 for the 1922 Browns, was one of the heroes of the team which finished only one game out of first place. Bill DeWitt assigned Tobin to the Browns' training camp at Burbank, California. Plans were made for him to move to San Antonio to help the Browns' Texas League club, and finally to the minor league camp at Pine Bluff, Arkansas. DeWitt pointed out that the Browns posted 28 defeats during the 1948 season by the margin of one run. "The games might have been won with a well-placed bunt for a sacrifice or squeeze play," said the Browns' president.[7] Tobin served as coach for the Browns through the 1951 season.[8]

Six. An Owner at Last

Meanwhile player contracts had been sent, and DeWitt was elated that he was receiving signed contracts so rapidly, especially the ones from his key players, third baseman Bob Dillinger, who received a substantial raise, and outfielder Al Zarilla. By March 2, only Jerry Priddy and Andy Anderson had not yet signed.[9]

Spring training went by rapidly, and on the eve of the Browns' opening game in 1949, DeWitt was honored by the Knights of the Cauliflower Ear, wishing him the best of luck for his first game as owner of the St. Louis Browns. He was saluted for his "determination to take each game as a new job, for confidently setting up of a high goal and the constant efforts to reach it."[10]

Unfortunately, the Browns' 1949 season began as it had for so many years. In May, the Browns traded one of their few stars, Al Zarilla, to the Boston Red Sox for outfielder Stan Spence and cash. Zarilla had been the Browns' leading hitter the previous year with an average of .329, while Spence batted .235 for Boston. Bill DeWitt said the deal was "an effort to give the Browns some additional power."[11]

After he was traded to Boston, Zarilla, in a newspaper interview, charged that the Browns were suffering from a "defeatist attitude." He stated that while he did not wish to hurt his friends on the Browns or Bill and Charley DeWitt, Zarilla felt that the club, instead of looking for that "good break" to carry them to victory, seemed to wait for the daily "bad break" that always managed to pop up and result in another loss. He could not understand why the Browns had abandoned the "holler they had when they won the pennant in 1944."

Zarilla also criticized Browns manager Zack Taylor for "cutting down the speed" on his ball club. Taylor defended the Browns by reminding him that this team, which often got behind early, couldn't afford to run the bases so freely. As for the team's morale, Taylor stated, "You can bet your life that we haven't a defeatist complex on the ball club."[12]

Prior to the June 15 trade deadline, the Browns suffered an 11-game losing streak. While the Browns were having a horrible road trip and finding it almost impossible to win a game, DeWitt was closely watching the progress of his neighbors, the Cardinals, and especially their aggressive new president, Fred M. Saigh, Jr. "I'm fascinated by Saigh's success," said DeWitt. "All in all, he's doing a wonderful job selling baseball to the St. Louis fans, something we've needed here for years."[13]

This was a change of attitude on DeWitt's part. The Cardinals had been outdrawing the Browns by as much as 5–1 for most of the 1949 season. DeWitt stated that he had been making note of Saigh's ideas, hoping he could try them out at some later date. He was amazed by the

Cardinals' public relations department, headed by James L. Toomey. "I'd like to see the Cardinals have a winning team to work with," said DeWitt. "Whatever the Cardinals and Saigh do now, the Browns and I will do later."[14]

Even while DeWitt was predicting how the Browns would eventually do well in St. Louis, Dan Daniel, New York baseball reporter, was writing that the Browns would vacate St. Louis during the 1950 season and "would be playing baseball in another city, backed by new capital." Without asking either Bill or Charley DeWitt, Daniel gave three reasons why it was impossible for the Browns to operate their team in St. Louis. First, the Browns were unable to continue to play in St. Louis with every season showing a drop in home attendance. Second, the club simply could not continue to dispose of star players each year to replenish the treasury and win with the remaining players, Finally, Fred Saigh would not object to paying a higher rent or even buying the park if they could have sole major league rights in St. Louis.[15] DeWitt responded that there was nothing to the Daniel story. "You can wager anything you want that we'll be doing business at the same old stand in 1950 and for many years to come."[16]

After a short period of friendlier exchanges, the war of words between Fred Saigh and Bill DeWitt resumed. Saigh told a sportswriter that wherever the Browns moved, they would have to win. "No city will support a constant loser and nobody should expect it." In rebuttal, DeWitt told the *Post-Dispatch* that "Saigh knows nothing about our club and it is none of his business what we do about the club or its finances."[17] J. Roy Stockton agreed with DeWitt, stating that the Browns, despite their record, were a St. Louis institution. He told Saigh that the city wanted the Browns to remain in St. Louis. He had a word of advice for DeWitt, "Don't you go to selling any more ball players for money."[18]

Eight years after he failed to move the Browns, Don Barnes still believed that St. Louis should be a one-club city, but he believed that the Cardinals, not the Browns, should move out of St. Louis. The city "might become educated to patronize the Browns," said Barnes, "if they were the only team here and showed improvement."[19]

The Browns ended the 1949 season winning only 53 games while losing 101, finishing in seventh place not the cellar, three games ahead of the Washington Senators. They were 44 games behind the pennant-winning New York Yankees.[20] The total attendance at home games was 270,936.[21]

The one bright spot for the Browns during the 1949 season was that Roy Sievers, a native St. Louisan, was voted the American League's

Rookie of the Year by the Baseball Writers' Association of America. This was the first year that this award was given.²² His batting average was .306, and he hit 16 home runs and drove in 91 runs, all for a team 48 games below .500.²³ No other Brown would win a major award.²⁴

During the 1940s, a group of loyal supporters of the Browns created "The Browns' Booster Club." In July 1949, DeWitt, in a lengthy and personal letter to Norman Handel, chairman of the new club, apologized for failing to contact him sooner, but acknowledged the devotion of the club. He also noted that "everyone from the president down to the bat boy, each and every

The Browns hit the jackpot when they signed Roy Sievers (seated), a native St. Louisan, in 1949. During his 20-year major league baseball career, five of them with the Browns, Sievers was Rookie of the Year, a five-time All-Star, and in 1957 led the American League in both home runs and runs batted in.

one of us, values the encouragement your club has given us from the first day of the season." DeWitt informed Handel that he intended to proclaim the night of August 16 "Appreciation Night" and asked him to invite all members of the Browns' Booster Club to be guests of the Browns that evening, providing four passes for each member.²⁵ Three months later, DeWitt invited Handel and a few of his friends for cocktails and a short meeting to "talk about the Browns."²⁶

In late October, DeWitt publicly announced that all Browns over 28 years old—even including Bob Dillinger and Jerry Priddy—were up for sale. Concurrent with this announcement, DeWitt stated that the Browns were reshuffling their farm system. Nine clubs were being dropped and three new ones—one each in Class A, B, and D—were to be added, leaving the Browns with a total of 14 farm clubs. Finally, DeWitt said the Browns were interested in acquiring "good ball players," but especially a shortstop and a pitcher.[27]

While the Browns patiently waited for offers for their players, they announced that manager Zack Taylor had been rehired for the 1950 season. DeWitt also announced the signing of coach Earle Brucker, released recently by the Philadelphia Athletics after nine years as their pitching coach. "He's a great handler of pitchers, and I'm sure he can help our ball club. Brucker joins the other three Browns' coaches, Johnny Tobin, Ralph Winegarner and Fred Hoffman."[28]

The Browns made a number of player deals at the December 1949 winter meeting in New York that also added a great deal of money to DeWitt's coffers. The Browns sent third baseman Bob Dillinger and outfielder Paul Lehner to the Athletics for veteran infielder Frank Gustine, rookie shortstop Billy DeMars, and outfielders Ray Coleman and Rocco Ippolitto. In addition, the Browns received $100,000.[29] For DeWitt, the $100,000 was the best part of the deal. "I can't make any money at the gate. I've got to make it selling my best players,." which, according to the press, he did in order to retire his debts.[30]

As the winter meeting concluded, the Browns made another major trade. DeWitt sent second baseman Jerry Priddy to the Detroit Tigers and in return, the Browns received right-handed relief pitcher Lou Kretlow and $100,000. Kretlow had come to the Tigers from their farm system, where he had won 25 games in 1948. Priddy had been a member of the so-called "million-dollar infield" of the Kansas City Blues, who came up to the Yankees along with Phil Rizzuto in 1941. With Joe Gordon playing second for the Yankees, Priddy could not break into the regular lineup as an everyday player, and he was dealt to Washington, where he remained until 1947, when the Browns acquired him. The Tigers had been trying for two years to get a second baseman, with Priddy one of their chief targets.[31]

DeWitt insisted that he was not turning his entire club loose and then transferring the franchise to another city. "We're selling ball players, but not clubs. We're not broke and we are not considering moving the franchise to Los Angeles." He pointed out again that the reason for selling players was simply because "we couldn't make expenses by drawing only 270,000 fans last season and selling is the only way we can make up the deficit."[32]

Unfortunately, this left DeWitt with a very weak team. When American League clubs came to St. Louis to play the Browns, they continued to play before small crowds. At the same time, the DeWitts claimed

Six. An Owner at Last

they were building a young club that would mature in the future. In fact, the Browns had the league's lowest attendance in 28 of the 40 seasons between 1910 and 1950.[33]

Occasionally a promotion to the majors represented a lower salary for the player than he had received in the minors. Pitcher Al Widmar starred for Baltimore of the International League, and in 1950 the Browns purchased his contract with a $2,000 pay cut. This was not unique; often a player was promoted to the major leagues and then told not to be disillusioned that he had "achieved any sort of stature within the game."[34] If the Browns wanted to pay its players a fair salary, DeWitt decided he would have to devise a plan to draw more fans to Sportsman's Park, and they would only come if the St. Louis Browns played winning baseball.

The Browns tried a new twist with the onset of the 1950 season. DeWitt hired the public relations firm of Robert A. Willier and Associates to "sell" the team to the St. Louis public. According to DeWitt, approximately five million fans lived within a radius of 150 miles of St. Louis. Willier assured DeWitt that he would rekindle and sustain their interest in the Browns but that he had no intentions of using Bill Veeck–type, minor-league tactics such as dressing the players in hula costumes to draw people. Willier's first plan was to use the Booster Club as a nucleus to achieve their goal. They were the ones who had to spread the news about the Browns.

DeWitt made it clear that he could not guarantee that the Browns would be a pennant contender in 1950. Willier understood and indicated his first plan was to sell his "client," the fans, that if they came out to the Browns' games, they would be seeing a high class of visiting teams, such as the Yankees and the Red Sox.

To appease the DeWitts, Willier assigned George Mora, a graduate of the University of Missouri Journalism School and the assistant publicity director of the St. Louis Chamber of Commerce, the responsibility of handling the Browns' public relations. In order to attract women and younger fans to the games. Willier appointed Mora's wife a vice president of Willier, and gave her that responsibility.

The Willier organization did the best they could, but no campaign of public relations could increase the attendance at the Browns' games. Nor could Willier's company help the Browns move up in the standings; attendance dropped to under 250,000. It was becoming more obvious that St. Louis could not support two major league baseball teams.[35]

Jack Fournier, who discovered such Browns as Johnny Berardino, Bob Dillinger, Les Moss, Fred Sanford, and Al Zarilla, couldn't come to terms with the club on a two-year contract and resigned as head scout.

DeWitt made it clear that there were no hard feelings between the two. In fact, DeWitt gave him the highest of recommendations. Freddie Hoffman, who served as coach and part-time scout, became a full-time scout.[36]

Before Bill DeWitt could even think of spring training for 1950, he had to make sure he was able to sign his players quickly and have a full roster in Burbank, the team's spring training site. He was surprised when he faced a definite holdout in Roy Sievers, the American League's Rookie of the Year. DeWitt met for a second time with Sievers, but the talks were not very productive. DeWitt declined to disclose the salary Sievers was offered or to give any information on how far apart the two were.[37] He was successful, however, in reporting that outfielder Dick Kokos, first baseman Hank Arft, and third baseman Charles Grand had come to terms. Jack Graham and Frank Gustine were the only two infielders who remained unsigned.[38]

The Browns announced that the team had finally filled Charley DeWitt's vacant position as the team's traveling secretary. William Durney, athletic director for St. Louis University, was to join the Browns as traveling secretary beginning March 15.[39]

Twenty Browns were under contract after three pitchers agreed to terms. They included Dick Starr, who had won only one game the previous year while losing seven because he was handicapped with appendicitis; Sidney Schacht, drafted from Scranton in the Eastern League; and Vernon Taylor, who had won five and lost eight at Baltimore. All were right-handers. Roy Sievers, whose 1949 salary was the major league minimum of $5,000, had turned down $8,000 for 1950 but did eventually sign.[40]

Only one player remained unsigned, and he probably frustrated DeWitt more than any other—pitcher Al Widmar. Widmar was a minor leaguer who had to prove to DeWitt that he could make the grade in major league baseball. The Browns acquired him in 1947 from the Boston Red Sox. In 1948, he won two games and lost six for the Browns and was optioned to Baltimore, where he compiled a 22–15 record.

He sent Bill DeWitt a letter and an unsigned contract in March 1950, telling his boss, "I could make more money selling automobiles than pitching for the Browns."[41] A few days later, Widmar returned a third unsigned contract believed to be for $7,500, and according to DeWitt, "a final offer."[42] Widmar then had a telephone conversation with DeWitt, explaining that he could not afford to waste time on baseball at the salary he had been offered. "We're so far apart on salary it's laughable."[43]

Widmar claimed that the Browns were preventing him from making a living. His Baltimore manager told his young pitcher that if he could show some patience, "We think you'll be back in the big time soon." Widmar, however, threatened to sue the Browns over the reserve clause, claiming that the Browns would not pay him a reasonable salary nor would they permit him to earn a living with another club.[44]

J. Roy Stockton, who usually was sympathetic towards the players, showed little compassion for Widmar. "Most baseball men will agree," wrote Stockton, "that the Browns were more than fair with Al Widmar. He just didn't want to play with the Browns."

Widmar eventually accepted a Browns contract. DeWitt refused to answer all questions concerning Widmar's salary. Widmar, however, said he was very happy with the contract. "I don't think I could have got a better one." As to the suit against baseball, Widmar said, "I sure am dropping it. I don't know law—I only know how to play baseball."[45]

A year earlier, Zack Taylor had publicly acknowledged that many Browns seemed to have a defeatist attitude. During spring training in 1950, DeWitt made headlines when he hired Dr. David Tracy to use hypnosis to help players on a losing team relax, feel as if they were winners, and improve themselves. This would go a long way to getting them out of the baseball cellar.

The hiring of Dr. Tracy went back to the summer of 1949 when Tracy, an athlete himself, was at Yankee Stadium watching the Browns drop a doubleheader to the Yankees. Later he called on the two DeWitts and explained how he thought he could help the club.[46]

Tracy was not only an athlete, he was an author, lecturer and specialist in psychological problems. He convinced the DeWitts that he could do things toward building the players' confidence and boosting their morale. They hired him for four weeks of the 1950 spring training season. He told them, "After I teach the players emotional stability, they will automatically climb higher in the league race. With my treatments, the club should finish fifth and may even climb to fourth."[47] Vice president Charley DeWitt told his players that the hiring of Dr. Tracy was "no gag." He felt that there were members on the team that had inferiority complexes, and that Dr. Tracy would "instill a winning spirit in them."[48]

At the end of May, Dr. Tracy said that he was severing his connection with the Browns. He had been hired by the club to boost the players' morale and confidence through the application of psychology. When he began his work, the Browns had finished in seventh place in the American League the previous year. When he left the Browns, the team was in the cellar. Dr. Tracy blamed "lack of cooperation from the management." Zack Taylor was opposed to Dr. Tracy from the very beginning, telling the doctor to stay away from the playing field and clubhouse. In particular, he had not been allowed to speak to the players prior to the game, although Dr. Tracy felt that it was pre-game talks that were most important in inspiring each player to do his best. Taylor ridiculed Tracy when his massive hypnosis failed to boost playing performances. The manager felt that a healthy Roy Sievers was infinitely more valuable to the team than the psychological insights of the "whammy man."[49]

In early May, Bill DeWitt turned down a cash offer to buy the Browns and transfer them to another city. The DeWitts had constantly received offers to purchase the Browns, but Charley said that those truly interested in buying the team should understand that the very least amount of money that the Browns would consider would be $3,350,000 and it was doubtful if even that amount would be sufficient to "swing a deal."[50] While the DeWitts kept insisting that the Browns were not for sale, Stockton realized that owning the team fulfilled a life-long ambition of the DeWitts. Nevertheless, he wondered if the team would be better off if the owners could put up with small crowds and small income long enough to make the team sufficiently competitive to build a winning club. "The ideal situation." reasoned Stockton, "would be for both St. Louis teams to be contenders."[51]

The unfortunate situation was that no St. Louis group had made the DeWitts a firm bid. "The only people who have made serious bids are groups that would insist on taking the Browns to California or Texas or somewhere else. Charles and I bought [the team] because we wanted the Browns," lamented Bill DeWitt.[52]

Meanwhile, the Browns and the Yankees closed a seven-man deal, but this one included no Browns front-line players. The Yankees received southpaw Joe Ostrowski, right-hander Tom Ferrick, and third baseman Leo Thomas. In exchange, the Browns acquired second baseman George Stirnweiss, outfielder Jim Delsing, and pitchers Duane Pillette and Don Johnson. DeWitt estimated the player value of Ostrowski and Ferrick at a total of $250,000; he assumed that the other new players were worth $50,000 each—making it a half-million-dollar deal. According to DeWitt, Stirnweiss was the big catch. "He'll settle our infield problems," said DeWitt.[53]

Once again Bill DeWitt renewed his plea for better support from the St. Louis Browns fans. Although he reiterated that he did not want to move his team out of St. Louis, he told the St. Louis Advertising Club, "We may have to someday unless we receive better support at the gate."[54] He indicated that the mayor of Baltimore, Thomas D'Alesandre, had outlined a program of several advantages for the Browns to move to Baltimore. The mayor guaranteed 750,000 fans and added that flight travel

Six. An Owner at Last

from Baltimore would be half of what it was from St. Louis. DeWitt also told the group that Dick Burnett, the millionaire owner of the Dallas Eagles of the Texas League, had also made an offer to move the Browns to Dallas.[55]

Up to now, Commissioner Chandler had made few comments. When the owners of the International League Baltimore team became more vocal, Frank Shaughnessy, president of that league, said that talk about moving the Browns to Baltimore had cut down attendance considerably for the Orioles. According to Shaughnessy, Baltimore baseball fans were mistaken that the present Baltimore ownership was thinking of moving in order to bring big league baseball to Baltimore. "It's the worst case of tampering I ever heard of. Something should be done to stop DeWitt," said Shaughnessy, who also called DeWitt's recent remarks "cheap publicity." While Chandler understood Shaughnessy's concern, he merely suggested to DeWitt that it would be more appropriate to discuss such matters during the off-season.[56]

Not everyone was pessimistic about the future of the St. Louis Browns. Metropolitan Opera star and St. Louis native Helen Traubel declared she had always loved the Browns, and she bought a "nice chunk" of stock "mostly to 'satisfy a sentimental urge,'" admitting that the Browns "were her first recollection of baseball." Her father, a St. Louis druggist, was an avid Browns fan, and she recalled stars such as George Sisler, "Babydoll" Jacobson and Urban Shocker. "I have faith in them," she said. "This is not a gamble, not a whim. This is an investment—in faith and in sentiment."[57]

Although rumors persisted, Bill DeWitt denied that Branch Rickey was going to the Browns as the new president and owner in a deal financed by the American League. According to the newspaper *The Daily Compass*, American League tycoons were ready to purchase a controlling interest in Browns stock and turn it over to Rickey in order to acquire his services. Bill DeWitt vehemently denied the rumors, stating that the Browns had not planned any changes in the operation of the club and that Rickey was not buying it. "It is not for sale," emphasized DeWitt.[58]

The Browns finished in seventh place in 1950 with a record of 58–96, 40 games behind the pennant-winning Yankees.[59] Attendance dropped another 23,000. Ned Garver was the mainstay of the pitching staff. His record was 13–18, but he completed 22 of his 31 starts. He and Bob Lemon led American League pitchers in complete games that year. Garver also had one of the lowest ERAs in the American League, 3.39.[60]

Rumors that Zack Taylor would not be rehired as manager in 1951 were put to rest when the DeWitts announced in late October that Taylor would return. "Zack has done a nice job with the Browns and I am well satisfied with his work." said DeWitt. He refused to disclose salary terms.[61]

The remaining months of 1950 were filled with rumors and speculation. Since Branch Rickey was out of a job, he was still the subject of much speculation. He conferred often with Bill DeWitt, and supposedly he was to meet with Cardinals owner Fred Saigh. The puzzled Saigh bluntly said, "I haven't the slightest idea why he'd want to see me. I have no appointment with Rickey." He was scheduled to meet with Bill DeWitt, supposedly just a social call. There were also rumors that he was going to the Pittsburgh Pirates organization in some capacity.[62]

While the rumors made for interesting speculation, the Browns were preparing for the 1951 season. Having signed Zack Taylor to lead the team, the Browns kept their coaching staff intact by renewing the contracts of Earle Brucker, John Tobin, and Ralph Winegarner. DeWitt said that Taylor was quite pleased with the return of his coaches.[63]

Charley DeWitt read a report in the *Cleveland Ohio Plain Dealer* that Bill Veeck might return to baseball as an owner of the St. Louis Browns. DeWitt scoffed at the report, referring to it as "just some ridiculous journalism." Charley said that he and his brother, Bill, hadn't seen or talked to Veeck in more than a year.[64]

Bill DeWitt returned home after a month's vacation in Florida, and immediately denied the story that Veeck would buy the Browns. "I really shouldn't dignify such a ridiculous rumor with a reply," said DeWitt. "We're trying hard to build up the Browns, and these reports emanating in other cities certainly aren't designed to help us."[65]

Despite Bill DeWitt's statements, rumors about efforts to purchase the Browns continued. Early in 1951, Fred Miller, millionaire Milwaukee brewer, expressed an interest in bringing major league baseball to Milwaukee. Miller claimed that he had sent a contract to the DeWitts, offering to purchase the Browns. Bill DeWitt reiterated, "We are St. Louisans by birth, like our hometown, and are convinced that the Browns must remain a definite part of St. Louis and should not be moved to Milwaukee, Los Angeles or any other place. It is our hope that St. Louis fans will rally behind our club and come to our games next summer."[66]

The Browns began the work of signing their players for the 1951 season. Thirty-four-year-old infielder Johnny Berardino inked his contract, followed by a pair of rookies, Bill Pilgrim and Rocco Ippolito, bringing to nine the number of players who had come to terms with the club.[67] The Browns solved their number one problem when they received the signed contract of their 25-year-old star pitcher, Ned Garver. In addition, the

Browns were successful in re-signing pitcher Duane Pillette and infielder George Stirnweiss.[68]

For quite a while, it was common knowledge that the St. Louis Browns were in a financial bind. They decided to borrow money to pay off debts and provide additional working capital for the club. Bill DeWitt said that there were plans to mortgage Sportsman's Park in St. Louis and Mission Stadium in San Antonio to secure the loan. The team's financial condition had figured in repeated reports, often denied by DeWitt, that the Browns might be sold and the franchise might be moved to some other city. Their home attendance in 1950 was down again: 247,131 compared with 270,936 in 1949.[69] DeWitt announced that the $600,000 they expected to borrow would be repaid over a period of ten years. "That will still leave a balance in the club treasury of $135,000 for extra working capital."[70]

It came as no surprise when the baseball scribes, assessing the teams for the upcoming season, felt that the Browns looked like the weakest team in the majors. They wondered how long the American League could afford to deal with a club that drew so few fans in 1950 and could easily draw fewer in 1951, especially when they saw absolutely no improvement from the previous year. As for bringing in money through player deals, the only players on the 1951 roster who could be "snapped up for big money" were Ned Garver and outfielder Don Lenhardt. Despite their poor showing in spring training games, when Bill DeWitt, the eternal optimist, insisted that he was not disturbed by the Browns' failure to do well during the spring. DeWitt may not have lost any sleep about his team's showing in spring training, but Zack Taylor certainly had. The Browns' victory against their San Antonio farm club was only their fourth win during spring training and broke an 11-game losing streak.[71]

The closer the teams came to leaving spring training to begin the 1951 season, the stronger the reports predicting that the Browns would be moved to Milwaukee. Red Smith, Milwaukee Brewers business manager, was quoted as saying that he and Fred Miller would buy 57 percent of the St. Louis club's stock by August. He further predicted that the team would be transferred to Milwaukee, with Charlie Grimm as the team's 1952 manager. Once again, the DeWitts denied Smith's report. "The Browns are not for sale," Charles DeWitt said. His brother Bill, at San Antonio, said, "If these Milwaukee people want to play an April Fool's joke, they'd better try it on somebody else."[72]

Bad luck or unfortunate breaks for the St. Louis Browns seemed to follow the team on or off the field. Frank Saucier was Minor League Player of the Year in 1950 and the last of the major league holdouts.

He was given an ultimatum in a letter from Bill DeWitt—if he had not signed his minor league contract by March 5, he would be suspended.

Saucier was supposedly the Browns' top rookie and had had a fantastic rookie year, leading the Texas League with a .343 batting average. He told the Browns that he realized that a rookie coming up to the majors was generally expected to take the $5,000 minimum salary, but he told the Browns, "Frankly I'm earning more than that in the oil fields." DeWitt's reply was succinct: "If Saucier [does] not sign his contract by Monday, [I will] notify the American League and request that Saucier be placed on the ineligible list."[73] Saucier signed his contract, and in 1950 he was named *The Sporting News* Minor League Player of the Year.[74]

In the summer of 1951, the Browns promoted Saucier to the parent club where he appeared in 18 games with 14 plate appearances. Saucier had one hit for a batting average of .071, with one run driven in. He never played professional baseball after that season.[75]

But Saucier's lackluster career with the St. Louis Browns took a back seat to events taking place off the playing field. Between 1946–1950, the St. Louis Browns had been last in attendance in the American League every year. That they would finish the season either in seventh or eighth place was guaranteed. It was also assumed that the DeWitt brothers would soon put the team up for sale. The only two unanswered questions were: who would purchase the team, and would they remain in St. Louis? The DeWitts, of course, insisted that the team would remain in St. Louis under their present ownership, but rumors persisted that the club's poor attendance might force its transfer to another city. It made no difference that the DeWitt brothers owned 58 percent of the club's stock.[76]

Bill DeWitt said that he preferred not to move the Browns to another city, but he was discouraged to have such small crowds at the games after all the work he had done to keep the Browns in St. Louis. He noted that Milwaukee, one of the American League's original members, had been longing for major league baseball for several years. He emphasized that the city was constructing a new ballpark with an ultimate capacity of 70,000.[77]

St. Louis Cardinals owner Fred Saigh would benefit by the transfer of the Browns to Milwaukee, as it would give him the opportunity to acquire Sportsman's Park. Milwaukee already had a professional baseball team, the AAA Milwaukee Brewers in the American Association. The two owners of the Brewers were Charlie Grimm and Bill Veeck, Jr., whose father had been president of the Chicago Cubs in the 1930s. Grimm and Veeck had taken a financially strapped franchise in 1941 and tripled the team's attendance by numerous promotional events. During the five years Grimm and Veeck owned the team, the Millers won three pennants.[78]

After the minor league ownership, Veeck purchased the major league Cleveland Indians, where he continued using his promotional skills. Veeck also increased attendance there and reached the ultimate achievement, a World Series win in 1948. Unfortunately, a year later, because of a settlement term in his divorce, Veeck was forced to sell the Indians.[79]

Meanwhile, rumors of the possibility that the DeWitts might sell the Browns because of poor attendance increased. In 1951 this possibility became more likely, and to intensify matters, Veeck was eager to return to baseball as a team owner. He began to negotiate with DeWitt early in May 1951. One month later, Veeck obtained an option on the DeWitts' shares of the Browns. There was an excellent chance that Veeck would transfer the Browns to Milwaukee.

Fortunately, at least one man wanted to keep the Browns in St. Louis. He was Mark C. Steinberg, a local investment broker, who obtained a second mortgage on the controlling interest of the Browns by purchasing a note from Richard Muckerman. The note was due in 1954 and was said to be for $700,000.[80] This note represented approximately 56 percent of the Browns' stock.[81] Steinberg was happy that at least the Browns would remain in St. Louis. "I know the DeWitt brothers," he said. "I have no desire to control the club. I only have one interest and that is to keep the Browns in St. Louis."[82]

Early in June, the newspapers reported two player deals involving the Browns. First, they obtained outfielder Paul Lehner from the White Sox and infielder Kermit Wahl from the Athletics, along with some cash, in a three-way deal. Don Lenhardt, who was used both in the infield and outfield by Zack Taylor, went to the White Sox.[83] The following day, the Browns released pitcher Cliff Fannin, who had won 34 games and lost 47 over five seasons with the Browns. He was sent to the Toronto club of the International League but could be recalled on 24-hour notice. Fannin welcomed the opportunity to work himself back into winning form.[84]

Anyone following baseball would normally be reading about player moves as the season progressed. That was not the case, however. In St. Louis, box scores and statistics took a back seat to a more pressing question—what is the future of the St. Louis Browns? For nearly a month, local newspaper coverage concerned that topic. Ultimately, two rumors concerning the future of the St. Louis Browns remained. One rumor had the Browns sold to a syndicate headed by Bill Veeck. The other rumor had the Browns already transferred to Milwaukee. Bill DeWitt vehemently denied both rumors.[85]

When two newspapers reported in front page stories that the Browns already had been sold to Veeck and associates, Bill DeWitt said, "We have had no substantial offer for the Browns. The ball club is not for sale. If someone comes to us with a firm and attractive offer, we would—as businessmen—have to consider it. But so far, no such offer has been made."[86]

Four newspapers, including one in St. Louis, reported "on good authority" that Veeck and DeWitt had made the deal. Three of the papers wrote that Veeck would keep the franchise in St. Louis, while the *Cleveland Press* reported that he might shift the club to Los Angeles. In St. Louis, DeWitt repeated what he had said many times, "There is absolutely no truth to the story that the club has been sold."[87]

Four days later, according to the press, all objections to the sale of the Browns to Bill Veeck had been removed, and the league owners were to meet in a few days to approve the deal. The present owners, Bill and Charley DeWitt, needed the consent of the American League club owners because one of their loans was made from the league in 1949 and they had not yet paid any of it back. It was understood that whichever deal was finalized, the DeWitts would remain with the Browns.[88]

Bill DeWitt insisted, "no deal had been completed for the sale of our stock in the Browns." He reiterated that he had not been forced to sell or negotiate, although he and his brother owed the American League $300,000. "It is a personal loan, not due until February 1, 1954." He denied the veracity of stories which said he was "debt ridden."[89]

On June 21, 1951, Donald Barnes announced that Veeck had agreed to buy the Browns if enough other stockholders besides Bill and Charley DeWitt were willing to sell their stock to Veeck and his partner, Sidney Solomon, Jr., St. Louis insurance man. Barnes emphasized that the club would remain in St. Louis.[90]

Veeck felt that he had taken on a sales job and that he had no intention of moving the team to another city "now or in the foreseeable future." Veeck felt television would help "sell the product" to Browns fans and that, unlike other club owners, he was in favor of televising as many games as possible. Veeck also announced that Bill DeWitt would stay with the Browns as a vice president and that none of the leading Browns players would be sold or traded prior to the sale of the team.[91]

Veeck had 12 days to buy 75 percent of the 114,000 outstanding shares of common stock in the club. The shares had climbed and were now valued at $7 a share, but Veeck was confident that he would have no difficulty purchasing the required stock. He also released his first plan for the Browns, indicating that he intended to make things lively when he gained control of the Browns. "I always believe in having fun at the

Six. An Owner at Last

Bill DeWitt adjusts Bill Veeck's recently acquired hat.

ballpark," said Veeck. "The more enjoyable you make it, the better people are going to like it. That's why I say let's have some fun doing it."[92]

DeWitt had no doubts that Veeck would succeed. "Whenever we tried to do certain things to add color to our games, we were criticized; with Veeck, it will be sensational." He promised to do anything Veeck wanted and assured him that together, they should help improve the Browns. "I will give him the benefit of my knowledge of the game in making deals or transacting whatever business we have at hand."[93]

On Tuesday, July 3, just 12 hours prior to the deadline set for acquiring 75 percent of the Browns' stock, Bill Veeck clinched the deal. Herbert W. Waltke, a member of the Browns' board of directors, changed his mind as the deadline neared and decided to allow Veeck to buy his stock.[94] Veeck formally took control of the team by appointing Rudie Schaeffer the new general manager. Schaeffer was an old cohort from the days when he was building up baseball teams in Milwaukee and Cleveland. Former president Bill DeWitt remained as the team's vice president, but Charley DeWitt left the team to devote his time to his insurance business. Zack Taylor remained the team's manager "until we find a fellow that is more suited to our operations," Veeck said.[95]

Veeck was the front man for a baseball syndicate of 16 investors. His personal representative, Sidney Salomon, Jr., predicted that the

"P. T. Barnum of baseball" would make St. Louis "the Mecca of Baseball."[96] The day Bill Veeck obtained controlling interest in the St. Louis Browns, the team he had purchased was 23½ games out of first place.[97]

At a late-afternoon news conference, Veeck announced that his goal was to build a winning team, and that African Americans would be given every opportunity to play for the Browns. Neither St. Louis team had black players in 1951, although the Browns had brought up two in 1947. Both were released before the season concluded. The Cardinals had never had a Negro in their lineup. Veeck concluded the conference by announcing that in addition to his position as team vice president, Bill DeWitt would assist him in making player trades, and he would also direct the team's farm system.[98]

The DeWitt brothers officially departed as Browns owners on July 11, 1951. "Naturally, I hate to get out of baseball," said Charley DeWitt, "but the only reason my brother Bill and I decided to sell was because our good friend and adviser, Don Barnes, told us we should. Our club was in its best financial shape in years; that's why we had no trouble selling it."[99]

Bill DeWitt was sorry to see his brother retire from baseball, but said he was accepting his new role, telling Veeck that he would do any job Veeck wanted him to do. "He has indicated that he wants me to supervise the Browns' minor league systems, the club's scouting and its player acquisitions. All I want personally is a good front row seat where I can watch the show and see the fireworks."[100]

Seven

A Three Ring Circus

When Bill Veeck took over the Browns in mid-summer of 1951, the sportswriters who loved to poke fun at him for his antics immediately released a flood of comments. John Lardner wrote, "Many critics were surprised to know that the Browns could be bought because they didn't even realize that the Browns were owned."[1] Columnist Arthur Daley of the *New York Times* wrote that the Browns "have no tradition and no hope." Jim Murray of the *Los Angeles Times* called the Browns the most feckless club in the history of the game. "Every season was one long steady retreat, out of the race by Mother's Day."[2]

Veeck himself felt there was really little he could do to improve a team he called "the worst looking collection of ball players I've ever seen."[3] Nonetheless, he decided to begin his ownership with the kind of promotions and stunts he had used before. The fans who attended games when Bill Veeck ran the team soon became accustomed to special events, often unannounced, such as giveaways or exploding scoreboards to entice them into attending Browns games. Two events in particular set the example, and both occurred in August 1951, within the first six weeks Veeck owned the team.

On August 19, in a game against the Detroit Tigers, Veeck sent midget Eddie Gaedel to pinch-hit for the leadoff batter, Frank Saucier. Gaedel wore the uniform of the Browns' bat boy, Bill DeWitt, Jr., with "1/8" as the number on the back. When the team's vice president, Bill DeWitt, Sr., told his son that a midget was going to come to the plate for the Browns but that the team did not have a uniform for him "because he's kind of small. Your uniform is a pretty close fit, so we need to borrow it." DeWitt Jr., responded, "Great."[4]

Between the games of the doubleheader that day, the 3'7" Gaedel popped out of a large cake brought to the ballpark to celebrate the birthdays of both the American League and the team's sponsor, Falstaff Brewery.[5] Browns manager Zack Taylor assured the home plate umpire, Ed Hurley, that the Browns had a contract for Gaedel, and after much discussion and a protest from Tigers manager Red Rolfe, Gaedel was allowed to bat. Tigers pitcher Bob Cain walked him on four straight pitches, and Taylor then removed Gaedel from the game for a pinch-runner. The following day, American League president Will Harridge ordered that Gaedel's contract be annulled and that any mention of his appearance in the major leagues be forever deleted from the record books.[6]

Veeck's second memorable stunt happened just five days later, on August 24. Theorizing that almost every fan secretly wants to manage a team, Veeck initiated Fan Manager for a Day. When the fans arrived at Sportsman's Park, some were given signs that said such things as "Take," "Swing," "Run," "Steal," etc. The designated fans sat together in a section behind third base, with Browns manager Taylor seated in a large rocking chair in front of them. The fans were told that the team had to obey their instructions on the signs. Athletics manager Jimmy Dykes threatened to protest the game if the fan voting delayed the game. All in all, the Fan Managers made good decisions, and the Browns won the game. Veeck was disappointed that fewer than 4,000 fans turned out for the game.[7]

The Browns finished the 1951 season with a record of 52–102, in eighth place, 10 games behind the seventh-place Washington Senators.[8] Before the year ended, DeWitt made a two-for-one transaction with the Boston Red Sox. The Browns gave the Red Sox their strong-armed right fielder, Ken Wood, for Bosox outfielder Tom Wright and one-time Browns catcher Les Moss, who returned to the Browns as "the player to be named later" in his original deal.[9] DeWitt also arranged a one-year working agreement between the Browns and the Class A Eastern League Scranton (Pennsylvania) Miners, making Scranton the 14th team in the Browns' expanding minor league chain.[10]

In 1952, Bill Veeck began his first full year of ownership of the St. Louis Browns. In February, he completed a seven-player trade with the Detroit Tigers in one of that winter's largest baseball deals. The Tigers sent the Browns pitchers Gene Bearden and Bob Cain, (who had pitched to Gaedel) and first baseman Dick Kryhoski in return for catcher Matt Batts, outfielder Cliff Mapes, pitcher Dick Littlefield, and infielder Benjamin Taylor.[11]

Veeck was confident that St. Louis would not support two major league baseball teams, and he proceeded to try to run the Cardinals out of town. He was convinced he had two advantages. First, Cardinals owner Fred Saigh was under indictment for income tax fraud. Second, the Cardinals had not been a real threat on the field since their appearance in the World Series in 1946. In his battle with the Cardinals, Veeck also made several moves he hoped would taunt Fred Saigh. Before spring

Seven. A Three Ring Circus

In 1952, Rogers Hornsby (right), new Browns manager, huddles with Bill DeWitt, Sr., to discuss the possibility of signing players who might help them in the following season.

training began, he hired the hard-boiled ex–Cardinal, Rogers Hornsby, as manager to replace Zack Taylor. He obtained a new shortstop, former Cardinal Marty Marion.[12] He also hired other former Cardinals, including Harry Brecheen as pitching coach and Dizzy Dean to broadcast the Browns games.[13]

While the Browns were spring training in California, Bill DeWitt was 3,000 miles away in Florida camps, searching for talent. DeWitt wanted to get together with the Yankees and Dodgers, the only two clubs with extra talent. "Our biggest problem," said DeWitt, "is to erase the defeatism complex which has plagued the club." But he warned his superiors that "this business of trying to swing a deal is getting tougher with every inflationary spiral. Clubs aren't interested in money. They'll hang on to their players unless they can get talent in return. Money means nothing."[14]

DeWitt was impressed by the crop of rookies training in Florida. Veteran baseball observers called the Grapefruit League the best group in ten years. "If we can spot a prospect on some other club before he makes the grade," said DeWitt, "chances are we can get him at a cheaper figure than if we wait a year or two."[15]

While DeWitt was making his way through Florida seeking talent and bemoaning the clubhouse attitude, Veeck and his coaches were pleased with the club's outlook and work in California. He wanted old-fashioned, two-fisted baseball, and the players were giving it to him. He clamped down on smoking during workouts, and he outlawed beer in the clubhouse. He bluntly admitted that he intended to lift the Browns from last place to first place in one season. "Who wants to play if you don't win?" he said.[16]

As the 1952 season was about to begin, the question asked was, "How tough will the St. Louis Browns be?" The consensus was that the team would finish around fifth. Jim Rivera, George Schmees, and Nieman would probably be their starting outfield. The bespectacled Clint Courtney was penciled in to work behind the plate, and the rest of the infield would consist of Marty Marion, Leo Thomas, Bobby Young, and Dick Kryhoski. Ned Garver, Earl Harrist, Bob Cain, and Gene Bearden were slated to be the team's starting pitchers.[17]

Throughout the month of May, Bill DeWitt attempted to improve the team's record by making judicious trades. DeWitt offered the Detroit Tigers his ace pitcher, Ned Garver, in return for third baseman George Kell. Several other players were also to be included, but the trade never came to fruition.[18]

On June 10, the Browns fired manager Rogers Hornsby. It had been hoped that his managerial style might help the club contend for a trip to the World Series, but it never materialized. His autocratic personality never resonated with the players, and he could never get the team to live up to his expectations.[19] At the time the Browns fired Hornsby, the club was 22–29, in seventh place.[20]

Marty Marion succeeded Hornsby but unfortunately, he could do no better than his predecessor. The Browns finished in seventh place again with a record of 64–90.[21] The club's 1952 attendance of 518,796 was, however, higher than the Browns had drawn in their pennant-winning season of 1944. Interestingly, the Cardinals drew fewer than a million patrons for the first time since the conclusion of World War II.[22]

Bill Veeck estimated that for the Browns to remain in St. Louis, the franchise would have to draw at least 850,000 fans merely to break even.[23] Veeck's promotions were bringing fans to the ballpark, but not quickly enough. In order to acquire needed funds, Veeck proposed to the American League club owners that they share both radio and television revenue with visiting teams. They immediately realized his motives and voted down his proposal, 7 to 1, informing Veeck that each team should be able to negotiate separate deals. An angry Veeck opted to retaliate against the other owners by refusing to sign releases allowing the televising of any game in which the Browns were visitors. The rest of the league struck back hard by changing the schedule to eliminate all night games in St. Louis, realizing full well that night games were financially more profitable than day games.[24]

Veeck's financial situation was worsening. The Browns owner was deeply in debt, and he entered the 1953 season with no television contract and a very limited radio network. To make matters worse, he had a local brewery anxious to sponsor Browns TV games for the 1953 season, but the only TV station in St. Louis was not willing to air them. In the late spring, another station would begin broadcasting in St. Louis and agreed to pick up the Browns games, but the income Veeck would have realized was minimal.[25]

Any hope Veeck had of the Browns remaining in St. Louis was thwarted when Cardinals owner Fred Saigh was not only fined for income-tax evasion, he was also sentenced to 15 months in jail. Saigh was ordered to dispose of his assets, including his ownership of the Cardinals. "There is no way I can stay in baseball," he said, and under pressure from Commissioner Ford Frick, put the Cardinals up for sale.[26] When August A. Busch, Jr., head of St. Louis Anheuser-Busch Brewers, indicated that he wanted to purchase the team from Saigh, Veeck realized that he could not stay in St. Louis and compete against the brewery.[27]

In February, Veeck announced that he intended to move the Browns out of St. Louis before the 1953 season began. No major league ballclub had relocated since 1903, nor had either the American or National Leagues added a team.[28] Veeck had two cities in mind—Milwaukee and Baltimore—the only cities that had publicly owned stadiums and adequate facilities to host major league baseball. Milwaukee was his first choice, but unfortunately for Veeck, Lou Perini, the owner of the Boston Braves, was about to move his team to Milwaukee.[29]

Before the 1953 season began, Veeck asked the American League owners for permission to move the Browns to Baltimore. Jerry Hoffberger of the National Brewing Company of Baltimore offered Veeck $300,000 for the rights to sponsor the Browns in Baltimore. The American League owners promised that at the winter meetings in Tampa, they would give Veeck quick approval to move there. However, when the meeting occurred, the owners voted, 6–2, to oppose his move to Baltimore, claiming it was too close to the opening of the 1953 season. Yet the very next morning, the National League owners voted unanimously to give Perini permission to transfer his team to Milwaukee immediately.[30] The Browns, still under the ownership of Bill Veeck, were forced to play the 1953 season in St. Louis.[31]

When Veeck heard that the owners had turned down his request to move, he felt it was simply a case of collusion against him. The truth was that the bulk of the baseball owners did not like Veeck's constant publicity-seeking methods of operating a baseball team. Most of baseball's other executives were much more sedate than the rambunctious, high-spirited Veeck, and his often-outlandish promotions bothered them. They also tired of his constant wrangling over radio and television rights, and his scheduling night games created enemies. His propensity to calling them "idiots" certainly did not help.[32]

More than just disliking Veeck, many of the baseball owners were legitimately concerned that the competition between Philadelphia and Washington would be exacerbated by adding a third team to the area. Finally, there was a minor league team in Baltimore, and the teams in that league were afraid that removing the Baltimore team would have a devastating financial effect on them.[33]

DeWitt was certain that Veeck was determined to move the Browns out of St. Louis, and he wondered how this move would affect his professional and his family life. As the Browns vice president, DeWitt worked for Veeck, and he was unhappy with the rumors that 1953 might be the last year the Browns would play in St. Louis. He and Margaret had established an easy-going, home-centered family environment in their large house in St. Louis. According to their daughter Joan, they had many friends, and were especially close with Don Barnes' family. Bill, his wife and children went to Barnes' house for dinner every Sunday and often entertained their many friends and baseball associates at their home. Bill DeWitt, Jr., remembered that a typical social evening with friends was dinner followed by bridge and poker.[34]

It was no surprise that there were rumors that DeWitt had been angling with the new owner of the St. Louis Cardinals for a job as general manager. But DeWitt would have difficulty in obtaining the job. Bill Walsingham, nephew of the late Sam Breadon, had spent all his adult life in baseball and appeared to be the top candidate for the post. He had been general manager of the Cardinals when Fred Saigh owned the team.[35]

When the 1953 season began, Veeck became a "lame duck" owner since the public was well aware of his intention to move the Browns out of St. Louis. Veeck had really worked himself into a corner. He had alienated the other baseball executives by his antics both on and off the field, and by 1953 he had also isolated himself from both the fans and the press. Fans boycotted Browns games, and he was hanged in effigy throughout the city.[36] Yet Veeck had been so sure that the other owners would allow him to move to Baltimore that he had spent more than $400,000 for prospects he had expected to showcase in Baltimore.[37] To recoup that money, Veeck sold Sportsman's Park to the Cardinals for $800,000. He also sold his ranch in Arizona and peddled pitcher Virgil Trucks and outfielder Bob Elliot to the White Sox for $90,000.[38]

At the winter baseball meeting in Florida in March 1953, the first item on the agenda was the transfer of the Boston Braves to Milwaukee. With little fanfare, Warren Giles, president of the National League, announced that the Braves' transfer had been approved. He emphasized that there was no chance for the American Association to block the transfer, saying, "It's a question of a voluntary withdrawal from Milwaukee or a major draft of the territory." Brewer Frederick Miller would buy into the club, but Giles quoted Perini as saying, "Not one share of stock is for sale."[39]

Bill DeWitt, vice president of the Browns, whose similar transfer application was rejected by the American League, was in the hotel for the meeting and commented, "Baseball history has just been made and, as usual it was made by the National League…. This was a wonderful move for baseball, and I am here as a good sport to congratulate Perini and the National League."[40]

While the meeting was taking place, *The Sporting News* reported that it had learned from an unimpeachable source that Bill Veeck had shifted his plans to move to Baltimore after the Milwaukee deal fell through. The source reported that Veeck and DeWitt had been in contact with major and minor league bigwigs for ten days.

Browns general manager Rudie Schaffer, who made a hasty trip out of St. Louis and returned two days later, denied he had gone to Florida and said that he had no idea if the Browns were headed to Baltimore. He indicated, however, that he would make a formal announcement within a few days.

Meanwhile, in Hollywood, Florida, Orioles owner Jack Dunn III at first denied he was aware of any negotiations but finally admitted that he had been approached with a proposal to move the Browns to Baltimore. It was no secret that in Baltimore, plans had already been approved for the double-decking of Memorial Stadium, which presently seated 31,000 fans and would ultimately seat 62,000.[41]

Near the end of March, there was still no official report of a St. Louis Browns sale nor any valid indication that the team might move out of the city. St. Louis Mayor Joseph Darst had to assume that the Browns would remain in St. Louis, telling St. Louisans that he was deeply pleased that the citizens had been so vigorous and successful in their response to the threatened loss. He added, "I am extremely hopeful that the people will not permit their enthusiasm to wane and will evidence their support by attending as many [Browns] games as possible."[42]

Vice president Bill DeWitt joined Veeck in Texas, ostensibly to help him set up the squad and send some of the rookies elsewhere. But his main reason for coming was to sign pitcher Don Larsen, a promising right-handed recruit, recently discharged from military service, to a Browns contract.

Larsen had been training with the Browns as a member of their San Antonio farm club, and he made such a fine showing that the club decided to keep him. Larsen became the fifth ex–GI on the Browns' roster, joining pitchers Clarence Marshall and Mike Blyzka, and outfielders Rocco Ippolito and Dick Kokos. Each club could carry five ex-servicemen over its 25-man limit once the teams were organized.[43]

DeWitt was extremely high in his praise of his new pitcher. "Larsen is acquiring poise fast. The big thing is that he has the 'mentality' to pitch in the big leagues after making the big jump from A ball. He has the confidence and could be a terrific pitcher by the end of the year." Manager Marty Marion rated Larsen as the best-looking rookie pitcher in the league.[44]

Later in the season, Bill DeWitt predicted that another of the Browns' pitchers, Bob Turley, presently in the army, would join the Browns before the current season ended. DeWitt said he keeps in close touch with all of the players currently in their minor league system, and he was elated with what he had seen. Ever the pre-season optimist, DeWitt predicted that Turley might be called to the majors even before the end of the season.[45]

J. Roy Stockton was growing weary of the antics of the team and their keeping the baseball fans in St. Louis guessing what plans the Browns' front office had for the future of the team. He stated that the DeWitt brothers ran the club strictly as a capital gain project and that the American League helped finance the DeWitts and Muckerman by holding their note for more than $600,000. Stockton understood that the DeWitts had had to sell some assets prior to the notes coming due, and that ballplayers were the only commodity the DeWitts had. Stockton summarized that they had "beat the bell" by selling the team to Veeck and his associates.

Stockton summed up his indignation about the secrecy of the Browns' intentions by asking why the team's St. Louis fans should "go all out for the Browns at the box office without some assurance that they are not merely oiling the machinery for a transfer of the franchise to some other city?"[46]

As the season continued, everyone in St. Louis realized that the Browns would be transferred but most simply asked, "Where?" DeWitt's right-hand man, general manager Rudie Schaffer, would not even hazard a guess as to whether the team would go east to Baltimore or west to Kansas City or the Pacific Coast. Even Bill DeWitt, who at one time was in the midst of the negotiations for the move to Baltimore, said he had no idea what was going on.[47]

To no one's surprise, the Browns ended the 1953 season with an embarrassing record of 54–100, finishing in eighth place.[48] One of the very few highlights of the season was Bobo Holloman's 6–0 no-hitter over the Athletics in his first major league start on May 6. The win, Holloman's only major league complete game, came on a rainy night, witnessed by 2,473 fans in the stands. For the entire 1953 season, the Browns played at home before a total of 297,238. In the final game the Browns played in St. Louis, the Chicago White Sox defeated the Browns, 2–1, in 12 innings. The Browns had run out of fresh baseballs, and the final out in the game was recorded with a recycled baseball.[49]

Shortly after the season ended, Bill Veeck sold his interest in the Browns to Clarence Miles, who would become chairman of the board of the new Baltimore team. The American League approved the sale contingent on Veeck's exclusion from the new administration and ownership of the team. Removing Veeck from any participation was key in the eyes of the other American League owners. The primary new Baltimore owner was Jerry Hoffberger, president of the National Brewing Company, who agreed to have his firm advertise on Washington's games on radio and television. After the move, Clark Griffith, owner of the Washington Senators, would lose air rights in Baltimore, but Hoffberger agreed to cover Griffith's losses.[50]

Baseball magnates patted each other on the back. By forcing Veeck to sell the Browns and leave baseball, they had accomplished three objectives. First, Boston and St. Louis, which could each support only one major league team, now had that team—the Red Sox in Boston and the Cardinals in St. Louis. Second, the major leagues now had teams in Milwaukee and Baltimore, two strong minor league cities. And finally, the close-knit major league magnates had rid themselves of Veeck, their most troublesome outsider.[51] No one seemed to object when the new owners asked Bill DeWitt to come to Baltimore with the team.

Eight

Interregnum

In 1953, owner Bill Veeck sold his remaining stock in the St. Louis Browns to Baltimore investors. On September 29, the American League owners voted unanimously to approve the transfer of the Browns franchise, with the team to remain in the American League as the Baltimore Orioles.[1]

The Orioles began operations immediately, utilizing their newly acquired farm system which included approximately 300 players on 12 teams from Class AA to Class D. Most importantly, the new franchise also included Bill DeWitt, Sr., the Browns' director of farm operations, who moved with the stock transfer to Baltimore. DeWitt stated that he would continue operations, keeping his headquarters in St. Louis until his contract ended in July 1956. Clarence Miles, chairman of the board of the new Orioles, confirmed the agreement with DeWitt, admitting, "I don't know right now anything about the farm system. We've got a lot to learn." DeWitt was not only to continue as director of farm operations, he would serve as temporary general manager until the team hired a permanent GM.[2]

In his brief stint as general manager of the Orioles, DeWitt made a few minor deals. He acquired 27-year-old southpaw Jim Post from Toronto of the International League, 23-year-old outfielder Karol Kwak, who led the Class B Tri-State League with a batting average of .359, and two right-handed pitchers, Vachal Perkins and Ryne Duren. Perkins and Duren were brought up from San Antonio, one of the former Browns minor league affiliates.[3] A few days later, DeWitt signed an African American outfielder, Ernest Duncan Johnson of the Kansas City Monarchs, announcing that Johnson would be assigned to the Orioles' farm club at Wichita in the Class A Western League. DeWitt was so impressed with Johnson that he said, "He may be playing for the Orioles someday." Johnson led the Negro American League in home runs and RBIs in 1953.[4]

In late October, the Orioles hired Arthur Ehlers as their general manager, replacing Bill DeWitt. From 1947–1950, Ehlers was the director of the Philadelphia Athletics' farm system, and he became their general manager in 1950 when Connie Mack retired. His contract with the Athletics had expired, and he agreed to a three-year pact with the Orioles. The Orioles announced that Bill DeWitt would become the full-time director of the team's farm system.[5]

The Orioles made their final personnel move for the year when they named Jimmy Dykes field manager to replace Marty Marion, who had left the Browns to manage the Chicago White Sox. Dykes managed the team for one year and then was replaced by Paul Richards, who led the Orioles from 1955–1961.[6]

On October 29, 1953, in the brokerage offices of Stein Bros. and Boyce, the Baltimore Orioles legally and officially became a member of the American League after 50 years of absence from major league ball, and the St. Louis Browns ceased to exist. The ceremony lasted one hour, and after all the speeches were given and all the legal papers signed, American League president William Harridge presented Clarence W. Miles, president and chairman of the board of the Baltimore Orioles, Inc., with the franchise certificate. Mayor Thomas D'Alesandro thanked Harridge effusively for his help and closed with a warning: "We'll take those Yankees' scalps."[7]

Shortly after the St. Louis Browns moved to Baltimore, Bill DeWitt was appointed a vice president of the team. He held that position for approximately six months. In April 1954, Roy Hamey, assistant general manager of the New York Yankees, became GM of the Philadelphia Phillies. Yankees co-owner Dan Topping offered the vacant post to Bill DeWitt, who quickly accepted. "I made a satisfactory adjustment of my salary with the Baltimore club," said DeWitt. He added that the Orioles were very fair.[8]

Veteran *Washington Post* sportswriter Shirley Povich praised the Yankees for hiring DeWitt. According to Povich, the Yankees first admired DeWitt's shrewdness when he sold them losing pitcher Fred Sanford for $100,000 and came to admire DeWitt's ability to deal with ball players, scouts, and farm clubs. Few baseball men had more experience than DeWitt, Povich wrote, and he earned respect in St. Louis for his ability to barter and keep the Browns going on a shoestring, sometimes even showing a profit. Asked many times how he felt joining the Yankees, a club that almost always defeated his Browns, DeWitt's answer was simple: "I suppose if you can't beat 'em, it's best to join 'em."[9]

No one touted DeWitt's ability more than Yankees co-owner Dan Topping, who told the press about "'his new employee.' Bill DeWitt probably knows more about the American League than anyone except

Bill DeWitt, Sr., meets and greets the three men from the Yankees for whom he will be working: (left to right) owners Dan Topping and Del Webb, and general manager George Weiss.

[Yankees general manager George] Weiss."[10] Topping was also impressed by Bill DeWitt's skill at twice finding buyers for the Browns, the American League's worst team—Don Barnes in 1936 and Richard Muckerman in 1945. Topping was also captivated by DeWitt's ability to make deals which helped keep the Browns afloat. He cited DeWitt's sale of Vern Stephens and Jack Kramer to the Red Sox for $300,000 in cash. Yankees manager Casey Stengel joined Topping in praising Bill DeWitt.[11]

The Orioles didn't often acknowledge the assets the Browns brought to their team. One of DeWitt's finds was 21-year-old Bob Turley, who pitched for the Browns in 1951 and 1953, winning a total of two games. He began to show his talent in 1954, when Turley won 14 games for the Baltimore Orioles. At DeWitt's urging, the Yankees obtained Turley from the Orioles. Turley pitched for the Yankees from 1955–1962, posting a record of 84–52.[12]

The Yankees were disappointed to come up short in the 1954 pennant race, despite statistics that would have elated most teams: more runs (805) than any team in the major leagues, and a record of 103–51.

Eight. Interregnum

The Cleveland Indians' 1954 record was 111–43, however, and Cleveland won the pennant, finishing eight games ahead of the Yankees.[13] The National League champion Giants swept the Indians in the World Series, four games to zero.[14]

Late in 1954, George Weiss announced that Bill DeWitt would be the Yankees' trouble-shooter during the winter months. DeWitt left on his first project in his new role in November. The club announced publicly only that he would "be away for two weeks on miscellaneous duties." Actually, his agenda included conferences with regional scouts in the West and visits with pitchers Allie Reynolds and Johnny Sain. Sain had told the Yankees he wanted to return in 1955 if "proper arrangements" could be made. Reynolds had confided that he was considering retiring from the game.[15]

When the 1954 major league season ended, the Philadelphia Athletics, formerly owned by Connie Mack, were sold to industrialist Arnie Johnson. Johnson moved the team to Kansas City, the home of the Kansas City Blues, a minor league affiliate of the New York Yankees. Johnson named Parke Carroll, general manager of the Blues, vice president and business manager of the new Athletics. DeWitt met with Del Webb, not only co-owner of the Yankees but also a contractor, to help relocate the Yankees' minor league affiliate in Kansas City and find a replacement for Carroll.

In addition to being Weiss' trouble-shooter, DeWitt quickly assumed numerous and varied duties.[16] Like most assistant general managers, DeWitt signed players to their contracts and helped negotiate player deals with other American League clubs. Besides the usual tasks, George Weiss loaded DeWitt with other jobs: the supervision of personnel for West Coast scouting and the responsibility for working out spring training schedules and arranging the details for games. Weiss also wanted DeWitt to gather information about other major league clubs and their personnel, and often sent him to visit the Yankees' minor league affiliates, consulting with the managers and players.[17] With all the responsibilities assigned to DeWitt when working for Branch Rickey and George Weiss, as well as for what he learned running his own team, Bill DeWitt was establishing himself as one of baseball's most knowledgeable executives.

Near the end of 1954, DeWitt was the guest speaker in St. Louis at the annual B.P.O. Elks, No. 9 Sports Celebrity Night. Ever the optimist, he predicted that the Yankees had the 1955 pennant "in the bag," and that since he made his home in St. Louis, he hoped that the Yankees and Cardinals could meet in the 1955 World Series. DeWitt modestly admitted that he had been "somewhat involved" in the Yankees obtaining former Browns pitchers Don Larsen and Bob Turley, by advising Weiss to "go after" them.[18]

In December, Bill DeWitt gave the team's 1954 annual report on the status of the club's farm system. The Yankees sold the American Association franchise from Kansas City to Denver, leaving the Yankees owning only one farm club: Binghamton in the Class A Eastern League. Even in Binghamton, the New York organization did not own the ballpark. "In fact," said DeWitt, "the Yankees do not own a single park, not even their own stadium." In its heyday, the Yankees' farm system consisted of "22 clubs of which no fewer than 14 were owned outright."[19] DeWitt attributed the loss of so many minor league affiliates to many factors, but he stressed that the shrinking of the minor league chain had been caused by the determination of major league teams not to sign young players unless they showed prospects of becoming major leaguers. "Reduction of the Yankee farm system," emphasized DeWitt, "and liquidation of all real estate holdings in the minors, has added to the unrest in baseball."[20]

After the first of the year, DeWitt began the task of signing his players for the 1955 season. Center fielder Mickey Mantle reportedly received a $3,000 raise, increasing his salary into the $20,000–$25,000 bracket. Normally tight-lipped, Mantle announced, "I'm satisfied with my contract and I'm coming to camp this time with nothing bothering me. I feel great in every respect."[21] That same day, DeWitt held the signed contracts of his catchers, Charley Silvera, Lou Berberet, Yogi Berra, and Elston Howard.[22]

At an early March meeting of all Yankees executives, one of their chief topics was the increase in players' salaries. Bill DeWitt had a very gloomy view of the situation, insisting that the day of "reckoning" was not far off. "Many older players are pricing themselves out of baseball," he insisted. He cited the case of Ralph Kiner, whose demand for a salary of $80,000 was turned down by the Pittsburgh Pirates. Kiner then went to the Cubs, who refused to pay the $65,000 he asked for. He eventually went to the Cleveland Indians, who agreed to pay him $50,000.

"Do you realize what that salary to Kiner means for the general payroll of the Cleveland Indians? Maybe as much as $200,000, altogether, in increase," said DeWitt. "Kiner is advertised at $50,000, so what happens? One of the great pitchers is next in line for a contract, and he has to get $55,000, because if the 'new man' is entitled to 50 the pitcher certainly merits 55."[23]

Early in March 1955, DeWitt was sent to Phoenix to "check out" the Arizona division of baseball spring training. After looking at the Cubs in Mesa, Arizona, he headed to California to meet with his scouts.

DeWitt's uncanny ability to appraise young talent caused some baseball pundits to rate him an American League Branch Rickey. On this trip, DeWitt claimed that he had "no trades at all in mind," but added, "We could always use another starting pitcher."[24]

DeWitt traveled many miles each year performing his job. "Last year I was in California twice, Los Angeles and San Francisco, New Orleans, Kansas City, Chicago, Columbus, Binghampton [NY], and Indianapolis." This past trip was different from almost all his other business travel, because his wife and two of his children, Dee Dee (age 17) and Bill Jr. (age 13), accompanied him. DeWitt stated that being a St. Louis resident with a New York job added to his traveling, and he was considering renting a small apartment in New York.[25]

Weiss would often send him to the Yankees' affiliates for updates and to offer help to the team if necessary. In 1955, the Yankees had two AAA farm clubs, one in Richmond, Virginia, managed by former Yankees pitcher Eddie Lopat, and the other, the Denver Bears, managed by another former Yankee, catcher Ralph Houk. The Yankees organization considered their Denver players the cream of their upcoming talent. Denver's roster included future major leaguers Bobby Richardson, Woodie Held, Marv Throneberry, Darrell Johnson, and Don Larsen.

By late May 1955, the Denver Bears had a horrible record of 7–25, and the Yankees execs wondered if they had made the correct decision in selecting Houk as the manager. Assistant general manager DeWitt, of course, was sent to Denver to suggest that the Bears purchase some players from the major league clubs in a few days when teams were required to trim their rosters from 28 to 25 players. DeWitt and Houk met at a Denver hotel, and after listening to DeWitt's suggestion, Houk bluntly told him, "Bill, I don't want any new ballplayers. I just want time to work out our problems with the ones we have. I picked these players in the spring and I believe in them. I don't want any help."

DeWitt was bewildered. He had never encountered a manager who refused help from a front office that offered to improve his team. When he returned to New York, DeWitt reported Houk's words to Weiss. "Okay, so be it," Weiss responded. "Let's see what we can do." As the summer wore on, the Bears played over .600 ball the remainder of the year and finished at 83–71. A pleased New York organization re-signed Houk for the 1956 season, adding to the team's roster two additional stars, shortstop Tony Kubek and pitcher Ralph Terry.[26]

DeWitt's early optimism was justified. New York won the American League pennant in 1955 with a record of 96–58, finishing three games ahead of last year's winner, the Cleveland Indians. The Yankees met the

Brooklyn Dodgers, the National League pennant winnerby 13½ games over the second-place Milwaukee Braves.[27]

The Yankees started the 1955 World Series with two quick wins at Yankee Stadium. In the third game, the Brooklyn Dodgers started southpaw Johnny Podres, whose season record was a mediocre 8–12. Podres pitched a complete-game victory perhaps, inspiring the Dodgers, who won the next two games as well. Needing only one more game to win the World Series, the Dodgers were stymied by southpaw Whitey Ford, who held them to one run and four hits. The Dodgers won the deciding seventh game, thanks to another winning performance by Johnny Podres and to Gil Hodges, who drove in the only two runs in the game.[28]

When the World Series concluded, general manager George Weiss, manager Casey Stengel, and almost the entire Yankees team set out on a tour of the Orient. Left behind was assistant general manager Bill DeWitt, whose instructions were to start looking for players who would immediately help strengthen the team. "If anything should develop here before I return," said Weiss, "Bill DeWitt will be in the office to handle things. No matter where I will be, Bill will be able to get me on the telephone."[29]

Weiss and DeWitt were in constant contact during the Orient tour. They arranged a list of players who might be used as "trade bait" at the upcoming winter meeting. DeWitt leaked no names to the press, but rumors circulated that shortstop Billy Hunter, shortstop/second baseman Jerry Coleman, and first baseman Eddie Robinson were very likely among the expendables. Pitchers Don Larsen, Jim Konstanty, Bob Wiesler, Tom Sturdivant, and Tom Morgan also could go. What the Yankees were seeking was another frontline pitcher who would allow Bob Grim to be used as a full-time bullpen pitcher.[30]

Despite all the rumors, Bill DeWitt continued to insist that the Yankees had no deal cooking. "Just because the Indians and the White Sox have made moves, I don't feel the pressure is on us to make any moves." He did add, however, that he would listen to any offers from the White Sox regarding a deal involving pitcher Billy Pierce.[31]

In addition to rumors involving major league players, there was talk that Bill DeWitt, "the experienced baseball man," would succeed Clarence Miles as president of the Baltimore Orioles. Miles, who led the campaign to return baseball to Baltimore, resigned early in November amidst reproach of his unsuccessful $700,000 campaign to rebuild the Orioles by signing "bonus babies." Paul Richards, who held the dual function of field manager and general manager, called Miles' resignation "a shock and a surprise."[32]

Bill DeWitt was one of five men mentioned for the Orioles job,

Eight. Interregnum

and it was felt that he was the logical man to succeed Clarence Miles, since Miles suggested that the new president "be an experienced baseball man." DeWitt certainly had the experience since he had held just about every type of front office job in baseball. DeWitt did not seek the post, and he made it clear that he had another year to run on his New York contract. He also made it clear that "nobody from Baltimore has approached me." The selection of the new Orioles president was James J. Keely, a contractor.[33]

During the final weeks of 1955, DeWitt was still searching for starting pitching. When the Red Sox picked up pitcher Bob Porterfield from the Washington Senators, DeWitt admitted that the Red Sox's addition could make things tough for the Yankees in 1956 because Porterfield would fit right into their starting rotation. Undeterred, DeWitt declared, "These clubs aren't squeezing us out of the trade market. On the contrary, we've found that everybody still wants to deal with us because we can give them more good players than anybody else."[34]

As 1955 was nearing its close, Yankees executives prepared for the annual major league meetings in Chicago. Other clubs made offers to trade pitchers to the Yankees but at what the New Yorkers considered extremely high asking prices, and the Yankees made no pitcher deals. Both Weiss and DeWitt were still looking for that pitcher, but they expected no action until after the holiday season.[35]

Prior to spring training in 1956, educator and author Dr. Rufus Early Clement, who was also a leader in community relations and an advocate of human rights, held an event recognizing Branch Rickey as the man responsible for integrating major league baseball. Unable to make the event, DeWitt sent a telegram praising Rickey and congratulating Dr. Clement for his selection. In the telegram, DeWitt stated that Rickey had been his inspiration and ideal since he first knew him 40 years ago. "I am happy to join with his many friends in paying tribute to him on this occasion," concluded DeWitt.[36]

A week later, Rickey sent DeWitt a telegram expressing regrets that his protégé was unable to make the Dr. Clement's dinner, but the remainder of the telegram clearly demonstrated how the relationship between the two men had continued to grow. "You have known me," wrote Rickey, "perhaps better than any other person in baseball, and I want you to know that when your telegram was read out loud, I was deeply moved. You are more than a friend of mine. It goes deeper than that. I wish you were my son, for I feel that relationship as a very real one."[37]

Baseball was now in its annual contract period. DeWitt signed three of his stars by February 1. Hank Bauer flew to New York from Kansas

City, had a checkup, and then inked his 1956 contract for $25,000.[38] Yogi Berra had a brief conference with DeWitt and signed a $50,000 contract. "I got what I wanted in dough," he said.[39] Mantle also signed, but not before he had a hassle with DeWitt. When he was first offered $25,000, he returned the contract unsigned. But he eventually accepted an additional $10,000 and signed his $30,000 pact in a room filled with the press.[40] In the past couple of seasons, George Weiss, with rare exceptions, delegated salary negotiations, but that now became the almost exclusive task of Bill DeWitt, as assistant general manager.[41]

On February 9, 1956, baseball lost one of its noblest statesmen, Connie Mack, who passed away. Bill DeWitt, who was long associated with Mack in the American League, said, "He was more a real part of the game than any other man I know. Like the thousands of friends he had, I'll miss him very much."[42]

On February 9, 1956, the Yankees finally obtained the southpaw pitcher that had been mentioned in rumored deals all winter, Maury McDermott. In return, the Washington Senators received outfielder Dick Tettlebach, pitcher Bob Wiesler, catcher Lou Berberet, second/third baseman Herbie Plews, plus a fifth man to be sent prior to April 1, presumably from the Yankees' roster.[43]

After DeWitt signed 26-year-old right-hander Bob Grim, only three pitchers remained unsigned—the Bombers' ace southpaw, Whitey Ford, and two relief pitchers—Jim Konstanty and Tom Morgan.[44] Morgan, Ford, and outfielder Irv Noren were the next Yankees to accept their contracts, leaving Konstanty and Billy Martin, hero of the New York Yankees' 1953 World Series victory over Brooklyn, the only unsigned 1956 Yankees. Martin, who was considered the most stubborn, threatened to hold out, insisting that the team was well aware of what he wanted. "The next move is up to them," said Martin.[45]

Weiss asked manager Casey Stengel to intervene and get Martin to agree to his contract. Normally Stengel avoided getting involved in player negotiations, but Martin had always been referred to as "Casey's boy," so DeWitt decided to let Stengel give his "peppery youngster" a bit of fatherly advice.[46]

During spring training, George Weiss sent DeWitt west to help strengthen the 1956 roster. "I'm on one of my many missions for the Yanks. Mr. Weiss, Casey and our coaches know what they want, and it's up to me to do the 'leg work,'" DeWitt said prior to his departure. "I enjoy my work because making contact with the other clubs is pleasant business.... You can truthfully say, I suppose, that when the new season gets under way, you won't be able to tell a lot of players without a scorecard."[47]

While a major function of spring training is to prepare the team for the upcoming season, it also gives team officials the opportunity to make trades to fill major gaps on their roster. Bill DeWitt and Baltimore manager Paul Richards passed up a scheduled exhibition game to discuss a possible trade. The Orioles had a desperate need for a second baseman, while the Yankees were still looking for more depth in their starting pitching. The Orioles had two right-handed pitchers to offer: Jim Wilson and Ray Moore, last season's 10-game winner for the Orioles, while the Yankees had a plethora of second basemen in Billy Martin, Gil McDougald, Bobby Richardson, and Jerry Coleman. Despite prolonged discussions, no deal was consummated.[48]

The pitching woes of the Yankees continued throughout most of 1956. Mickey Mantle and Yogi Berra were a one-two attack, the Yankees' best since Ruth and Gehrig, but they received far too little help. There seemed to be no available pitchers of note to help the Yankees' ace, Whitey Ford.[49]

During the baseball season, the usual rumors of player trades or retirements at the season's end emerged. In July, one of the hottest rumors was the possible retirement of American League president Will Harridge, who was in his 25th year in that post. His present 10-year contract would expire at the end of the 1958 season, but because of illness in his family, it was rumored that he would retire at the end of the present season. Two names were mentioned as possible successors, Frank Lane of the St. Louis Cardinals and Bill DeWitt.[50]

Despite the Yankees' concerns about their pitching, the Bronx Bombers won the American League pennant for the second consecutive year, again beating out the second-place Cleveland Indians. Once again, the Yankees faced the Brooklyn Dodgers in the World Series.[51]

During the regular season, Yankees pitching might have been a concern, but four pitchers compiled double-digit victories—Whitey Ford 19, Johnny Kucks 18, Tom Sturdivant 16, and Don Larsen 11. Moreover, five players posted double-digit home runs—Gil McDougald 13; Bill Skowron 23; Hank Bauer 26; Yogi Berra 30; and Mickey Mantle 52. Mantle also notched a batting average of .353 which, along with his 130 RBIs earned him baseball's Triple Crown.[52]

This year, when the Yankees again faced the Brooklyn Dodgers in the World Series, the results were different from 1955. The pattern of victories and defeats was virtually the same, with one major difference. In both years, the Dodgers won the first two games and lost the next three. In 1955, Brooklyn won Game Six to tie the series at three games apiece and went on to win Game Seven. In 1956, the Dodgers also won the sixth game to the tie the series, but the Yankees won the last game to become the World Champions.[53]

Adding to the excitement of the 1956 World Series was the accomplishment of Yankees pitcher Don Larsen. Not only did he shut out the Dodgers, 2–0, he accomplished a feat still unique in World Series history—a perfect game. He retired all 27 batters he faced without allowing a single Dodger to reach base. Except for two close outs, one in the second inning and another in the fifth, the other 25 Dodgers at-bats were routine outs, and Don Larsen had made World Series history.[54]

By 1956, the number of minor leagues had been reduced to 28, and there was fear that the number might drop further. Numerous suggestions were offered to help the minors. Walter O'Malley, president of the Brooklyn Dodgers, suggested that a series of major league all-star games be played in a dozen top minor league cities as fund-raising events. The minor league operators immediately turned thumbs down on this proposal.

When the major leagues met on August 2, 1956, Commissioner Ford C. Frick set up a "Save the Minors Committee" to develop plans to help the members of the National Association of Professional Baseball Leagues. Kansas City's president, Arnold Johnson, was named chairman of this committee. Joe Cronin, general manager of the Boston Red Sox, and George Medinger, vice president of the Cleveland Indians, represented the American League, and Horace Stoneham, president of the New York Giants, Gabe Paul, Cincinnati's general manager, and Bob Carpenter, president of the Philadelphia Phillies, represented the National League.[55]

The committee recommended that a "stabilization fund" be established, and on October 11, Commissioner Frick announced that at a special meeting held during the World Series, the major league owners had agreed to creating a fund totaling $500,000, primarily for clubs and leagues in lower classifications. The fund was financed by contributions of $31,250 from each of the 16 big league clubs.[56]

Once the money was raised, Frick asked John Quinn, general manager of the Milwaukee Braves, to head a special committee of major and minor league executives to help allocate the money raised by Johnson's committee. Frick also asked Bill DeWitt to accept the job of administrator of the fund.[57]

The offer to leave the Yankees and assume this newly created position came at an opportune time in DeWitt's professional life. According to Bill DeWitt, Jr., "Yankee owners [Del] Webb and [Dan] Topping had recruited my Dad by telling him Weiss was going to step down 'soon' and that he would become Yankee GM. When it became clear that Weiss had no intention of leaving, my Dad realized the owners had misrepresented his plans in the hopes that Weiss would resign."[58] At that point, the 54-year-old DeWitt realized that he was unlikely to advance any further with New York. He was honored by Frick's offer and accepted the opportunity to become the head of the minor leagues with the official title of baseball coordinator. He would operate his office out of St. Louis, another benefit of the new job.[59] DeWitt officially assumed his duties on January 1, 1957.[60]

The six-man allocation committee with whom DeWitt was to work had been appointed by Commissioner Ford Frick and included, in addition to chairman Quinn, Walter Briggs of the Detroit Tigers, Joe L. Brown of the Pittsburgh Pirates, Grayle Howlett of Tulsa, Claude Engberg, president of the Pioneer League, and interestingly, DeWitt's former boss, Yankees general manager George Weiss.[61]

Weiss called Bill DeWitt's new position as Coordinator of the $500,000 minor league fund "the no. 3 job in all of baseball"—ranking right behind that of the commissioner and the National Association president. "We are very sorry," said Weiss, "to lose Bill DeWitt from our organization, but we never have prevented anyone with our club from improving his position in baseball. We send Bill our very best wishes for a very highly successful career as baseball coordinator."[62]

Even before the committee could begin its mission of helping the minor leagues, skeptics were predicting few if any positive results. One of the most vociferous skeptics was Robert Creamer, respected sportswriter, author, and editor of *Sports Illustrated*. Creamer stated bluntly that in the long run, the minor leagues had no reason to exist except to serve the major leagues. To substantiate his opinion, Creamer asserted that Commissioner Ford Frick was a major league man whose primary loyalty was to the major league club owners.

The minor leagues' man was George M. Trautman, president of the National Association of Professional Baseball Leagues, who knew more about the plight of the minor leagues than anyone else. According to Creamer, Trautman had been preaching for years that a successful minor league operation depended greatly on the executive who actively worked to promote his team. "But," wrote Creamer, "lack of any economic progress is one of the reasons why baseball is attracting so few capable young men into its business operation."

Creamer felt that the appointment of Bill DeWitt gave the minor leagues hope. Maybe the majors really meant it this time, he speculated. One minor league general manager brusquely stated that he did not like Bill DeWitt, but "people who know him better than I do say he has one of the best baseball brains in the business and if he can use some of the money to set up a group that could go around and look at a minor league club and make suggestions ... he could be the greatest thing to happen to baseball since Branch Rickey."[63]

DeWitt called a meeting of the six-member board, telling them that he hoped the grant of $500,000, which was intended to be for one year's operation, would last for several years. He also indicated that he would be at the call of the special committee. "This committee will set the policy," said DeWitt, "and I will execute it. I plan to contact a lot of people throughout baseball to get their ideas so that when we move—and we plan to move slowly—it will be in the right direction."

While preparing to set up his headquarters in St. Louis, DeWitt announced that he had appointed as his field man, G. E. "Eddie" Gilliland, former assistant vice president of the Browns. Gilliland had been president of the Florida State League, president of the Toledo American Association club, farm director of the Detroit Tigers, and general manager of the Miami Sox of the Florida State League. DeWitt, discussing his field man's duties, said, "Eddie will visit the various clubs that might want counsel and advice, look over their set up, confer with league presidents and then report back to me. He is thoroughly schooled in all phases of baseball, particularly the promotional end."[64]

DeWitt received no calls the first four months from the minors for financial aid. Finally, at the beginning of May, the Wenatchee club in the Class B Northwest called, asking for help. "My job," said DeWitt, "is to help stabilize the minor leagues. I will try to assist them in promoting minor league baseball and advise clubs on operational problems."[65]

Shortly after DeWitt was appointed Coordinator, he made it quite clear that he did not want to be perceived as a "generous and rich uncle" whose function it was to dispense money to struggling minor league teams. To clarify his committee's policies, DeWitt again explained the ground rules for receiving financial aid from this body. Basically, minor league clubs owned by a major league team or by a league were not eligible for funds. Minor league clubs that could not open the 1957 season without funds from the committee were also ineligible. Funds were not loaned but would be given on an outright grant basis. Finally, grants would be made only to clubs that responded within a "reasonable length of time" to the committee's requests for financial statements and other information.[66]

George Trautman questioned some of the restrictions placed on minor league teams seeking financial aid. He argued that many minor league teams had suffered bad breaks because of the weather and that these clubs needed and deserved immediate assistance. "The transfusions," said Trautman, "will be of no value after the patients have died." Trautman said that DeWitt's office had told him it was investigating clubs which had asked for help. "And I am hopeful," Trautman concluded, "that the help will be forthcoming."[67]

Eight. Interregnum

On October 16, 1957, the Cleveland Indians board of directors voted 10–2 to oust their general manager, Hank Greenberg. The board felt the need to do something to deal with a tremendous slump in the Indians' attendance. Only the American League Senators and National League Giants drew fewer fans the past season. Ironically, Greenberg owned 20 percent of the Indians' stock, and he indicated he would retain his shares. The rumor mill immediately began mentioning Bill Veeck, Al Lopez, Paul Richards, Bucky Harris, Muddy Ruel, and even Bob Feller as Greenberg'

DeWitt left the Yankees to become baseball coordinator to help reorganize the minor leagues He conducted his work in St. Louis, allowing him to watch games from his seat perched behind home plate while enjoying his favorite hot dogs—those from St. Louis.

successor. Everybody's unofficial list also included Bill DeWitt, who answered inquiries by saying, "I'm very happy in my present position but a fellow always needs to improve himself."[68]

From the moment Greenberg was removed as the Cleveland Indians' general manager, nearly every newspaper reported that DeWitt would most likely succeed him. Although no candidates for the post were mentioned at the team's directors' meeting, one official told *The Sporting News*, "We have a high regard for DeWitt. We know his baseball background and it's excellent."[69] Despite his continuing denials, on October 31, the Indians flew DeWitt to Cleveland, where he interviewed for ten hours with Indians executives. Before flying home, he told the *Cleveland News* that he had not been offered the GM job, nor did he apply for it, but "I definitely would take the job under the right conditions."[70]

The same story appeared in nearly every nation's sports section, indicating that as soon as William R. Daley, chairman of the Cleveland Indians' board of directors, returned from Europe, Bill DeWitt would be chosen as the team's new general manager, Further, the press speculated that his first order of business would be to hire Lou Boudreau to the Tribe's coaching staff as batting instructor. On November 11, however, the directors selected 62-year-old Frank Lane, currently the GM of the St. Louis Cardinals, as the new general manager of the Cleveland Indians. He was given a three-year contract reportedly at $60,000 a season. Meanwhile, the Cardinals, at a hastily called press conference at Busch's brewery, announced that Lane's assistant, Vaughan "Bing" Devine, would replace Frank Lane.[71]

The choice of Frank Lane shocked most Cleveland baseball fans, especially since every local Cleveland newspaper had insisted, from the moment Greenberg was fired, that Bill DeWitt was the one candidate to replace him. The only newspaper locally or nationally to predict that Frank Lane would succeed Greenberg was the *Chicago American*.[72]

While Cardinals fans were shocked to read that Lane had accepted the post in Cleveland, those in the Cardinals organization were not. Known locally as "Trader Lane," he loved to make player deals, some good and some bad. If a deal he made didn't pan out, Lane was never apologetic or remorseful. If he received attention from a trade, he was satisfied. Eventually, Cardinals owner Gussie Busch heatedly objected to a trade Frank Lane insisted on making, sending Ken Boyer and Harvey Haddix to the Phillies for outfielder Richie Ashburn and another player. When Busch refused to make this trade, Lane quit as Cardinals general manager and ended up in Cleveland.[73]

Early in 1958, DeWitt lost his assistant, G. E. Gilliland, who accepted a position as director of development for the Stetson Law Center at St. Petersburg, Florida. "We hate to lose Eddie," said DeWitt, "but he could not pass up the opportunity. He will take over his new duties on January 15."[74] To offset the news that DeWitt was temporarily without an assistant, the committee overseeing baseball realignment voted to extend the fund for relief of the minor leagues for another year.[75]

Once DeWitt knew his fund was replenished for another year, he began conducting a survey of all minor league cities to determine the "health" of each ballpark and its host city. Is the park adequate and in good repair? Is the town able, willing, and interested in continuing to host professional baseball? Are the present stadium operators of the club financially responsible? He also wanted the survey to include data that would help determine the optimum number and classification of minor leagues, as well as the number of clubs in each league necessary to supply players for the major leagues.

DeWitt stated that he and his committee would attempt to assemble all available information about operations and problems of the minor league teams and make this information available to the major league teams to inspect. From this data, DeWitt explained, "We hope to outline steps taken by the more successful organizations as methods to solve the losers' problems."[76] *The Sporting News* praised DeWitt for his survey and his smart approach to problems. The paper felt that DeWitt's survey was an effort to get all the facts on which intelligent action should be based.[77]

While DeWitt was trying to solve the financial problems of the minor leagues, he received the news of his mother's death. Mrs. Lulu M. DeWitt, Bill's mother, died of a heart attack at the age of 80. In addition to Bill, Lulu DeWitt had only one other immediate survivor, Bill's older brother Charley.[78]

The same month his mother passed away, Bill DeWitt was sworn in to practice law in the Federal Courts throughout the United States. He had been enrolled to practice law in the circuit courts of Missouri since 1931. DeWitt made it clear that he felt it was to his advantage in his baseball position to become thoroughly acquainted with federal law. "I have no intention to practice law," said DeWitt. "I plan to stay in baseball."[79]

DeWitt's major success in his job as minor league coordinator was the realignment of the American Association, but even in success, he quickly learned that there was no way to please everyone. Based on his detailed survey, DeWitt drew up a plan that would help to equalize the financial structure of the resultant leagues and provide examples of successful minor league teams to serve as guides to the clubs that needed help. Unfortunately, virtually every specific in his proposal met with both acceptance and vociferous opposition. For example, DeWitt presented a realignment plan that the American Association and the Texas League adopted. The plan moved three Texas League franchises to the American Association, resulting in a 10-team American Association, divided into Eastern and Western divisions. The reduction of teams in the Texas League was offset by that league's interlocking schedule with the Mexican League. Opponents argued that these moves would start a chain reaction that would affect several other leagues. One such effect was the virtual elimination of the Arizona-Mexico League, much to the chagrin of Charles "Chuck" Hollinger, president of the A-M loop, who blamed DeWitt for wiping out his league.[80]

In January 1959, John J. McHale resigned as general manager of the Detroit Tigers to become vice president of the Milwaukee Braves. The two front-runners to fill the vacancy were Paul Richards, current manager of the Baltimore Orioles, who had caught Detroit's last World Series victory, and Bill DeWitt. It was not until the 1959 season ended that the Tigers, in a drastic shake-up of their front office, publicly announced that Bill DeWitt would become Tigers president. DeWitt looked forward to leaving a job that had been frustrating during his entire time in that position. The 57-year-old DeWitt's predecessor was Harvey Hansen, a Detroit lumberman; Hansen remained on the Tigers' board of directors. In other changes, Charley Gehringer, a former Tigers second baseman, ended his long association with the club, failing to win re-election.[81]

On September 30, 1959, when DeWitt officially became president of the Detroit Tigers, the major leagues discontinued DeWitt's minor leagues fund and drew up an entirely new plan. A new fund of $1 million, twice the size of the assets DeWitt was given, was to be raised to finance both player development and a promotional program for leagues in the National Association.[82] John W. Galbreath, Pittsburgh Pirates president, was one of the chief promoters of the new fund, which proved to be a boost for the minors. Big league executives worked closely with National Association president Trautman to distribute financial aid to the various minor league circuits during the critical 1950s and 1960s. Although it seemed that Bill DeWitt's work had been ignored, knowledgeable baseball observers felt he deserved a great deal of credit for developing the necessary groundwork for this new plan.[83]

In his new role as president of the Detroit Tigers, Bill DeWitt took over a baseball team that had not been a contender for post-season play since 1950. His first job was to determine the team's strength and weakness. "We have to work hard and build ourselves up," says DeWitt. The owners told DeWitt that he had complete freedom to spend money where he saw fit, e.g., to hire scouts and to pay bonuses. DeWitt made it clear that spending money was what he intended to do.[84] He had accepted the job as president of the team because the owners assured him that they were more interested in building a winner than in making a profit.[85]

DeWitt became the fourth man to head the Detroit Tigers in four years. John Fetzer, chairman of the board, who hired DeWitt to a three-year contract, admitted that the board had decided on a new policy. Under the new setup, no stockholder would hold office. "All we want," said Fetzer, "is a winning team."[86]

DeWitt and his wife had continued to live in St. Louis even when Bill's job was elsewhere, but for this position they decided to move to the Detroit area. After Bill and Margaret spent a day house-hunting, DeWitt sat down with a reporter for *The Sporting News* to discuss some of his

Eight. Interregnum

plans for the Tigers. He wanted to enliven Briggs Stadium, the Tigers' home field, with promotions even though Detroit had a tradition going back to the late W. O. Briggs of baseball without elaborate trimmings. DeWitt, however, believed that fans liked a little extra entertainment, including fireworks displays at night games. He was also happy to hear that the Tigers had revived Ladies' Day during the 1959 season.

Without equivocation, DeWitt stressed that his number one project was having the Tigers finish above fourth place in 1960. After meeting with general manager Rick Ferrell and manager Jimmy Dykes, DeWitt agreed that the club needed better players and more scouts. He added that he was a firm believer in interleague trading. DeWitt immediately sent Ferrell to visit both Cuba and Puerto Rico, and the team appointed a scout for each island. "The Tigers must spend their money wisely in acquiring new talent, and a good investment is acquiring experienced scouts," said DeWitt.[87]

Although his predecessor, John McHale, left Detroit for a comparable general manager's job in Milwaukee because the Tigers limited his budget, DeWitt felt they had been very accommodating to him so far. "The Tigers are still better off than some clubs. Let's call them a high medium. But the money isn't available like it used to be."[88]

As each day passed, Tigers fans were beginning to learn more about the Detroit Tigers president, his philosophy, and his plans for the Tigers in 1960. DeWitt would often be seen in the Detroit clubhouse while indicating he would not interfere with Jimmy Dykes; he liked first-hand information, and the best way to get it was in person. "When I was assistant general manager of the Yankees," said DeWitt, "I was in the clubhouse and the dugout every day. I'd talk to the manager, the trainers, coaches, players. I'd talk to everybody."[89]

At the end of the 1959 season, DeWitt announced his team's schedule for the 1960 season. The Tigers would schedule 24 night games as compared with 21 the previous year, and five of these games would be with the New York Yankees. When the late Walter O. Briggs owned the Tigers, Sunday doubleheaders had virtually disappeared from the schedule. In contrast, DeWitt arranged nine Sunday twin-bills while eliminating Monday games. Monday dates in Detroit would take place only on holidays. "The most convenient time for the fans to see the Tigers is at night and on week-ends," said DeWitt. "That's when we are going to play more of our games. We are merely following a national trend to more night ball."

DeWitt also announced he would maintain the 1959 ticket prices and starting times for the upcoming season at Briggs Stadium. To avoid being perceived in Detroit as a "one-man gang," DeWitt gave GM Rick

Ferrell, vice president Jimmy Campbell, and others a free hand to do their jobs as usual.[90]

Before DeWitt headed for spring training, he invited the press and radio to a briefing session. Every reporter and columnist appeared elated by what they heard from DeWitt. "He seems to have organized his front-office team," one journalist observed. "If he does as well in straightening out the team on the field, the Tigers may start going places in 1960." One of the senior writers among the press corps was convinced that the Tigers "should immediately do better under the new administration."[91]

DeWitt spent the first few weeks in 1960 preparing for spring training and trying to get all his players signed before leaving for Florida. Several players were squawking about what they called penny-pinching tactics by the front office. DeWitt, of course, denied these allegations and promised that by the time the season started on April 19, everyone would be signed and in uniform. "I do know," stated DeWitt, "players have come to expect too much and that the Tigers have been exceedingly generous in the past."[92]

By March 7, Charlie Maxwell, a slugging outfielder. was the Tigers' only holdout. At issue was $1,500, the difference between Maxwell's salary demands and what DeWitt called the final offer. Maxwell was seeking a salary of $25,000, but he ultimately signed his 1960 contract for $24,000, a $6,000 increase over his 1959 salary.[93]

In order to improve Detroit's defensive play in the infield, DeWitt hired former shortstop and future Hall of Famer Luke Appling as a Tigers coach. DeWitt rattled off a group of infield double play combinations—Rizzuto and Coleman; Fox and Aparicio; Rizzuto and Gordon; Groat and Mazeroski—as the type of infield combinations that play on pennant contenders. "I note that for the last two seasons the Tigers have been last in the American League in double plays," said DeWitt. "It must be fixed. I never saw a contending club with a poor double play combination."[94]

In a Tigers front office move, Bill DeWitt took over the job of general manager, at the same time dropping that specific title. He named former GM Rick Ferrell his special assistant who would head player personnel. DeWitt stated that the general manager was generally in charge of the entire operation, but Ferrell did not particularly care for office-type paperwork. "This will give him more time in the playing end of the business. The move is welcomed by Rick and will give us a broader operation at the executive level."[95]

While the Tigers were nearing the end of their spring training in Lakeland, Florida, the *Detroit Times* baseball writer Joe Falls, published

Eight. Interregnum

a report that the Tigers' manager, Jimmy Dykes, "could possibly follow Rick Ferrell, the defrocked general manager, into the limbo of the unwanted—perhaps sooner than anyone expects." DeWitt called the story ridiculous and called Dykes a "good manager and a solid guy." When the *Times* accused DeWitt of being an executive who "does not always seek out his manager's opinion," DeWitt insisted that he always consulted with both Dykes and Ferrell, adding, "They're in on everything. We've discussed the ball club and plans for it about every day.... I'm not pushing anyone around and there's no pressure on the manager."[96] When asked for his opinion, Dykes stated, "I have no complaints and there have been no disagreements. I've looked over my contract and it's all legal and in good order. I intend to fulfill my part of it."[97]

The Brooklyn Dodgers moved to Los Angeles in 1958, and the New York Giants moved to San Francisco the same year. New York Mayor Robert Wagner appointed attorney William Shea to lead the effort to bring an existing franchise to New York. Unsuccessful, Shea proposed establishing a third major league, the Continental League, with one of the teams located in New York.[98] Shea had the backing of Branch Rickey, who had resigned as president of the Pittsburgh Pirates to become president of the newly established league.[99]

On April 15, 1960, Charles F. Hurth, former president of the Southern Association, was introduced as the general manager of the New York Continental League franchise. Hurth was a nephew-in-law of Branch Rickey and had begun his baseball career in the 1930s, working for the St. Louis Cardinals' farm teams in Ohio. Hurth was not Rickey's first choice to run the New York team, and Rickey, to avoid any charge of nepotism, made that point quite clear. His first choice was Bill DeWitt, who was not only a strong backer of Rickey but a proponent of a third league. It was a moot point, however, for before the end of 1959, DeWitt had accepted his job with the Detroit Tigers.[100]

Bill DeWitt served 14 months as the Tigers' president, participating in three significant trades with the swap-happy Cleveland Indians GM, Frank Lane, during the 1960 season.

His first trade took place on April 12, when he swung one of the most successful trades in Tigers history. DeWitt obtained first baseman Norm Cash, considered a future star, for seldom-used infielder Steve Demeter. Demeter's first year in the majors had been with the Tigers in 1959, and he would appear in only four games with the Indians in 1960, his last year as a major leaguer.[101] Cash won the batting title in 1961 with a .361 mark; he also led the American League in hits with 193, and his .487 on-base percentage also topped the league. In 11 seasons, he hit 22 or more home runs (including 41 in 1961), for a total of 377 career-home runs.[102]

On April 17, 1960. five days after the Cash deal, DeWitt made his second noteworthy trade. In a one-for-one deal considered controversial at the time, DeWitt sent the reigning American League batting champion, Harvey Kuenn, who hit .353 in 1959, to the Cleveland Indians for Rocky Colavito. Colavito had hit 42 home runs in 1959, tying Harmon Killibrew for the American League's home run championship. While Kuenn lasted only one year in Cleveland before being traded to the National League and never again hitting above .308, Colavito played four seasons in Detroit and continued to hit the long ball, slugging 139 home runs, an average of nearly 35 per season.[103]

While *The Sporting News* did not assess the two DeWitt deals, it noted that there could be no doubt that Bill DeWitt was calling the shots at Detroit, especially trades. Although DeWitt admitted that while he informed the club owners of his intention to make the two trades, he stated that there was a clause in his contract which gave him authority to make all trades. "We have an executive committee of five who run the Tigers—Harvey Hansen, Harry M. Sisson, John E. Fetzer, Kenyon Brown, and me," De Witt explained. "And I'm the chairman," he said with a smile.[104]

If Bill DeWitt needed a pat on the back or words of encouragement, he certainly got them when in early May 1960, he received a letter from someone who had a "little baseball experience"—Ty Cobb. Cobb, who now lived in Menlo Park, California, sent DeWitt a three-page, beautifully handwritten letter from the 73-year-old Hall of Famer. The letter contained a little advice and much praise for DeWitt's work with Cobb's Detroit Tigers, his team for 22 of his 24 major league seasons. He highly praised DeWitt for obtaining Colavito and urged him to "go easy" on his recent acquisition.[105]

Near the end of June, DeWitt answered Cobb, apologizing for the delay in replying, saying it would be an honor and a pleasure if Cobb were to visit Briggs Stadium. After asking Cobb to send him an autographed photo, DeWitt made one additional request: "If you see any good looking young ball players in California that you think might develop into major leaguers, I hope you will tell us about them."[106]

DeWitt's third trade in 1960 involved no players. On August 3, 1960, DeWitt and Frank Lane completed one of the most unusual trades in the annals of major league baseball. DeWitt dealt Jimmy Dykes, manager of the Detroit Tigers, to Cleveland for their manager, Joe Gordon. Gordon would only last the final eight weeks of the 1960 season before he resigned with a record of 26–31.[107] This would not be the first time that Joe Gordon resigned while wearing a Detroit Tigers uniform. In 1956 Gordon, a coach with the Tigers, resigned because of front-office interference. At his resignation as manager, he said, "I knew the Tigers were a bad team but I didn't think they were this bad."[108] The managerial swap originated three weeks earlier as a joke but was resumed seriously when both clubs fell on tough times. "When your club goes bad," said DeWitt, "You do one of two things. You either get a lot of new players or you get a new manager. We got a lot of new players and that didn't help, so we got a new manager."[109]

Less than a week after the managerial swap, Dykes ripped his former boss, saying he resented DeWitt's clubhouse visits, his suggestions on how to run the team, and the way DeWitt ignored his advice on trades. He also resented calls from DeWitt when the club was on the road, having DeWitt recommend the lineups, and suggesting which players to use. Informed of Dykes' statements, DeWitt said, "I'm not going to say anything until I have had a chance to digest the article. I don't want to blast the guy [Dykes] and lower the boom on him."[110]

When the 1960 baseball season was well past the halfway mark, DeWitt began looking forward to the 1961 season. He expected better performances from hitters like Al Kaline and Rocky Calavito, as well as considerable help from the powerful American Association farm club in Denver. He admitted that 1960 had become a season of transition and that many of the moves he made didn't turn out as expected. "I'll say one thing for our players," said DeWitt. "They've had good hustle. They've tried hard."[111]

DeWitt also admitted that his managerial trade didn't work out as anticipated. It seemed likely that the Tigers would wind up with a minimum of 82 defeats, the poorest record since 1954, when Fred Hutchinson's club dropped 86 games. DeWitt had established the goal of improving on 1959's 76–78 record, but he admitted that was impossible. He still felt that the club could bounce back the next year with more consistent hitting.[112]

DeWitt also bemoaned the fact that he had invested $25,000 in gimmicks designed to entice more customers to Briggs Stadium. That program was not a success either. For the 1960 season, the Tigers were on their way to posting attendance down by approximately 40,000. DeWitt admitted that the Veeck-like pre- and between-game shows, including a five-piece Dixieland band playing for 37 games, fireworks, shows by well-known baseball clowns Al Schacht and Jackie Price, and trampoline acts didn't encourage the Detroit Tigers to play better ball.

The Tigers completed the 1960 season with a record of 71–83, finishing in sixth place. They had employed three managers during the season: Dykes, Joe Gordon, and one of their coaches, Billy Hitchcock, who won the one game he managed while waiting for Joe Gordon to settle in as the Tigers' third manager in 1960.

When the season ended, DeWitt predicted that the Tigers would undergo a "house cleaning" for next season. Ironically, the cleaning began with the firing of coach Billy Hitchcock, who had been with the Tigers since 1955. The veteran coach was told ahead of time that he would be gone when the season ended, but he remained with the club until then. "When you've had a season like we've had, you have to make changes," DeWitt commented. He added that it was likely there would be more changes during the winter.

DeWitt did not have to wait very long for the changes to continue. On October 4, 1960, Detroit manager Joe Gordon quit the Tigers after only two months on the job. Gordon bluntly stated that he wanted a free hand in running the Tigers, and he did not feel he had it under president Bill DeWitt.[113]

Bob Broeg, *St. Louis Post-Dispatch* sports editor, was in New York covering the 1960 World Series between the Pittsburgh Pirates and the New York Yankees, when he heard rumors from World Series headquarters predicting that Bill DeWitt would be fired after serving only one season as president of the Detroit Tigers. Ordinarily Broeg would dismiss such rumors, but he knew the Detroit writers were not given to making wild statements unless there was some semblance of truth to the rumor. Broeg, after covering the Browns for many years, knew DeWitt quite well and was aware of both his strengths and weaknesses.

Broeg also knew that in his one season as president of the Tigers, DeWitt had not ingratiated himself with the press, the public, or the players. Broeg noted in one of his articles some of the mistakes DeWitt had made in his first weeks on the job. He had stripped Rick Ferrell of his general manager's title, an unnecessary and meaningless gesture since the president was hired to run the front office. He also had interfered with both Jimmy Dykes' and Joe Gordon's field leadership. Finally, Broeg concluded that DeWitt needed a completely trusted right-hand man like Frank Lane or Bing Devine, who could reliably handle the detail work and never be the source of malicious gossip.[114]

What Broeg termed a rumor quickly became a reality. John E. Fetzer, a one-third owner of the Detroit Tigers, announced that he had made a large purchase of the ball club's stock, bringing his holdings to two-thirds of outstanding stock and controlling interest. Fetzer, a wealthy Kalamazoo, Michigan, radio executive, announced that DeWitt's status with the Tigers would remain unchanged for the time being, but if DeWitt remained with the Tigers, he would have no say in choosing the new manager. Fetzer added, "I'm not pushing the panic button on Bill

Eight. Interregnum

DeWitt or anyone else. I'm not rushing into action regarding any of our Briggs Stadium personnel."[115]

On October 20, 1960, Bill DeWitt officially resigned as president of the Detroit Tigers Baseball Co., after declining an offer by Fetzer to become assistant to the club president. DeWitt had two years remaining on his three-year contract that paid him a reported $50,000 annually.[116]

DeWitt admitted that he had considered Fetzer's offer to become assistant to the president of the Detroit Baseball Company but rejected it. He had come to the Tigers as president and started a rebuilding program which he had to relinquish due to the change in ownership of the club. Even if he took the job, he felt his program would still not be executed according to his plans. In a courteous farewell message, he said he had enjoyed his stay with the Tigers. Further, he wished Fetzer and the club nothing but success and the best of luck in the future. In return, Fetzer told DeWitt he had the highest regard for him, calling DeWitt one of the most knowledgeable men in baseball. Pro forma, Fetzer expressed regrets that DeWitt had chosen to leave. "John Fetzer and I are parting as friends," said De Witt, adding that his future was "indefinite" but that he intended to remain in baseball.[117]

NINE

A New Team, Another World Series

For the first time since he was 16 years old and working for the St. Louis Cardinals, Bill DeWitt, Sr., was not employed in baseball. In late 1960, however, DeWitt, who had bounced around considerably in major league baseball executive posts, was back in the National League as general manager of the Cincinnati Reds, replacing Gabe Paul. Paul, after a disappointing 1960 season, had resigned to become the first general manager of the expansion Houston Colt .45s.[1]

On November 3, 1960, DeWitt was formally hired by the Reds' principal owner, Powel Crosley, Jr., who unfortunately was in Savannah, Georgia, recuperating from a mild heart attack. Crosley announced that DeWitt would also become a vice president and member of the board of directors.[2] During the ten years DeWitt spent with the Yankees, Bill and his family always maintained their St. Louis residence. He and Margaret bought a home in Detroit, but when DeWitt began working for the Reds, the Detroit home was sold, and he and Margaret began house-hunting again with the intention of moving to Cincinnati permanently.[3]

DeWitt's appointment was heartily endorsed by two of major league baseball's icons, Branch Rickey and Warren Giles. Rickey's immediate reaction was, "Crosley could not have picked a better man." Giles had served as president and general manager of the Cincinnati Reds from 1937–1951. He was appointed president of the National League in 1951, holding the position until he retired in 1969. "I compliment Mr. Crosley very highly," said Giles, "on the appointment of DeWitt. I have known Bill for nearly 40 years and consider him one of baseball's most able executives."[4] DeWitt spoke glowingly of Giles, whom Crosley consulted when filling the post vacated by Gabe Paul. The friendship of DeWitt and Giles dated back to 1920, when the two met in Branch Rickey's office in St. Louis. "I was employed by the Cardinals then," said DeWitt, "and Giles was running the St. Joe club in Missouri."[5]

One of DeWitt's first statements to the press, as he was getting settled, was that he would confer with manager Fred Hutchinson about any needed changes in his staff, or any problems in the team's makeup. He also wanted Hutchinson's input regarding the interleague trading period, which would begin November 15. DeWitt endorsed Hutchinson as an excellent manager who had the "right" personality, really knew his baseball, and had the respect of his players. "That's 60 percent of the battle," said DeWitt.[6]

DeWitt became general manager of the Cincinnati Reds, who won the National League pennant in 1961. He and manager Fred Hutchinson helped Reds fans celebrate their victory.

DeWitt had inherited a team that finished the 1960 season in sixth place with a record of 67–86, 28 games behind the pennant-winning Pittsburgh Pirates.[7] The Reds were an aging team, fifth in runs scored and sixth in ERA. Five regulars were 29 years old or older, and three of the starting pitchers were over 30.[8] Hutchinson and DeWitt spent three days analyzing the 1960 Reds, fine-combing the performances of each player and exploring possible changes for 1961. Hutchinson promised DeWitt that his team would play much better in 1961. "When you finish sixth there is no alibi," said the team's skipper. "It's because you play like sixth placers." He told DeWitt that his players knew the fundamentals … but somewhere they forgot them. "I'd say it's a case of carelessness."[9]

Even before spring training began, *The Sporting News* praised DeWitt as an excellent baseball man who should succeed with the Reds. The paper claimed that he should not be judged by his actions in Detroit, where he had to answer to a group of owners. In Cincinnati, he had only one owner to whom he must account, and fans who had proven their patience in the past.¹⁰ *Cincinnati Enquirer* reporter Lou Smith also felt that owner Powel Crosley, Jr., had picked the right man in Bill DeWitt, making sure the front office was in good hands.¹¹

DeWitt made some trades during his first winter meeting as the Reds' GM, and one involved a player with whom he was quite familiar, selling second baseman Billy Martin to the Milwaukee Braves.¹² DeWitt admitted that he sold Martin to the Braves as a last resort. "We exhausted the market," said DeWitt, "and just weren't able to trade him to any other club."¹³

Ten days later, DeWitt completed a far larger trade in a three-team deal. First, DeWitt dealt his slick-fielding shortstop, Roy McMillan, to the Braves. In exchange for the National League's top defensive shortstop for the past few seasons, the Braves sent the Reds pitchers Joey Jay and Juan Pizarro, both promising hurlers. The Reds then shipped the newly acquired Pizarro and another pitcher, Cal McLish, to the Chicago White Sox for third baseman Gene Freese.¹⁴

After the deal had been completed, Bill DeWitt said in Cincinnati, "We hated to part with McMillan, but the club felt it had to because we needed more hitting and feel Freese can furnish it." Freese had previously played for the Pittsburgh Pirates, St. Louis Cardinals, and Philadelphia Phillies; he had hit .273 in 1960 with the White Sox. He also clouted 17 homers and drove in 79 runs in 127 games for Chicago, following an early-season slump.¹⁵

Before spring training, DeWitt wanted to become more familiar with the Cincinnati Reds' fans. A local organization, The Cincinnati Ballplayers of Yesterday, held their annual dinner late in January. At the dinner, he introduced his plans to visit cities in Ohio, Kentucky, West Virginia, and Indiana in late January/early February. The Reds drew many fans from this area, and his visits were well-received.¹⁶

Back in Cincinnati, DeWitt announced that he had set up a supervised conditioning program for the players who wintered in the Greater Cincinnati area. These included outfielders Frank Robinson and Gus Bell, infielder Willie Jones, and pitcher Joe Nuxall. Players who wintered elsewhere had tactfully been advised that it would be to their advantage to report to camp in peak physical condition. "Baseball, like any other competitive activity, sometimes makes great demands on the player," said DeWitt, "and it is his response to these demands that makes him either an asset to the game or just another player."¹⁷

On March 29, 1961, Powel Crosley, Jr., principal owner of the Reds since 1934, who had been hospitalized recently for a heart condition, died at his home in suburban Mount Airy at the age of 74. When he purchased the club, it was in ownership difficulties, and Crosley was able to keep the team in Cincinnati despite constant rumors that the franchise would be moved. Months prior to his death, Crosley directed that ownership of the Cincinnati Reds be held by a non-profit foundation, and funds earned by the foundation be used for charitable, scientific, educational, and literary purposes. The trustees of the foundation were Mrs. Stanley E. Kess, Crosley's daughter, and her husband; Crosley's sister; a brother, who was vice president of the club; Powel Crosley's personal secretary; and Crosley's investment counselor. At a meeting of the board of trustees, Mrs. Kess was named president of the Reds, and Bill DeWitt the team's vice president and general manager, was given complete charge of the baseball operation in accordance with Crosley's wishes to have "baseball men run the baseball business."[18]

The Sporting News called Powel Crosley, Jr., one of baseball's most prominent men, who also was one of baseball's most humble individuals. He loved his team and his city, revealing before his death that he planned to have his ball club controlled by a Board of Trustees with all profits from Crosley stock going to local charities. According to the press, Powell never interfered with the operation of his ball club, preferring to remain in the background and allowing competent men to run the club. "He has had four of the best—Larry MacPhail, Warren Giles, Gabe Paul and now Bill DeWitt. Mr. Crosley left a monument of service to baseball and to his community."[19]

No sooner had DeWitt officially assumed his duties as general manager and vice president of the Cincinnati Reds, than the National League was faced with the issue of distributing players to Houston and New York, the two new National League teams making their debuts in 1962.

The rules for the clubs choosing the new players were complicated. Not only was each existing National League team required to contribute players to the two new teams, each club could freeze only five players on their 40-man rosters, and then the new teams would be allowed one full round selecting one of the 35 remaining players from each established club.

A furious William DeWitt could not comprehend why the new team could be allowed to reach the first division in its first year. "How am I going to explain that to the people here in Cincinnati? It could be a very embarrassing situation." DeWitt favored the plan adopted by the American League, where each team made 15 players available from the winter roster.

DeWitt also blasted ex–Yankee George Weiss, now president of the National League's New York team. Weiss advocated a liberal expansion draft, arguing that it takes approximately $400,000 to grow one big league player. DeWitt told his fellow executives, "I can remember his words when he was with the Yankees and everybody was saying 'break up the Yankees. It's going to take [the Reds] some time to build and get out of the second division, so I see no reason why we should be forced to weaken ourselves further."[20]

The press in Houston, the home of one of the two expansion teams, excoriated DeWitt for his comments regarding each existing team having to risk some of its best players to develop rosters for the new teams. The *Corpus Christi Times* sarcastically asked DeWitt why a man who spent several years in baseball's "poor house" could not find a little sympathy in his heart for those who might soon be in the same boat. "You might consider how we would explain to the people in Houston and New York why they were saddled with a bunch of baseball hangers-on whose only relation to major league status is the lettering across the front of their baseball shirts."[21]

Once the season began, DeWitt continued to seek the players he would need to win the pennant. Near the end of April, he sent catcher Ed Bailey to the San Francisco Giants for second baseman Don Blasingame, catcher Bob Schmidt, and a player to be named later. DeWitt was elated to get Blasingame, a player he described as "a great little hitter," and a spark plug on the Giants who would add speed to the Reds. "And don't forget," he added, "Schmidt is a catcher who is younger than Bailey."[22]

Three weeks after the trade was completed, Blasingame's batting average was lingering around the .150 mark, and many Reds fans wondered if DeWitt had made a good trade. He assured the fans that although Blasingame's average was lower than he had anticipated, he felt Blasingame was an asset to the team. "Don's covered a lot of ground around second base," said DeWitt. "I'd say most people liked our trade with the Giants. After all, Ed Bailey was the regular catcher for several years when the club wasn't going anywhere. You just can't stand still."[23]

Just before the Blasingame trade, Bill DeWitt became a grandfather for the first time. He had waited nearly a week in St. Louis for his daughter Donna (Mrs. Robert Bell, Jr.), to make him a grandfather. According to the proud grandpa, William Randolph, an eight-pounds, 12-ounce "bonus prospect," finally arrived at 2 a.m., April 22, 1961, at St. Louis Maternity Hospital. "And they named it after me," Bill gloated.[24]

On April 30, the Reds won the second game of a doubleheader from the Pittsburgh Pirates to begin a nine-game winning streak. A month later, the Reds had a six-game winning streak to improve their record to 26–16. At the All-Star Game break, the Reds' record was 55–30, and they were in first place by five games over the Dodgers. After the break, the tables were turned; the Dodgers got hot and the Reds struggled. In mid–August, the Reds had six more losses than the Dodgers and trailed by 2½ games. On August 15, the Reds traveled to Los Angeles for a three-game, two-day series, which they swept, leaving Los Angeles with a half-game lead. The Dodgers eventually lost 10 consecutive games, while the Reds stayed in first place the remainder of the season, winning the pennant on September 26 by beating the Chicago Cubs, 6–3, in a day game while the Dodgers lost to the Pittsburgh Pirates, 8–0, in the second game of a doubleheader.[25] The Reds had compiled a record of 93–61, winning the 1961 National League pennant by four games over the Dodgers.[26] Bill DeWitt had put together a team that went from sixth place to the National League pennant in just one year.

Most baseball mavens attributed the Reds' success to trades made by DeWitt, but he modestly shared the credit. DeWitt pointed out that some of 1961's outstanding players were there when he became general manager. He did take credit for filling large gaps with his much-needed acquisitions from other teams. DeWitt added Joey Jay to the starting rotation and Gene Freese at third base. Don Blasingame had solved his second base problem, though he couldn't replace Ed Bailey behind the plate. He also acquired first baseman Gordon Coleman and pitcher Howie Nunn in trades.[27] The Reds' 1961 pennant was only their fourth in the 20th century, and their first since 1940.[28] DeWitt also acknowledged that during the prior year, "Gabe Paul and Fred Hutchinson started bringing up youngsters that gave us a running start in 1961."[29]

DeWitt also had kind words for two men once associated with the Reds: Gabe Paul, former general manager, and Birdie Tebbetts, former manager. Tebbetts quit as Reds manager near the end of the 1958 season to manage the Milwaukee Braves, and Gabe Paul went to the Houston Colt .45s, one of the two expansion teams in the National League. Players like Jim O'Toole, Bob Purkey, Vada Pinson, Frank Robinson, Bill Henry, Gus Bell, Wally Post, Jay Hook, and Jim Maloney were acquired when Paul and Tebbetts were running the team.[30]

Even before the season ended, the Reds announced that Fred Hutchinson's managerial contract had been renewed for both 1962 and 1963. The experts had predicted that Cincinnati would be a sixth-place team in 1961, but Hutchinson, a former pitcher himself, helped recruit the pitching the Reds had long needed to make the club a pennant contender. DeWitt did not disclose Hutchinson's salary terms, but both acknowledged, "It was sweetened a little."[31]

Of course, the team's success was due in large part to the players who performed so admirably on the field. Joey Jay, who won 21 games, Jim O'Toole, with 19 victories, and Bob Purkey, winner of 16 games, all had banner years. Their outstanding bullpen included Jim Brosnan, who won 10 games and saved 16 more, and Bill Henry, who also saved 16 games.

Offensively, the Reds were a powerhouse. The lineup included Vada Pinson, who batting .343 with 16 home runs, Gene Freese, who notched a batting average of .277 and belted 26 home runs, Gordy Coleman, a .287 hitter who also hit 26 home runs, Frank Robinson, with a .323 batting average and 37 home runs, and the team's reliable pinch-hitter, Jerry Lynch, who finished the season with an average of .315 and 13 home runs.[32]

Regardless of his modesty. primary credit for the team's success in 1961 must, of course, be given to general manager Bill DeWitt. Described by those who knew him as "hard-working and ambitious, and demanding with his employees," DeWitt was the first to admit he was a baseball junkie with no hobbies or interests outside of baseball. He was one of a handful of baseball executives who had no other financial resource—his business was baseball. When he took over the Reds in 1961, the team had little hope of improving greatly on their mediocre 1960 season. They had questions marks at nearly every position, and their pitching staff was weak. It seemed as if their roster was comprised of players past their prime or young and needing more major league experience. But he made some excellent trades which, at the time, generated little enthusiasm, yet ultimately proved to be excellent acquisitions. When DeWitt's Reds won the pennant in 1961, Bill DeWitt became the first general manager to win the pennant in both leagues.[33]

Having won the pennant, the Reds now faced the formidable task of opposing the New York Yankees in the World Series. As Reds pitcher Jim Brosnan said, "We didn't think we could beat the Yankees so we just decided to have fun. The World Series was a party for us."[34]

The Yankees manager in 1961 was Ralph Houk, who had succeeded the legendary Casey Stengel after the 1960 season. Stengel had won seven world championships for the Yankees, and Mickey Mantle said, "The pressure on Houk had to be like having an elephant sitting on your chest." If there was any pressure on Houk in 1961, he must have kept it to himself. The Yankees dominated the American League in 1961, winning 109 games, the most by the franchise since 1927. Roger Maris broke Babe Ruth's home run record with 61, Mantle contributed 54, and the Yankees, as Mantle said years later, "went sailing into the World Series like Slim Pickens riding the guided missile in Dr. Strangelove."[35]

The Yankees were favored to win the World Series even though Mantle missed the entire Series because of an injury. He developed an abscess on his hip from getting a bad injection from a quack doctor near the conclusion of the season. The injury was so severe that he was forced to watch most of the games from the bench with blood seeping from his uniform.[36]

The Yankees won the first game, 2–0, thanks to Whitey Ford's complete-game, two-hit masterpiece. The Yankees had only six hits, but two of them were home runs, one each by Elston Howard and Bill Skowron. The Reds came back to win the second game, 5–2, as Yogi Berra's two-run homer for the Yankees in the fourth inning was all the scoring New York could muster. Games Three, Four and Five were all played in Cincinnati, but the Yankees were not concerned with the Reds' home-field advantage. The Yanks won Game Three, 3–2, scoring single runs in the seventh, eighth, and ninth innings.

After the close loss in Game Three, the Reds never again threatened. In the fourth game, Ford held the Reds to four singles until he was removed in the sixth inning because of an ankle injury. Reliever Jim Coates preserved the shutout as the Yankees won, 7–0. The fifth and final game of the 1961 World Series was no contest. The Reds scored five runs on Frank Robinson's three-run homer and Wally Post's two-run shot, but the Yankees scored 13 times against eight Cincinnati pitchers for a crushing 13–5 defeat of the National League champions. The Reds used a record-tying seven relievers to try to stop the Yankees' onslaught but to no avail. "The Yankees weren't cocky and didn't do anything to show us up," said pitcher Jim O'Toole. "They just went about their business and kicked the shit out of us."[37]

Despite the World Series loss, Bill DeWitt received multiple honors. He was named "Major League Executive of the Year" by United Press International's board of baseball experts. This was the second time DeWitt had been named the No. 1 executive, having received the same award from *The Sporting News* in 1944. At that time, he was general manager of the Browns, who won the only American League pennant in the history of that franchise. DeWitt attributed his success in 1961 to a Rickey motto he always kept on his desk: "Take care of getting ball players and the rest will take care of itself."[38]

DeWitt received still another honor when the Knights of the Cauliflower Ear, composed of leading St. Louis Sportsmen, selected DeWitt as their honoree at their annual Spring Training Party in February 1962.[39] Finally, DeWitt learned that the St. Louis Baseball Writers announced that he and retiring star infielder (and presently a full-time Redbirds coach) Red Schoendienst, would share the group's highest accolade, the Dr. Robert F. Hyland Award for meritorious service in sports. For many years, Dr. Hyland had served as the team physician for the St. Louis Cardinals.[40]

Finally, Bill DeWitt was named president of the Cincinnati Reds at the club's annual stockholders and directors meeting, filling the vacancy created by the death of Powel Crosley, Jr., the previous March. Named to succeed Crosley as chairman of the board of directors was Stanley Kess, Crosley's son-in-law.[41]

DeWitt's first order of business in 1962 was signing his players as quickly as possible. He was relieved when one of his key players for 1962, Frank Robinson, agreed to terms in January. In past years, Robinson had been one of the most difficult players to sign. Although DeWitt refused to reveal any figures, he did admit that Robinson received a "substantial and well-deserved raise." Unofficial estimates put the salary figure at $55,000. Robinson, who hit .323 with 37 home runs and 124 runs batted in, was a runaway winner of the National League's Most Valuable Player Award. When he inked his contract, Robinson said, "I hope I can do something to repay the club for its faith in me by having a good year and helping the Reds win the pennant again, and this time the world championship."[42]

DeWitt was concerned that he would have a problem signing one of his star pitchers, Jim O'Toole. O'Toole publicly announced that "Bill DeWitt [is] going to be a little shook up when the two of us sit down to discuss my contract." O'Toole had good reason to believe he had the upper hand in any discussion about a raise. He won 11 of his last 12 starts and finished the 1961 season with a record of 19–9, third in wins after his teammate Joey Jay and Milwaukee's Warren Spahn. But the 25-year-old hurler signed his contract for an estimated $24,000. "I'm very happy," said O'Toole.[43]

A key member of the 1961 Reds, Jerry Lynch hit .315 in 96 games, primarily as a pinch-hitter. As a pinch-hitter, he hit .404 to help the Reds win the pennant. He announced that he wanted plenty of "cold cash" in return. To prove his point, he sent back his first two salary offers unsigned and then went to Cincinnati in person to plead his case before DeWitt, who listened to Lynch. The two agreed on a salary estimated at $23,500. This was one of the highest salaries in history for a pinch hitter.[44]

No Cincinnati Red gave DeWitt more trouble about his 1962 contract than pitcher Joey Jay, who was disgruntled at the $26,000 offered him by DeWitt. Jay, who won 21 games in 1961 and was the only Reds pitcher to win a game in the World Series, offered DeWitt five times the salary offered him to buy up his contract. "I think I deserve a better salary than he's offering me," Jay contended.[45]

DeWitt responded that Jay, the last Reds holdout, could sit out the entire season if he wanted, but that the club would not budge from its original offer. Eventually, Jay ended his salary dispute by accepting an estimated $12,500 raise for 1962, giving him a salary of $27,500. Jay said he was "satisfied with the contract and primed for another good season." Manager Fred Hutchinson was jubilant, saying, "I'm glad he's back. I feel like we've picked up 21 more games." DeWitt explained, "I gave a little, and he gave a little. Now I hope Joey has another good year so he can get another good raise next time."[46]

The Sporting News, which usually avoided sides in salary disputes between players and management, did state its position on the squabble between Jay and DeWitt. The situation went "beyond the normal realm," the paper wrote, that when Jay demanded the right to buy his contract if his terms were not met, he accused DeWitt of "not knowing what is fair." The Sporting News reprimanded Jay and stated that the Reds' general manager had been signing players to contracts for more than 25 years, and he had a good idea of what was fair. "Jay has had one good season," said the newspaper, "and wanted to wreck all the rules and destroy the budget balance of the ball club. Now that Jay has accepted terms, it is to be hoped that all rancor is vanished, and Joey will direct all his efforts to another 20-win season."[47]

Even before spring training began, DeWitt was asked the same questions numerous times: Can the Reds repeat and win the National

Although Frank Robinson was Cincinnati's star player, DeWitt considered him expendable, and he was traded to Baltimore for some much-needed pitching (National Baseball Hall of Fame Library, Cooperstown, N.Y.)

League pennant again? As expected, DeWitt refused to answer directly, but instead would point out changes he had already completed to make improvements. The Reds acquired several veteran pitchers, including Johnny Klippstein and Dave Sisler from the Washington Senators, Dave Hillman from the Boston Red Sox, and Mo Drabowsky from the Cubs. He also noted that talented rookies Tommy Harper, Chico Ruiz, and Cookie Rojas, would challenge veterans for playing time. He added that other rookies were expected in camp, including pitcher Sammy Ellis, catcher Don Pavletich, and third baseman Cliff Cook.[48]

One of the changes Bill DeWitt didn't announce until spring training was nearly over was that he had begun negotiations to purchase the Cincinnati Reds, an action he had considered since joining the team as general manager. He would have financial help in purchasing the club, but he could not name his partners at the present time.

The transaction went quickly. On March 23, 1962, a new corporation headed by Bill DeWitt purchased the Cincinnati Reds from the Crosley Foundation for $4.6 million. The ownership of the club had been in the control of the foundation since Powel Crosley, Jr.'s, death in March 1961. DeWitt immediately promised to keep the Reds in Cincinnati, a requirement Crosley had specified in his will. The new owner announced that he would also push for a new, modern, municipal stadium.[49]

DeWitt had come back to Cincinnati to announce the sale. "This agreement will be submitted to the stockholders for their approval at a special meeting called for April 5," DeWitt stated. He also announced that the transfer required ratification by three-quarters of the nine other National League clubs. DeWitt was quick to mention that the sale had the approval of Warren Giles, president of the National League, who said, "I feel a foundation is not the proper organization to run a Major League ball club."[50]

The Sporting News applauded the sale of the Reds to Bill DeWitt, stating it was good for baseball. "We compliment DeWitt on this forthright action, ... and wish DeWitt many years of progress in the home of the champions."[51]

DeWitt's purchase of the Reds was approved by the club's stockholders with only one dissenting vote.[52] Yet, DeWitt was still constantly answering questions concerning the makeup of the financial partners who purchased the team. There were reports that two former owners of the Browns, Donald L. Barnes and Bill Veeck, would be associated with him. DeWitt absolutely denied that report and said, "I am investing my own capital in the Reds. Of course, a deal of this kind required a substantial amount of financing, and I am getting the money from

Nine. A New Team, Another World Series

Cincinnati interests. Later, if I decide to take in any other stockholders, they will be Cincinnati people." He assured these detractors that he was buying the Reds because he intended to live in Cincinnati the rest of his life. "I have faith in the club and in the city," he said.[53]

It appeared that every time Bill DeWitt spoke to the press or groups of Cincinnatians, he emphasized two points. He predicted that expansion would continue in the majors, and soon there would be four additional cities with major league ball teams. He also repeatedly reminded everyone who would listen to him that there was a definite need for a new home ballpark for the Reds. This caused many fans to ask themselves, "If DeWitt didn't get a new park soon, would he use that as an excuse to move the team out of Cincinnati?"[54]

It was rumored that Joseph F. Rippe, Jr., a local real estate developer, had offered $5.55 million to buy the Reds, overbidding DeWitt by close to $1 million. According to an Ohio newspaper, Ohio Attorney General Mark Elroy announced that he would award the club to Rippe's group on four conditions. First, Rippe would have to submit a written statement that he would underwrite the expense of an examination of the Reds' books and then state in writing if the books were satisfactory. The second requirement would be that Rippe would then offer to buy the team at a price substantially higher than that paid by DeWitt. The third condition would require another written statement that he would guarantee to keep the team in Cincinnati for a time to be negotiated later. Finally, Rippe would have to state in writing that one-half or more of his offer would be paid to the Crosley Foundation at the time of the sale. The whole incident became moot when the Crosley Foundation trustees stated that Rippe had not made a formal bid to them, and if he did, they would not consider it. They further agreed that the sale to DeWitt was in the team's best interest because DeWitt was best qualified to operate a baseball franchise and maintain a successful operation of the National League team in Cincinnati.[55]

To appease the Cincinnati Reds Board of Trustees, DeWitt temporarily gave the Board control of the baseball team and also agreed to keep the Reds in Cincinnati at least five years. He also promised Mrs. Kess that the Foundation would have the right to name a majority of the Board of Directors of the baseball club until the purchase price was completely paid off.[56]

On June 6, as the guest speaker before Cincinnati's Traffic Club, Bill DeWitt spoke about a variety of topics before the 300 people in the room—brushback pitches, the balk rule, Jerry Lynch's defensive problems as an outfielder, and expansion of major league baseball. He took a number of questions from the audience, and he finally answered the question everyone hoped would be asked: "The Reds are an institution in Cincinnati. I'm enthusiastic about this wonderful city and I have no idea of moving."[57]

Meanwhile, the fight continued between Attorney General McElroy and the Crosley Foundation. The members of the Foundation firmly believed their sale to DeWitt was fair and proper and what the late Powel Crosley would have wanted, and they hired Charles Sawyer as their legal counsel. Sawyer was a prominent Democrat and former U.S. Secretary of Commerce in the Truman cabinet. He was a member of the eminent Cincinnati law firm, Taft, Stettinius and Hollister, and a former director of the Reds. He denounced McElroy's order to transfer the baseball franchise to Rippe and called the actions of the attorney general "extraordinary and untimely." Bill DeWitt stayed as far as he could from the conflict, saying, "It's between the attorney general and the trustees."[58]

During the turmoil over ownership of the Cincinnati Reds, Bill DeWitt continued his fight for expanding the two major leagues to a total of 24 teams, and he wanted Commissioner Ford Frick to begin planning immediately. Feeling that neither the team owners nor the two leagues were capable of achieving this change, DeWitt insisted that it had to begin at the top, from Commissioner Frick. He even suggested a target date of 1964 and the simplest form of expansion—two leagues of 12 teams in each league. This timetable would give Frick 21 months prior to the opening games in the new cities. He also called for inter-league play that would count in the standings. "By bringing in some inter-league games, you give the fans in the one-league cities a chance to see all the stars."[59]

Frick definitely felt that DeWitt was moving too quickly. Frick tried to mollify him by agreeing that he favored having two 12-team leagues, but that going to 12 clubs would involve many fresh problems for each major league. "The two leagues have not yet perfected their current organization of ten clubs each," Frick reminded DeWitt. He also suggested not rushing into inter-league play. "I do not like the idea of too many playoffs," said Frick. "The time may come when we will have four major leagues of eight teams each, with a playoff system leading into the World Series. In the meantime, let's digest what we have eaten before tackling another big dinner." Frick added that it was definitely not up to him to initiate expansion.[60]

Late in the 1962 season, the Reds were three games behind the Giants with 13 games remaining. Cincinnati went on a nine-game road trip to New York, Philadelphia, and Pittsburgh, but won only three of the nine games, going 1–2 in each city. They finished the season in third place with a record of 98–64, 3½ games behind the pennant-winning San

Francisco Giants. Their 1962 winning percentage was .605, one point higher than their pennant-winning number in 1961. The team did have some bright spots. Frank Robinson had 208 hits, ended with a batting average of .342, hit 39 home runs, and drove in 136 runs. Pitchers Bob Purkey and Joey Jay both recorded more than 20 victories, and Jim O'Toole was not far behind with 16 wins.[61]

One of the Reds' bright spots in their bullpen was Jim Brosnan, who led the team with 14 (unofficial) saves in 1962. It was his action off the field that caused DeWitt's unhappiness with Brosnan. During a baseball season, major league players are forbidden by paragraph 3(c) of the Uniform Player Contract, which read : The player agrees that during the playing season he will not make public appearances, participate in radio or television programs or permit his picture to be taken or write or sponsor newspaper or magazine articles or sponsor commercial products without the written consent of the Club, which shall not be withheld except in the reasonable interests of the Club or professional baseball.[62] In 1962, Brosnan's journal of the 1961 season, *Pennant Race*, was published. The book received positive praise everywhere except in baseball front offices. DeWitt was unhappy with Brosnan's violation of one of baseball's governing rules.[63]

On July 10, 1962, Donald Barnes, former owner of the St. Louis Browns, passed away at the age of 68. He died of complications following an abdominal operation earlier in the day. Bill DeWitt and his entire family had had a deep personal relationship with Barnes, and his passing was a sorrowful event.[64]

At the conclusion of the 1962 baseball season, Frank Robinson announced that he planned to retire from baseball for "physical reasons." The 27-year-old outfielder indicated that he had no grievance against the team and there was nothing personal in his decision to leave the Reds. Robinson, in his seventh season with the Reds, and the National League's Most Valuable Player in 1961, admitted he might change his mind. "Well, if the Reds made me an offer I just couldn't refuse, I'd be awful crazy to turn my back on baseball completely." He added that he expected a substantial raise from the Reds for his performance and conceded the offers might go as high as $65,000, an estimated $10,000 increase over his 1962 salary.[65] DeWitt was aware of Robinson's plan to quit, and his only comment was, "Robinson is free and over 21. He can do what he wants."[66] Robinson's comments about a possible retirement and DeWitt's response caused an interest in Robinson's status with the Reds. DeWitt answered that the Reds had no "'untouchables,' but I can't conceive any club offering us what we'd want in return for a player like Frank Robinson."[67]

Between the end of the 1962 season and intensive planning for 1963, Bill and Margaret DeWitt took an extensive European vacation. Once back in the states, DeWitt received even more satisfying news: Ohio's Attorney General had withdrawn his suit seeking to have the sale of the Cincinnati Reds to Bill DeWitt nullified when a new agreement was put into the sale contract. It consisted of DeWitt's written guarantee to keep the Reds in Cincinnati for ten years and a proviso increasing the team's board of directors from three to seven members. The four new members of the board were prominent Cincinnati businessmen, and they represented the balance of power on the board. DeWitt, in effect, acquiesced to make the Reds something of a "civic enterprise."[68]

DeWitt was not anticipating any major disputes in signing his players for the 1963 season, but he was anxious to receive the signed contracts of key players he considered vital to any pennant hopes for the upcoming season. Early in January he signed one of his top pitchers, Bob Purkey, whose .821 winning percentage, based on 23 victories and only five losses in 1962, was the best in the major leagues. "Bob had a great season and deserved a very substantial raise," said DeWitt, who announced the signing. "I hope he has as good a season this year, and I expect him to be another 20-game winner in 1963."[69]

DeWitt anticipated another strong pitching staff with three Reds pitchers each winning a minimum of 20 games. A few weeks after he received Purkey's signed contract, he also got the signed contract of Joey Jay, a 20-game winner in each of the last two campaigns. Terms of his 1963 contract were not disclosed, but there were guesses it was for as much as $35,000. DeWitt called it a "very substantial raise," and Jay agreed. "That's about it. It's a nice raise."[70] The third member of the trio of expected 20-game winners was Jim O'Toole. His record for 1962 was 16–13 after winning 19 their pennant year. O'Toole was in Florida and was scheduled to meet with DeWitt in Tampa.[71]

In assessing his pitchers, DeWitt boastfully stated, "I wouldn't trade our pitching staff for any other in the league." A fourth pitcher that he predicted would help bolster his team was 23-year-old Jim Maloney, who showed DeWitt his maturity as well as his throwing skills. DeWitt also pointed out that southpaw Joe Nuxhall would be with the Reds for the full 1963 season. Nuxhall was 5–0 for the Reds the previous year after the Reds purchased him from San Diego.[72]

DeWitt was not only eager to sign his pitchers, but also everyday starters, beginning with outfielder Frank Robinson, who hinted he and DeWitt might have a little difficulty agreeing on his salary. The prior year Robinson was paid an estimated $40,000, making him the highest-salaried performer in Reds history. In early February Robinson showed up at DeWitt's office with his outfielder buddy, Vada Pinson. Bill DeWitt was delighted when both signed their 1963 contracts. Pinson's contract was thought to be between $25,000 and $30,000, and while Robinson's figure was never made public, the best guess was around $60,000.[73]

The Reds went to spring training in 1963 with one of the largest squads in the team's history. Fifty players were scheduled to show up in Tampa, including 11 members of the squad who were not listed on the roster. DeWitt was particularly eager to see two of the 11, Pete Rose and Tommy Helms, who formed a second base combination that he thought might very well be part of the team's infield in the near future. "They [will] make the fans in Cincinnati quickly forget the amazing exploits of Roy McMillan and Johnny Temple of a few years back," said DeWitt.[74]

Near the end of spring training, manager Fred Hutchinson felt that "Everything's coming up roses. We are set at every position and have speed and power." He praised the talents of Tommy Harper, the most sought-after player in the major leagues at the winter meetings. He felt his team had the best outfielders in Frank Robinson, Vada Pinson, Jerry Lynch, and Wally Post. He praised his reserve outfielders, Marty Keough and Ken Walters, labeled pitchers Bob Purkey, Joey Jay, and Jim O'Toole the most efficient starters in baseball, and lauded his late-inning relief artists, Bill Henry and Jim Brosnan. Dave Sisler and Johnny Klippstein were spot starters as well as relievers.[75]

With the 1963 baseball season close to half over, the Cincinnati Reds were still searching for relief pitchers. Their attempt to obtain Roger Craig from the New York Mets got nowhere. "We're trying, but there's nothing doing yet," said both DeWitt and Hutchinson.[76] The Reds had traded Jim Brosnan to the Chicago White Sox early in May. Brosnan claimed that DeWitt traded him because he wanted to shed his $30,000 salary, which was one of the highest on the team.[77] DeWitt vehemently denied Brosnan's claim, reminding him that in every player's baseball contract, there was a clause which prohibited players from writing for any publications without the club's permission. Brosnan wrote two baseball books, *The Long Season* and *Pennant Race*, both written during the baseball season and without submitting any drafts to DeWitt prior to publication. DeWitt made it plain that he believed that Brosnan spent too much of his time early in the 1962 season making public appearances to promote *Pennant Race*. More importantly, DeWitt maintained that baseball was secondary to Brosnan's writing even though the club was paying him to play ball.[78]

The Sporting News took Brosnan's side, commenting that while DeWitt was merely enforcing a clause in his pitcher's contract, he appeared to be overzealous when he attempted to silence Brosnan's book and magazine writing. The newspaper felt that Brosnan's comments were "straightforward and they speak the truth and they have been hailed as the most honest reporting on baseball that anyone has ever done."[79]

Brosnan was happy that he was traded to the White Sox, near his home in Morton Grove, a suburb of Chicago. "Now I will have more time to devote to my family as well as my writing." But if Brosnan thought he would be allowed more freedom than under DeWitt, he was mistaken. White Sox general manager Ed Short quickly announced that Brosnan would not be permitted to publish any newspaper stories or magazine articles, much less conduct a radio or TV show during the season. "We feel that our players' full attention should be given to the club."[80]

Brosnan appeared in 45 games for the White Sox, finishing the 1963 season with a record of 3–8 and 14 saves.[81] He balked at signing the White Sox's contract offer for 1964 which asked him to take a pay cut and continue the ban on his writing. The White Sox released him before the 1964 spring training camp opened. He received no offers from any other club, and the career of one of baseball's best relief pitchers was over. Brosnan passed away in 2014.[82]

During the 1963 season, things went much better for Bill DeWitt off the diamond than on. He and Margaret watched their son, Bill Jr., receive his diploma at Yale University's commencement exercises on June 10. Except for time lost recovering from surgery on his left shoulder because of an injury several months earlier, the 21-year-old spent most of the summer working in the Reds' accounting office. Bill Jr. was no stranger to baseball's executive quarters. "When I was growing up, my dad always kept me [his only son] around. Especially during the summer, he always had me go with him wherever he was going—ball parks, speeches, games, meetings, etc." In the fall of 1963, Bill Jr. entered the Harvard School of Business Administration.[83]

News relating to the Reds' personnel and performance in 1963 was mainly negative. In July, Fred Hutchinson announced that on orders from Bill DeWitt, Reds players were not to discuss with writers any of their injuries. Hutchinson told his players that DeWitt had been upset by stories quoting Reds players about their ailments.[84]

DeWitt was also unhappy about the Reds' performance on the field. His ace pitcher, Joey Jay, who had demanded a raise in salary based on his 1962 numbers, was having trouble winning games in 1963. He suffered his 15th loss early in August, coupled with only four victories. The Reds, now in fifth place, fell 8½ games behind the Los Angeles Dodgers. DeWitt and Hutchinson were growing weary of seeing runners stranded

Nine. A New Team, Another World Series 157

on third and attempted bunts rolling foul.[85] Reds were being given not-so-gentle hints by DeWitt that a shakeup was in store for 1964. "You'll need a scorecard to tell the names of players next year," DeWitt told a luncheon group.[86]

The Reds finished 1963 in fifth place, 13 games behind the pennant-winning Los Angeles Dodgers at 86–76. In assessing his team's disappointing finish in 1963, DeWitt said that a few Reds had had disappointing seasons. Joey Jay won only seven games, compared with 21 in 1962; Bob Purkey won 23 games in 1962 and could only win six in 1963; DeWitt also noted that the Reds could stand considerable improvement in their bullpen. "Unfortunately, clubs which have good relief pitchers want to keep them. You just have to develop your own." He also stated that he could not see any pitchers in his farm system that would "fill the bill."

In addition to pitching shortfalls, many hitters disappointed. Gordy Coleman hit only .247, while a season before, his average was .277; Leo Cardenas dropped from .294 in 1962 to .235; and although Frank Robinson hit a robust .342 in 1962, he ended the 1963 season batting only .259. The one player DeWitt praised was his catcher, John Edwards, who ranked third in the club in runs batted in. He even set a major league record for putouts by a catcher in a season, 971 putouts in 143 games, breaking the old mark of 877 registered by John Roseboro of the Dodgers in 125 games in 1961. Even here, DeWitt added a caveat. "We need to land an adequate second-string catcher during the off season."[87]

Once the World Series ended, DeWitt announced that the Reds had retained its three-man coaching staff. Reggie Otero would return for his sixth year with the Reds. Pitching coach Jim Turner, with nine years' pitching experience in the majors, returned for his fourth year with the Reds. First base coach Dick Sisler was a major league outfielder who had managed at Nashville and Seattle prior to coming to the Reds.[88]

The Reds also announced that they had renewed their working agreement with the San Diego club of the Pacific Coast League, the third straight year the Reds affiliated with the Padres. "We've received tremendous cooperation and we are very happy with the San Diego facilities accorded our players," said DeWitt. At the end of the 1963 World Series, 18 players on the Reds' current roster had played at San Diego.[89]

Nineteen sixty-three did not end on a happy note for DeWitt and the Cincinnati Reds, but it paled in comparison with the way 1964 began. In early January, the Reds owner sadly announced that his manager and close friend, Fred Hutchinson, was beginning treatment for chest cancer. There had been tears in DeWitt's eyes when Hutchinson called him with the news. "Fred is full of confidence and so am I," DeWitt

DeWitt discussing events at the Reds' camp with manager Fred Hutchinson.

said. "Both of us expect he'll be in Tampa when our club opens spring training on the 29th of February."[90]

While Hutchinson was fighting cancer, DeWitt was making plans for the 1964 spring training session. He ordered pitchers and catchers to begin workouts in Tampa on March 1, with the remainder of the squad to report on March 5. Determined to assemble the best roster possible, he ambitiously scheduled 29 exhibition games, beginning with a match against the Chicago White Sox at Sarasota on March 14. The Reds were scheduled to play seven National League clubs and six American League teams and then barnstorm north with the White Sox.[91]

DeWitt extended the Reds' executive staff by naming Phil Seghi assistant general manager, a new post on the Cincinnati club. Seghi moved from his job as secretary of the farm clubs to his new position working with the major league players. One of his first projects would be the traditional duty of player contract negotiations. "Seghi will be my eyes and ears in the major league player field. I have so many other duties involving fiscal affairs, that I can't do justice to both," said DeWitt. The 48-year-old Seghi began his baseball career as a scout with the Reds in 1956.[92]

One of the Reds' best pitchers and biggest headaches for both Hutchinson and DeWitt was Joey Jay. He won 21 games for the Reds in both 1961 and 1962, but he fell considerably short in 1963 with a record of only 7–18.⁹³ The Reds were convinced that his decreasing performance was caused by his outside businesses, especially his oil business in Spencer, West Virginia. After Hutchinson and DeWitt both denied him permission to leave camp, he took a chartered plane from Florida to his home in Cincinnati. "We can't tolerate any player walking out on us," said Hutchinson. "Both owner and manager agreed that his unauthorized departure would only exacerbate his problems with management."⁹⁴

In early May, Jay announced that he would quit baseball when the season concluded. He became especially miffed when the Reds moved rookie Sammy Ellis into the starting rotation. "They let a kid take my job," he declared. "When you're going bad around here, they avoid you." He described his teammates as "the best I've ever been with. It's the front office."⁹⁵ Despite his threats, Jay did not retire after the 1964 season. He pitched for the Reds in 1965 and part of 1966 before he was traded to the Atlanta Braves. He retired after the 1966 season, and during his 13-year career in the major leagues he compiled a 99–91 record.⁹⁶

During the 1964 season, DeWitt met with Cincinnati city officials to discuss the possibility of a new ballpark. DeWitt was distressed that attendance was dwindling, and baseball fans were complaining about traffic problems and the safety of their parked cars around Crosley Field. DeWitt estimated that a new 40,000-seat stadium would run $12 million in construction costs alone. There would be additional money needed for land costs and parking facilities. No decision was reached on the fate of the present 52-year-old ballpark.⁹⁷

Rumors persisted throughout the season that Hutchinson would issue a statement after the All-Star Game, resigning as manager of the Reds. These rumors surprised DeWitt, and he joined his manager in knocking them down. "This is news to me," DeWitt said shortly before the start of the All-Star Game. "Fred is doing fine and he's our manager until he says otherwise. We wouldn't think of replacing him."⁹⁸

The Cincinnati Reds were certainly doing their part in lifting the spirits of their ailing manager. After sweeping Milwaukee in a doubleheader, the Reds moved into third place, 3½ games behind the Philadelphia Phillies. Owner DeWitt was doing his best to keep up the momentum as he recalled two Cuban players from his San Diego minor league club, infielders Chico Ruiz and Tony Perez. DeWitt earlier had recalled Don Pavletich after John Edwards, Cincinnati's first-string catcher, developed a sore arm.⁹⁹ Unfortunately, after Hutchinson underwent additional tests, DeWitt agreed to a leave of absence for his manager. The club announced that during the upcoming road trip, coach

Dick Sisler would be in charge of the team.[100] In making the announcement, DeWitt was emphatic when he stated, "Hutch is still the manager of this ball team."[101]

In the middle of September, *The Sporting News* commended the Cincinnati Reds and their personnel for their actions during what they termed a "trying season." "The team, hardened pros that they are, are giving their all, a tribute to them, their manager, the coach in charge and the club president," wrote *The Sporting News*.[102]

Despite the laudatory comments, DeWitt was justly concerned over the club's poor home attendance this season. "You know, the Reds could win the pennant and still finish a poor ninth in attendance," he said. "And that's not healthy, especially in view of the fine brand of ball we're playing."[103] DeWitt was equally upset when a wire service report stated that Walter Alston would succeed the ailing Fred Hutchinson as manager of the Reds. An agitated DeWitt described the report as "simply preposterous." "We have no job open and Fred Hutchinson is our manager," DeWitt added.[104]

The Cincinnati Reds finished in a tie with the Philadelphia Phillies for second place in the National League. Both teams finished 92–70, one game behind the pennant-winning St. Louis Cardinals. Many consider the 1964 pennant race one of the most exciting in National League history. Three teams—the Cardinals, the Reds, and the Phillies—had numerous opportunities to win the pennant in the last two weeks of the season, but the winner wasn't decided until the last day of the season. With a month to go, the Phillies had a double-digit lead, but they suffered a major collapse. Unfortunately for the Reds, the Phillies defeated them in key games, including the final game of the year. This loss allowed the Cardinals to win the pennant by one game.[105]

Frank Robinson's .306 batting average was the highest by a starting Red, while Jim O'Toole's 17–7 record and 2.66 ERA were the best statistics for a Cincinnati starting pitcher. Sammy Ellis led the s team in saves with 14, and catcher Johnny Edwards won a Gold Glove Award. Bill Henry had a remarkable statistic—an 0.87 E.R.A. for a relief pitcher.[106]

Fred Hutchinson died November 13, 1964. Upon hearing the news, Bill DeWitt said, "Our relationship was employer-employee, but it was more on a man-to-man basis. His death was a tremendous personal loss."[107] Commissioner Ford Frick summed it up for all baseball with the heart-felt remembrance, "I am proud that I was Fred Hutchinson's friend." Ex–St. Louis great Stan Musial, who collected his 3,000th hit while Hutchinson was managing the Cardinals, said, "If you couldn't play for Fred, you couldn't play for anybody."[108] The Reds planned to wear black armbands the entire 1965 season in memory of their late

Nine. A New Team, Another World Series

manager. The team also installed a showcase on Crosley Field with photos of the highlights of Hutchinson's career.[109]

In getting his team set for the 1965 season, DeWitt first began assembling his coaching staff. He began with the not-surprising announcement that Dick Sisler would be the new manager and that Frank Oceak would join coaches Jim Turner, Reggie Otero, and Ray Shore, who had all been rehired. Oceak would handle the first-base coaching chores, and Otero would continue at third.[110]

As 1964 was closing, DeWitt began to think about his needs for the 1965 season. He

Because of his failing health, Hutchinson asked the Reds to relieve him of his managerial duties. Management chose coach Dick Sisler to manage the Reds in 1964.

also began to make a list of players who were untouchable. His greatest need was for a hard-hitting third baseman. After scanning the rosters of other major league teams, he concluded that the best third baseman who might be available was Houston's Bob Aspromonte. "We've got a young ball club," said DeWitt, "and Aspromonte at 26 would fit in with the players we have. He would give us protection we need at third base for three or four years." At the same time, he was dividing his players into two classifications. He listed players he called the "vulnerables." They included Jim O'Toole, Jim Maloney, Sammy Ellis, Billy McCool, and, surprisingly, Joey Jay. He also placed the word "untouchable" on catcher John Edwards, outfielders Frank Robinson, Vada Pinson, and Tommy Harper, and infielders Leo Cardenas and Pete Rose.[111]

Ever since DeWitt had moved to Cincinnati, he had been involved in the community and active in civic affairs. He was appointed to the board of governors of the Cincinnati Burns Institute of Shriners

Hospital for Crippled Children. He also was appointed to the City of Cincinnati Municipal Baseball Advisory Council.[112]

As an active Cincinnati citizen and as a team owner experiencing reduced attendance, DeWitt was concerned with improving the infrastructure around Crosley Field. DeWitt wrote to Wallace Power, director of public utilities of Cincinnati, informing him that local industries had promised that they would participate in the team's season ticket plans if DeWitt could get additional parking. DeWitt proposed a package deal—the Reds would spend $450,000 on Crosley Field during the next three years if the city of Cincinnati would spend $2.2 million for 2,130 new parking places. "The ball club's money would be spent on capital improvements for the comfort and convenience of fans. Improvements would include installing new modern, riser type contour seats to replace the old ones, and updating the present rest rooms." DeWitt's report showed that Crosley Field could be modernized, and approximately 10,500 seats could be added.[113]

Every club owner is optimistic about his team's outlook for the coming season. While Bill DeWitt would not go as far as predicting his team would win the pennant in 1965, he did admit that he had "never been more optimistic." DeWitt claimed that the Reds were well fortified at all positions. He agreed with his manager, Dick Sisler, that the Reds' pitching staff was the best in the league "both in quality and quantity." He was especially pleased with the trade he had made the previous winter with the St. Louis Cardinals, sending Bob Purkey to the Cardinals in return for relief pitcher Roger Craig and outfielder Charlie James. He was also eager to take a look at two promising youngsters training with the Reds: Tony Perez and Tommy Helms. All were graduates of the San Diego farm club. He was also eager to see Lee May, a 21-year-old first baseman who had had an outstanding year for Macon in the Southern League in 1964.[114]

When the 1965 season began, DeWitt could hardly keep from boasting that his team was probably the first club in history to have two complete sets of everything—pitchers, catchers, infielders, and outfielders. "This club," DeWitt pointed out, "has speed, savvy, and right- and left-handed batters who can be platooned and switched."[115]

Right-handed pitcher Jim Maloney proved that DeWitt was not exaggerating when he bragged about Cincinnati's excellent pitching. On a Monday evening in June, Maloney pitched a no-hitter against the New York Mets for 10 innings, only to lose the game, 1–0, when Johnny Lewis homered off Maloney in the 11th inning. DeWitt was unable to watch Maloney's gem because he was in St. Louis, where his son Bill Jr., was to be married. Nonetheless, he raised Maloney's salary by $1,000.[116]

On August 22, Jim Maloney's salary was raised another $1,000 when he pitched another no-hitter. This game also went ten innings, but this time Maloney was the winner. DeWitt explained that the additional payments had to be a part of the player's salary since baseball rules prohibited granting bonuses based on performances.[117]

Toward the end of the 1965 season, rumors circulated that unless the Reds won the National League pennant, Dick Sisler would be fired. Sisler replied to the rumors, "Those rumors don't help a bit when we're in the thick of the pennant race. I've made mistakes, but what manager hasn't?" Sisler headed for his home in Nashville, making no effort to conceal his bitter disappointment. "I don't think John McGraw could have won the pennant with this club after our pitching fell apart," he said.[118] "No comment," responded DeWitt, who said he would put off any announcement of Sisler's future until the end of the season.[119]

On October 4, DeWitt fired Sisler as manager of the Cincinnati Reds, offering him "another job" with the organization.[120] It was no secret that DeWitt was disenchanted with Sisler's managerial performance, since only a week earlier the Reds were contending for second place. The team ended the season in fourth place, however, with a record of 89–73, eight games behind the pennant-winning Los Angeles Dodgers.[121] Sisler felt he should have been given one more year to get his ball club going. "I don't know why these things happen," he said. "And I'm very, very, very disappointed."[122] Sisler was not entirely to blame for the Reds' fourth place finish. The team allowed more runs than any other National League club and was first on the undesirable list of men left on base. Even their team batting average of .273 could not overcome those statistics.[123]

While the Reds were looking for Dick Sisler's successor, Ford Frick announced his intention to retire as Major League Baseball Commissioner, a post he had held since 1951. When the club owners gathered to choose Frick's successor, the original list of 18 candidates had been reduced to five: Eugene M. Zuckert, secretary of the Air Force; Curtis E. LeMay, former chief of staff and head of the Strategic Air Command; G. Keith Funston, president of the New York Stock Exchange; Joe Cronin, president of the American League; and Louis Carroll, legal counsel for the National League. None of these five candidates was able to muster the necessary seven votes from each league.[124]

Even before the voting began, Bill DeWitt had his own candidate for the post—Gabe Paul, DeWitt's predecessor as general manager of the Reds. When Paul asked that he not be considered, DeWitt was disappointed. The owners decided to wait until their winter baseball meeting in December to make their selection. A prominent club owner who did not wish to be identified said, "Paul would be very much acceptable to the owners if he made himself available. I feel he can get the necessary votes."[125]

On October 26, Bill DeWitt announced that Don Heffner would be the new Reds manager; he had been signed to a two-year contract at an undisclosed salary. Beginning in 1934, Heffner played second base and shortstop, primarily as a reserve, with the New York Yankees, St. Louis Browns, Philadelphia Athletics, and Detroit Tigers, ending his playing career in 1944.[126]

In 1947, Heffner began his managerial years in the Browns' farm system in Aberdeen, South Carolina, where he led his team to two consecutive pennants. He returned to the major leagues as a coach with the Athletics and the Tigers from 1958–1961. Heffner then spent two seasons managing the Reds' top farm club, the San Diego Padres, winning the 1962 Pacific Coast League championship. In 1963 and 1964, he was the New York Mets' third-base coach. Although quite familiar with many of the Reds from his years in San Diego, "He's one of the few guys in baseball who did not apply for the Reds' managerial job," laughed DeWitt. "I had at least six who did."[127]

When DeWitt went to Florida to participate in the annual winter meetings, he admitted he had no plans to make any "earthshaking" deals because he was reluctant to tamper with a young club. The senior starter in the outfield was 30-year-old Frank Robinson. Center fielder Vada Pinson was 27, and right fielder Tommy Harper was only 25. Three of the Reds' starting infield were in their 20s—Deron Johnson 27, Pete Rose 23, and Leo Cardenas 26. Tony Perez, who platooned at first base with Gordy Coleman, was only 23. John Edwards, the Reds' first-string catcher, was 27, as was his back-up, Don Pavletich. At 31, Coleman, the Reds' left-handed-hitting first baseman, was the "old man." "Like I said," repeated DeWitt, "it's a young team."[128]

In assessing his pitchers, DeWitt emphasized that with the exception of Joe Nuxhall, "We've got a young pitching staff." The leaders of the Reds' pitching staff, Jim Maloney and Sammy Ellis, a 22-game winner since becoming a starting pitcher in 1965, were both 24. Jim O'Toole was 28; Billy McCool, the fourth starter, was only 21; and their fifth starter, Joey Jay, who compiled a 9–6 record in 1965, had just turned 30 in August. Despite the fact that DeWitt had an above-average pitching staff, he was well aware that pitching cost the team the pennant in 1965, and he admitted he was out to bolster the staff for the 1966 season.[129]

On December 9, Bill DeWitt obtained the pitcher he was seeking, although it came at a high price. In the biggest deal at the 1965 winter meetings, Harry Dalton, newly named general manager of the Baltimore

Orioles, sent pitcher Milt Pappas and two other players to the Cincinnati Reds for Frank Robinson. The two players thrown in the deal with Pappas never played a single game with the Orioles. Right-hander Jack Baldschun and outfielder Dick Simpson were acquired from the Phillies and the California Angels, respectively, a week prior to the beginning of the winter meetings.

One of the outstanding sluggers in the National League, Robinson drove in 113 runs for the Reds in the 1965 season while hitting 33 home runs and batting .296. For the Orioles, getting Robinson ended a lengthy effort to acquire a long-ball slugger. Conversely, the Reds considered Pappas the "big one" in the four-player deal. The 26-year-old right-hander had a 13–9 record in 1965 with the Orioles. Even Simpson, the outfielder in the Pappas deal, brought offensive clout to the Reds. Although he played most of the 1965 season with Seattle of the Pacific Coast League, he hit .301, stole 29 bases, and hit 25 homers.[130]

Bill DeWitt called the Robinson transaction "a million-dollar trade" and an even deal. "We needed pitching," said DeWitt. "We got a top-flight starter in Milt Pappas and a real good relief man in Jack Baldschun plus an outstanding young prospect in Dick Simpson, who has tremendous speed, a real good arm and has power."[131]

The Robinson deal is still considered by many the most controversial trade Bill DeWitt made as a baseball executive. Robinson had been a batting star for 10 seasons, while the three players DeWitt received from Baltimore were certainly not in Robinson's category. Robinson was 30 years of age, but DeWitt argued that the slugger was "not a young 30" and that he wished to keep the Reds young.[132] DeWitt continued to insist that the Reds needed pitching, and he did not feel secure enough to rely on the pitchers already on the roster. Finally, when DeWitt was reminded what a great player Robinson was, he answered his detractors by reminding them that in 1965 the Reds scored 200 more runs than the pennant-winning Dodgers yet ended the season in fourth place. "It means that scoring runs is not the whole answer to winning. We had Robinson here for 10 years, yet we won only one pennant with him."[133] James Enright, sportswriter for the *Chicago American*, agreed with DeWitt's strategy, noting that DeWitt denied getting rid of Robinson because of his "bad boy" reputation. Robinson, indeed, may have developed something of a reputation, at least in some quarters. He was a hard-charging player, especially on the base paths; a star who received the sort of attention that invited resentment; and a run-in with the law (someone pulled a knife and Robinson responded by showing the fellow his gun) had played out in the media.[134]

Despite DeWitt's negative assessment of Robinson's future,

Robinson went on to become a Triple Crown winner in 1966, the MVP, and the major force in helping Baltimore win three pennants, while Pappas delivered "workman-like but unspectacular pitching."[135]

Robinson's reaction to the trade was disbelief, even though he had heard rumors that he might be traded. Once he got over the first shock, he began to think that the trade was a pretty good deal. What rankled him was DeWitt's comments about his being old at the age of 30. "I didn't know what he meant," said Robinson, "and I never spoke to the man again."[136]

The Robinson deal with Baltimore was the major trade made at the 1965 winter meetings. The Orioles were elated that the Reds had made Robinson available, though DeWitt had offered Robinson to other teams first. The Cleveland Indians came within a whisker of obtaining the Reds star. DeWitt, Phil Seghi, and Gabe Paul, former Cincinnati general manager who was now GM in Cleveland, had numerous talks. According to a reliable source, DeWitt told Paul he wanted an everyday outfielder, an established relief pitcher, and one of Cleveland's starters. Paul agreed to the first two requests, but he refused to trade any of his starting pitchers. DeWitt then contacted the Orioles, and the Robinson trade was consummated.[137]

In the baseball world and for DeWitt personally, the year 1965 ended on a sad note. On December 11, Branch Rickey passed away. Five hundred people attended the funeral services in St. Louis. He was given a final tribute by just a few of the men who spoke of him as baseball's most brilliant and far-seeking executives. Among the executives Rickey helped start in baseball were National League president Warren Giles, Cleveland Indians president Gabe Paul, and Bill DeWitt. "He had a great impact on my education, my baseball career, and on my life," said De Witt. "I guess he was my closest friend for many years."[138]

Nineteen sixty-six marked Bill DeWitt's 50th year in baseball from the time he started as a peanut vendor for the St. Louis Browns to his present position as owner of the Cincinnati Reds. Many changes had taken place in baseball during those 50 years, including increasing the number of teams in both major leagues. He reminded other major league executives that when the American and National Leagues expanded in 1961 and 1962, respectively, there had been a minimal amount of advance work done.

All four expansion clubs were forced to play their games in inferior parks. "If they had had new parks to start with," said DeWitt, "I think there would have been a much healthier situation." DeWitt lamented the fact that not only were the expansion teams given little time to construct parks, they needed time to appoint front-office staffs and construct farm systems prior to competing with long-established teams.

DeWitt was always a proponent of expansion and preached that baseball should prepare for more. He suggested that a committee determine which cities had an adequate population and a financial ability to support major league baseball. "Do they have a park with adequate physical facilities, and if not, do they have plans to build one? What are the radio and TV possibilities?" DeWitt suggested that perhaps cities presently in the minor leagues might become major league cities, and if so, then the minor leagues would have to be realigned. "I have no idea when the next expansion measure might gain approval," concluded DeWitt, "but I want the possibilities surveyed, and the data studied and then make a decision."[139]

A more local issue was also absorbing DeWitt's attention. Ever since he became owner of the Cincinnati Reds, he had been pushing for a new stadium. Early in 1966, he announced that the Reds would play in any stadium built with public funds, promising to work with both the city and county in any way possible to help in the construction of a riverfront stadium. DeWitt had long opposed a site on the riverfront, but his willingness to occupy a new stadium built on the banks of the Ohio River pleased Charles W. Staab, chairman of the Stadium Steering Committee and president of the Greater Cincinnati Chamber of Commerce. Staab was also executive vice president and business manager of the area's largest newspaper, the *Cincinnati Enquirer*.[140]

In addition to all his off-the-field activities, DeWitt still needed to prepare for spring training and the 1966 season, He was optimistic about the upcoming season, praising his outfield, even without Frank Robinson. He still had Tommy Harper, Vada Pinson, Deron Johnson (who drove in 130 runs in 1965), and Gordy Coleman. He finally seemed satisfied with his pitching staff. "I have a lot of pitching," he said, "with Sammy Ellis, Joey Jay, Jim Maloney, Billy McCool, Joe Nuxhall, Jim O'Toole and the newly acquired Jack Baldschun and Milt Pappas."[141]

DeWitt was looking forward to having Don Heffner as his new manager. Heffner was quite familiar with the team's personnel from his years with San Diego. In addition, DeWitt was impressed with Heffner's temperament. "He's not just a nice guy or a real hard-nose," said DeWitt. "He's in between. He can be both aggressive and conservative. He's adaptable. We have a club, in my opinion, that at certain times needs to be aggressive, and other times needs to be cautious."[142]

Heffner might have been the manager of the Reds, but the team never forgot the late Fred Hutchinson. Before an exhibition game between the Reds and the Kansas City Athletics in Bradenton, Florida, a marble monument was dedicated to the memory of the late Fred Hutchinson in Anna Maria Island, where Hutchinson used to live. Both new Commissioner William Eckert and Bill DeWitt spoke at the dedication as uniformed members of both the Reds and Athletics stood behind the speakers. DeWitt called his late friend "a great, big bear with a soft heart, a partner rather than a business associate." The inscription on the monument said, "Dedication to the memory of Fred Hutchinson, baseball major leaguer and manager, who gave of his time, talent and means to the youth of Anna Maria Island."[143]

The feud between Frank Robinson and Bill DeWitt continued well into the 1966 season. Robinson maintained that if DeWitt traded him to the Orioles to strengthen his ball club, he could understand, but "that comment about me being 'an old 30' is hitting below the belt." Pappas, who could also be outspoken, made a comment that put a new perspective on the trade. The pitcher called it "the greatest break I've ever gotten in my life. I should win more games with a team able to get a few more runs for me. Robinson will have a harder time hitting in the big Oriole park."[144]

The Reds did not start the 1966 season with a bang. They lost six of their first seven games, while Robinson was hitting .417 for the Baltimore Orioles. "We're just not hitting," explained DeWitt, "but I don't think it's anything to get panicky about. I have confidence in the ball players we have. We're not going to make any drastic changes." When informed what Robinson was doing for the Orioles, DeWitt's reply was that it is not possible to evaluate a deal in seven days. "Let's wait until the season is over and see what the jury says then." He added that he was happy Robinson had gotten off so well. "I wish him the best of luck," added DeWitt.[145]

By the middle of June, the Reds were in eighth place, only one game ahead of the Mets. The Mets had beaten the Reds three out of four games in a weekend series at Shea Stadium, and the collapse of the Reds caused rumors that Heffner was planning to resign as manager. Heffner denied such rumors, and a positive DeWitt commented, "We've got a lot of ability on this club. I still believe everything will get squared away before long." DeWitt firmly felt he had a good club despite the fact that it was mired in the National League's second division.[146]

Heffner did not resign, but rather on July 13, Bill DeWitt fired him and replaced him with Heffner's third-base coach, Dave Bristol.[147] Bristol was a former minor league infielder and manager and became the third man to head the club since Fred Hutchinson's health forced him to resign late in the 1964 season. Bristol was not present when DeWitt announced the managerial change, but commented from his North Carolina home, "Heffner is a good friend of mine and I hate to see anybody get fired. But somebody's got to take over and I'd soon it be me as anybody else."[148]

Nine. A New Team, Another World Series

When Bristol came on board as manager, the Reds had just broken an 11-game losing streak by defeating the first-place San Francisco Giants. Even after this victory, the Reds were nine games below .500 and 15 games behind the Giants.[149] As the Reds continued their slide during the 1966 season, it seemed the media and baseball mavens equated the poor showing of the team with the trade of Frank Robinson. One exception was Milton Richman, sportswriter for the UPI, who noted how odd it was that so many "so-called experts" who continued to deride the Robinson trade were the same ones who had picked the Reds to win the National League pennant in 1966—without Robinson. Richman was amused that these "experts" who were calling Robinson a "superstar" with the Orioles had never called him that when he played for the Reds. "They always agreed he was a good ball player when he wore a Reds uniform, but no one ever put him in the superstar class before."

During the 1960s, the players chose which of their peers would make up the teams for the All-Star Game. Richman also pointed out that Robinson's fellow players never thought enough of him to name him to the National League's starting squad. In 1965 Robinson was on the NL All-Star team, but he was picked by the manager and made only one appearance as a pinch hitter.[150]

The Baltimore Orioles clinched the American League pennant on September 23, finishing with a record of 96–73, nine games ahead of their closest competitor, the Minnesota Twins. In the National League, the Los Angeles Dodgers finished first, 1½ games ahead of the San Francisco Giants. The Reds finished seventh with a record of 76–84, 18 games behind the Dodgers.[151] In the World Series, the Orioles swept the Dodgers, winning all four games.[152]

On September 26, Dave Bristol was officially hired as manager of the Cincinnati Reds, having served as interim manager since July 13. At 33, he was the youngest manager in the major leagues. His contract was for one year. Bristol's first managerial job was at Hornell, New York, in the Class D New York–Pennsylvania League. He received several promotions and became manager of the Reds' San Diego farm club in 1964. In 1966, he was the third-base coach for the Reds before he replaced Heffner as manager.[153] After he hired Bristol, DeWitt also announced, "We're going to make some trades this winter, but we're sure not going to rip this team apart in doing so."[154]

After the Orioles defeated the Dodgers in the 1966 World Series, the consensus was that Frank Robinson was the chief catalyst in the Orioles' sweep. DeWitt avoided commenting on the trade that many said won the pennant for the Orioles.[155] As it turned out, it was not necessary for DeWitt to answer any questions about the Orioles-Reds trade.

The usually taciturn Frank Robinson became quite garrulous during the World Series celebration, and he talked about his relations with Bill DeWitt. "Sure, I've been hostile," Robinson admitted. "I had a chip on my soldier big as a log. You grow up, though." He spoke of how he would carry a gun and was not shy about waving it around. He admitted that while playing in the National League he would "ram his way around" on the field with a violence that "created more enemies than Atilla." Nor did he deny that he had a reputation as a hothead, and that he was too independent for his own good. He even talked about an incident in a Cincinnati restaurant when, during an argument, he pulled a revolver and how that incident "humbled him."

Robinson realized that the press and other players agreed that he was hard to handle and that his hostility on the ball field and in the clubhouse had its repercussions. He realized that his actions and attitude were the reasons players selected Hank Aaron over him when the players selected the All-Star teams.[156]

One of the advantages of major league baseball is that any fan can become an armchair manager, allowing that fan to make virtual player deals. The Robinson trade to Baltimore in 1966 is one topic that is still the subject of debate by baseball fans. In 2010, a knowledgeable collector of baseball memorabilia strongly defended the Reds' trading Robinson to the Orioles. He argued that the 1965 season set the stage for the Frank Robinson trade. The Reds had the strongest team in the National League except for pitching. The consensus was that the Reds were one pitcher away from the World Series in 1966, making it necessary to trade one of their players for a starting pitcher.

There were only two options to acquire a front-line starter—Frank Robinson or Deron Johnson. Robinson was three years older than Johnson, he was involved in a contract squabble with the team at the time, he was the team's highest-paid player, and he had a history of off-the-field problems. The Orioles had just completed several trades and had an over-abundance of pitchers to offer in a trade.

Unfortunately, nothing worked out in the Reds' favor: Robinson had a career year in 1966; the Orioles won the World Series; the Reds finished near last in the National League; and the players the Reds received from Baltimore had miserable years. In hindsight, the Orioles definitely got the better end of the trade. Despite the Robinson-deal fiasco, however, DeWitt refused to become "gun-shy." "I made deals before that one," he said, "and I'll make some more."[157]

There was, however, no need for Bill DeWitt to make any more deals for the Reds, for on December 5, 1966, he sold the Cincinnati Reds for between $7–8 million to a syndicate of Cincinnati investors, made up of 13 individuals, including DeWitt's son. They elected Frank Dale, publisher of the *Cincinnati Enquirer*, president of the club. The new owners signed a 40-year lease with the city to occupy the new stadium planned for the riverfront.[158] "I agreed to the sale," said Bill DeWitt, Sr., "only after receiving a pledge that the purchasers would execute a 40-year lease to the new stadium, thus assuring that the Reds will be in Cincinnati where they belong for the indefinite future."[159] According to the terms of the deal, DeWitt was to continue running the club until the deal was approved by the National League, probably sometime in January. Manager Dave Bristol and the Reds' front office staff also would continue in their jobs.[160]

One can speculate on the reasons why Bill DeWitt chose to sell the Reds at that particular time. He may have been disillusioned by the quibbling over the new stadium, discouraged by a lack of success on the field—a replay of all his years with the Browns, when he was much younger—or simply a desire to take things a little easier. Regardless, he had committed to running the Reds for an indefinite period as the new owners began a search for a general manager. The name of Bill Veeck popped up regarding who might fill that post under the new ownership. Another name that was heard was Bob Howsam, currently the general manager of the St. Louis Cardinals. "I haven't heard a thing about it," said Howsam, "but it's nice to know you're considered highly by other organizations."[161] Dale, the Reds' new president, who was also president of the Ohio State Bar Association, said that not only would DeWitt continue to run the front office, he would be free to negotiate player trades during the interim, subject to the approval of the new owners. Most believed, however, that after the fan reaction to the Robinson trade, it was doubtful that DeWitt would become involved in any major player deals.[162]

The new owners of the Reds took over the baseball club as planned on January 9, 1967. On that date, DeWitt signed a contract for $25,000 to continue with the club for one year as a consultant. He would become the Reds' interim general manager, acting as spokesman on league matters until a successor was named. Indicating his continuing interest in the club, DeWitt provided financing for Bill Jr. to purchase 15 percent of the team's stock.[163]

DeWitt remained as acting general manager for less than a week. Two days after the new owners officially signed the contract, the Reds' president announced that Robert L. Howsam had been named general manager, succeeding DeWitt. Howsam had been general manager of the St. Louis Cardinals since August 1964, when he replaced Bing Devine. Dale also stated that Howsam would replace DeWitt as the

Reds' representative at National League meetings, but that DeWitt was continuing as a consultant for the time being.[164]

A *Sporting News* editorial lauded Bill DeWitt for demonstrating top-quality leadership for many years. The paper also commended him for his courtesy and manners when he sold the Reds to a local group, despite his unhappiness that he was leaving the ranks of major league club owners. *The Sporting News* continued that DeWitt deserved praise for selling the franchise to a combine of Cincinnati and Ohio businessmen who were signing a 40-year lease on a new stadium in Cincinnati. "DeWitt deserves the applause of Cincinnati citizens and the respect of baseball men and fans everywhere."[165]

When asked by many whether he intended to remain in baseball after he was no longer employed by the Reds, DeWitt replied, "It's pretty hard to say what you're going to do a year from now."[166]

As if to emphasize that things were changing for DeWitt, his brother Charley passed away on April 11, the day after the 1967 season began. Only 66 years old, Charley died in St. Louis of a heart attack. In the *New York Times* article about his death, Bill was referred to as Charley's brother, "now a consultant to the National League."[167]

DeWitt's successor as general manager, Bob Howsam, receives most of the credit for the success of the Cincinnati Reds during the mid-1970s, but his success in many ways can be attributed to Bill DeWitt. Howsam inherited not only three members of the "Big Red Machine"—Johnny Bench, Tony Perez and Pete Rose—but he can also thank DeWitt for his three ironclad operating rules. Build through the farm system as much as possible; pay no attention if the organization develops an abundance of the same types of players, for quality prospects can always be traded for needed players; and trade anybody once he reaches 30. Even though the third rule cost Howsam the services of Frank Robinson, he acquired excellent new players in his place, including Joe Morgan, Jack Billingham, and Bobby Tolan in trades for players on the Reds' roster DeWitt had obtained before he left.[168]

Ten

Elder Statesman

True to his word, DeWitt stayed on as a consultant to Howsam and the Reds for a short period. Soon after Howsam took office, he asked DeWitt to accompany him, farm director Jim McLaughlin, and farm department aid Herky Robinson to New York for the free-agent draft. The Reds were able to draft 14 players, nine more than the previous year.[1]

While DeWitt was in New York, his father-in-law, Fred W. Holekamp, died of a heart attack on his farm in St. Louis County. An only child, Margaret had been close to her father, a retired partner of Holekamp Lumber Company, and an owner, breeder, exhibitor, and show judge of saddle horses.[2]

Except a minority shareholder, by April 1967, DeWitt was no longer affiliated with the Cincinnati Reds, but he was far from retired. One of his first undertakings began in early 1968. Speaking before a conference of Erie County, New York legislators, civic leaders, press, and broadcasters, he stated that he was prepared to help Buffalo become a major league baseball city. DeWitt made it clear that he did not want majority-stock control. "The National League prefers that any new franchise be home-owned. I know that money will be no obstacle for this Buffalo group. They have it." There was no hurdle. Using data verified by his survey of potential major league cities, DeWitt emphasized that Buffalo could not expect a commitment in advance of the city's building a stadium.[3]

Following his advice, the Erie County Legislature passed a resolution of intent to build a new stadium, and Buffalo's bid for a National League franchise began in earnest. DeWitt even toured Florida spring training camps to solicit votes from the National League owners.[4]

Near the end of 1968, DeWitt's name was linked with another professional baseball team, this time an expansion major league team that replaced the original team of the same name—the Washington Senators. When the majority owner of the Senators, James Johnston, passed away, his estate put the team up for sale. Bob Hope, popular TV and movie comedian and a minor stockholder in the Cleveland Indians, was part of a group that bid $9 million for the Senators, and it was assumed that he would be in the new ownership group. Hope's group also included James H. Lemon, Sr., a co-owner of the team, and Bill DeWitt. DeWitt, who would have 10 percent of the purchase, would have been in charge of the club's operation as board chairman.

Unfortunately for the Hope group, the American League and the probate court awarded the entire franchise to Robert Short, a trucking and hotel magnate, who had previously owned basketball's Minneapolis Lakers.[5]

In May 1969, DeWitt was in St. Louis to pay tribute to Norman Handel, former president of the Brownie Booster Club. He used that occasion to talk about the future of major league baseball, particularly regarding expansion. DeWitt suggested replacing Branch Rickey's idea of a third league with inter-league play. "Let's reshuffle geographically the clubs into three divisions—an Eastern Division, a Western Division, and a Central Division, each consisting of eight teams."[6] Although DeWitt's plan was not adopted as he suggested it, many of his ideas—three divisions, inter-league play, and round-robin playoffs—are in use today.

DeWitt came back to St. Louis to attend the funeral of Margaret's mother, who passed away in February 1970.[7] Later that month, DeWitt could be found in Chicago, discussing the future of the Seattle Pilots. The expansion Pilots were having financial difficulties, and it was obvious that the team would not remain in Seattle much longer. The American League provided the Pilots with $650,000 to allow the team to play baseball one more year in Seattle, but after that, the team's future location would likely be Milwaukee or Dallas-Fort Worth. Majority ownership of the Pilots was in the hands of Bill Daley of Cleveland and brothers, Dewey and Max Soriano, of Cleveland, who owned 40 percent of the team stock.

Most American League owners blamed the franchise's troubles on Dewey Soriano, the Pilots' chief officer. He was embroiled in controversy with Seattle city officials, and he had little rapport with the business community. The other owners suggested that someone else should take charge of the team as the active head of the operation. The someone else they had in mind was Bill DeWitt, but he turned the suggestion down. He did offer to help on a temporary basis or as an adviser.[8] On March 31, 1970, the Seattle Pilots officially became the Brewers, playing their first game in their new home, Milwaukee, seven days later, on April 7.[9]

Although Seattle's major league team, the Pilots, now called Milwaukee home, Bill DeWitt and Rudie Schaffer, a former associate of DeWitt from the Browns, were attempting to stake out the Seattle area for a National League franchise. There were reports that the two men were asking about the availability of Sick's Stadium for an interim minor league team. Schaffer stated that regardless of what happened with the Pilots, Seattle considered itself a prime spot if the city built a new stadium.[10]

DeWitt was not one to wait around for opportunities to reach him. In March 1972, the National Hockey League announced that for $25,000, anyone could join a list of groups interested in becoming one of two expansion franchises in the 16-team NHL.[11] Bill DeWitt led the Cincinnati delegation to the Board of Governors, presenting the city's case for being awarded one of the two new franchises. In Cincinnati, he told the Board, the city's hockey facility would be hooked together by the plaza of the new Riverfront Stadium, home of the Reds. Even the $6 million per team price of entering the league was not a deterrent. DeWitt responded, "We have a youthful, aggressive group and we have the money."[12]

The Cincinnati contingent sported black lapel buttons that read: "We're ready for the NHL," but Cincinnati's bid for a National Hockey League franchise was rejected. Bill Sr. did join his son Bill Jr.'s successful attempt to affiliate his hockey team, the Cincinnati "Stingers," with the World Hockey Association (WHA), where membership was only $4 million per team. Unfortunately, their plans for a new arena were put on hold until 1974.[13]

Although August Busch, Jr., was widely viewed as the owner of MLB's St. Louis Cardinals, Busch's brewery, Anheuser Busch, Inc., was the legal owner of the team. In November 1975, Bill DeWitt, Sr., was hired by Anheuser-Busch to serve with Chase Manhattan Bank and the brokerage firm of Merrill Lynch, Pierce, Fenner & Smith Incorporated to help appraise the fair market value of the Cardinals in connection with the brewery's possible sale of the Cardinals to Busch. DeWitt cautiously told the *Post-Dispatch*, "I have a fiduciary relationship so I necessarily must be guarded in what I say, but I will tell you I would not take the appointment unless I was assured full cooperation of not only the Cardinals' front office and availability to the club's financial figures, but also the privilege to talk to other teams, if necessary, to help arrive at dollar evaluations of St. Louis players."[14]

In interviews with *The Sporting News*, DeWitt explained that his job "was to arrive at a lump sum for all the players, allowing Busch to decide individual values within the composite amount in setting up a depreciation schedule when he completed the deal for the Cardinals."[15] Spink was impressed with DeWitt's knowledge of player values, which he had learned as an emissary for Commissioner Bowie Kuhn and American League president Lee MacPhail when he obtained potential bidders for a possible Seattle franchise. "I've kept my fingers in the pie that way," chuckled DeWitt, "but I don't work 10 hours a day anymore."[16]

There was really no need for DeWitt to work 10 hours a day. A millionaire now, DeWitt didn't have to work at all. He had made a sizeable profit from the sale of the Reds in January 1967, and in recent years he had been investing successfully in oil and gas leases and other ventures.[17]

In late November 1975, Bill Veeck announced that he was back in Major League Baseball with the purchase of the Chicago White Sox. Further, he stated that Bill DeWitt, would be one of the larger investors in the Sox. In fact, DeWitt would be chairman of the board, representing the team at all major league meetings. "That's one of the things he does best," said Veeck. "He knows all the owners and he is an excellent representative." Veeck planned to be president and chief operating officer.[18]

DeWitt, who had held executive positions with five major league baseball clubs in the last 50 years, did not hesitate in accepting Veeck's offer. DeWitt made it clear that he was not expecting to make a lot of money, but that it would be a lot of fun. Out of baseball since 1967, DeWitt admitted that it would be nice to be back on the inside. "It's going to take a promoter like Bill Veeck to get people out to Comiskey Park, but he's the type of guy who stirs up a lot of excitement," said DeWitt.[19]

For DeWitt, this venture was akin to a business reunion. In addition to Veeck, DeWitt's good friend, Hank Greenberg, was part of the deal. Veeck and Greenberg had previously run the White Sox as partners. Paul Richards, who would be part of the club operation, had managed the White Sox from 1951 through 1954.[20] DeWitt stressed that he had no intention of starting a new career. All he wanted was a reasonable investment in major league baseball again. "I think it's a good idea. I expect to make some money. The White Sox own 32 to 33 acres of ground. They own the ballpark, too. The club is going to stay in Chicago."[21]

When DeWitt told his wife, Margaret, he was getting back into baseball, she wasn't surprised. "Whatever you want to do is fine," she said.[22]

On December 4, 1975, Veeck presented his offer to the American League team owners, general managers and president MacPhail. After six hours of discussion, MacPhail informed Veeck, "The league clubs

Ten. Elder Statesman 177

Playing with his grandchildren was one of DeWitt's favorite pastimes. Here we see Bill Sr. with a very young Bill III.

considered your proposal, financial information and financial structure, and found it did not meet league standards. There is too much debt and not enough cash." Veeck had to come up with an additional $1.2 million in debenture money for the sale to go through.[23]

One week later, Veeck arrived at the 1975 winter baseball meetings in Florida to announce that he had the additional cash the league had demanded. On the first vote, Veeck still fell one vote short for approval. Detroit Tigers owner John Fetzer, never a great fan of Veeck but an ally of DeWitt, made an impassioned plea to his fellow owners to take Veeck back as a major league owner. On the second vote, Veeck's purchase was approved, with "no" votes only from Oakland A's owner Charles Finley and California Angels owner Gene Autry. After the vote was announced, Veeck stated, "It's not often that a 61-year-old, one-legged man gets a new start in life."[24]

One hour after the American League owners approved Veeck's purchase, the White Sox completed a five-player deal with the Philadelphia Phillies. The White Sox traded shortstop Mike Buskey and 37-year-old Jim Kaat, a 20-game winner the previous two seasons, for three young Phillies—right-handed pitchers Dick Ruthven and Roy Thomas and infielder-outfielder Alan Bannister.[25] DeWitt, accompanied by Veeck, attended the 1975 winter meetings and expressed delight that the American League owners approved Veeck's purchase, which allowed the Sox to remain in Chicago. DeWitt recognized that if Veeck's offer had been rejected, the White Sox would very likely have been sold to a Seattle group that would have moved the team to Washington state.[26]

DeWitt always recognized that being a major league team owner or high-ranking board member gave an executive the stature to speak out on all issues affecting his team. For example, the major league teams were to vote on a four-year agreement between the club owners and the players. August A. Busch, Jr., president of the St. Louis Cardinals, was outspoken that the contract was "being railroaded" and "crammed down his throat." Busch had an ally in A's owner Charlie Finley. Three provisions vexed Busch. The first was the length of time before a player could re-enter the free agent field. The owners wanted seven to eight years, but the players wanted fewer; the players won that point. Next, the players wanted binding salary arbitration; they won this also. Finally, the owners wanted compensation for lost players, and Busch claimed, "We got a crumb, namely draft choices." But Bill DeWitt, speaking for the White Sox and much to the chagrin of the irate Busch and Finley, calmly told his fellow executives that the proposal was "a just and fine contract." "There's no question," he added, "it will be ratified."[27]

In addition to his role as an executive of the Chicago White Sox, Bill DeWitt, took an active role in other baseball-related boards and organizations. One of the most prestigious was his appointment as one of 12 members of the National Baseball Hall of Fame Veterans Committee, serving there from 1973 to 1981. He impressed Ed Stack, former chairman of the Hall of Fame a fellow committee member, who said of DeWitt that he was "very knowledgeable about baseball and business in general…. He was a leader of the flock. A take-charge person."[28]

The Veterans Committee usually met at the Tampa Airport Marriott Hotel once a year in March during Spring Training. Bill Sr. participated in the election of many prominent Hall of Famers, including Jim Bottomley, Billy Herman, Bucky Harris, Fred Lindstrom, Cal Hubbard, Al Lopez, Joe Sewell, Hack Wilson, Chuck Klein, and Johnny Mize.[29] DeWitt was always amused when someone suggested the Veterans Committee was selecting "too many" former St. Louis and New York players. DeWitt usually answered briskly, "I wonder how the hell they figured the Yankees and Cardinals, Dodgers and Giants won so many pennants if they didn't have exceptional players!"[30]

Edward W. Stack was Corporate Secretary of the National Baseball of Fame beginning in 1962. In 1977, he was named chairman of the board and president. Stack only saw Bill DeWitt in Tampa for the yearly meeting, but he remembered him well. "Bill really enjoyed his interaction with all of the baseball related people at the Tampa meetings. He was very knowledgeable about baseball and business in general. As I remember, he was a leader of the flock, a take charge person."[31]

In 1977, Bowie Kuhn selected Bill DeWitt for membership in one of MLB's most powerful committees. He was chosen as one of four additional members to baseball's Executive Council, along with Busch from the Cardinals; Ruly Carpenter, from the Phillies; and Ewing Kaufman, from the Kansas City Royals. They joined Commissioner Kuhn, League presidents Lee MacPhail and Chub Feeney, the Detroit Tigers' John Fetzer, Ed Fitzpatrick of the Milwaukee Brewers, the Montreal Expos' John McHale, and Walter O'Malley of the Los Angeles Dodgers.[32]

In late 1979, Veeck and DeWitt Sr. considered a possible sale of the White Sox to Marvin Davis, an oilman who had been anxious to bring big league baseball to Denver. DeWitt questioned whether the American League would vote to abandon the Chicago market by allowing the White Sox, a 1901 charter member of the League, to move.[33] DeWitt's uncertainty was justified, but the opposition came first from the Sox board of directors, which refused to sell to anyone who would move the team out of Chicago.[34]

The following September, Bill Veeck admitted that he was no longer capable of competing financially in the current baseball community. On August 22, 1980, Veeck announced that he had agreed to sell the team to Edward J. DeBartolo, Sr., for $20 million. DeBartolo was a successful developer of shopping malls in Youngstown, Ohio, as well as several racetracks. His family owned the San Francisco 49ers in the National Football League and the National Hockey League's Pittsburgh Penguins. One of the White Sox board members who voted to accept the DeBartolo bid indicated that he was swayed by his plans to stay in Chicago and to make the team competitive as quickly as possible.[35]

Commissioner Bowie Kuhn was adamant in his opposition to DeBartolo, saying that his ownership of three racetracks in Illinois was a problem. DeBartolo, however, suspected that Kuhn's real reason was his Italian ancestry, a charge which Kuhn claimed was "contemptible, irresponsible, and false."[36] DeWitt defended Veeck's action when he said, "I can't agree on his judgment on a lot of things, but he is a most thoughtful person."[37]

The proposal received only eight of the ten votes needed when the American League met in Chicago to vote on the team's transfer from Veeck to DeBartolo. At the winter meetings in Dallas, the American League again met to discuss DeBartolo's offer to buy the White Sox. It was defeated again, this time by a vote of 11–3, with only Oakland, Cleveland, and the White Sox voting for DeBartolo. Veeck called the action of the American League teams "capricious, ghastly, and unfair. I've never been ashamed to be a member of the American League before—but I am now."[38]

On January 8, 1981, Veeck sold the Chicago White Sox to a local group headed by Jerry Reinsdorf, also a real estate investor, and Eddie Einhorn, a television executive. It was essentially the same offer made by DeBartolo; it allowed Veeck and his partners to exit baseball with a profit. Three weeks later, the American League owners voted unanimously to allow the sale of the team to Reinsdorf and Einhorn, with a signing ceremony at Sears Tower.[39]

DeWitt had spent more than 50 years in baseball, holding administrative positions with seven major league clubs. He was the first to be named Major League Executive of the Year in both the National and the American Leagues, while general manager of the St. Louis Browns in 1944 and the Cincinnati Reds in 1961. He also served as a member of the Veterans Committee for the Hall of Fame.[40]

DeWitt was highly respected by his peers. Bill Veeck noted, "Bill DeWitt forgets more about baseball in a week than most people remember in a lifetime." DeWitt was assistant general manager for the Yankees for three years under George Weiss. Before he died in 1972, Weiss said of him, "Anybody who could hold the Browns together with his expertise and baling wire for all those years had to be the smartest guy in the game."[41]

Branch Rickey had the most influence on DeWitt. After performing a number of perfunctory jobs for him, DeWitt was "adopted" by Rickey, who took him on as his administrative assistant. "It was the greatest break I could have had," said DeWitt. "I learned at the feet of the master. Branch Rickey was the greatest mind baseball has ever known. I just hope some of it rubbed off on me."

Rickey was the one who insisted DeWitt complete his education and even encouraged him to obtain a law degree. Although DeWitt never used the degree in the traditional ways, he admitted later, "I'm sure glad I had it because I needed it to translate all the legal language in the contracts I negotiated."[42]

When DeWitt became more experienced himself, he was always willing to reciprocate the help he had received by mentoring other young men trying to make baseball their livelihood. William "Bill" Bartholomay always credited Bill DeWitt for playing a major role in his baseball career. In 1961, Bartholomay began his first venture in baseball when he and six partners bought a 46 percent share in the Chicago White Sox from Charlie Comiskey.[43]

Bartholomay, however, wanted to be a majority owner, and in November 1962, the 34-year-old led a consortium that purchased the National League Milwaukee Braves from Lou Perini. When the Braves went to Cincinnati to play the Reds, Bartholomay frequently met with Bill DeWitt and his wife Margaret, who was especially fond of him. "I looked forward to having dinner with Bill and Margaret when our team came to Cincinnati."

Although the Braves were very successful in Milwaukee, setting league attendance records, DeWitt had always felt that MLB should have a team from the southeast and that Atlanta was ready. Milwaukee's stadium lease would expire in 1964, and Atlanta banks were prepared to help finance the move. The city had already built Fulton County Stadium, and Atlanta was prepared for "social issues," as they termed integration.[44]

DeWitt introduced Bartholomay to Branch Rickey, who helped serve as an adviser. "But it was DeWitt who really guided me in the move and mentored me as much as Rickey had mentored DeWitt. I was the youngest owner in the majors, and DeWitt was with me every step of the way."[45]

Bill DeWitt underwent surgery for cancer shortly after the White Sox were sold. His daughter Joan came back and stayed with her parents to spend time with her ailing father. She recalled that her father had kept letters, old newspapers, and financial records. He even had a thank-you letter from Stan Musial for arranging room and board with one of the Cardinals' coaches when he first came to St. Louis. DeWitt arranged his files and directed that they should all go to the Browns Hall of Fame. Unfortunately, most of the files were discarded.[46]

One year later, on March 3, 1982, the 79-year-old baseball executive died at his home in Cincinnati. His body was flown back to St. Louis, and funeral services were held for him at the Lupton Chapel. He was buried at Oak Grove Cemetery in St. Louis. Services were also held for him in Cincinnati.[47] Bill DeWitt was survived by his wife, the former Margaret Holekamp, two daughters, Mrs. Donna DeWitt Perkins and Joan DeWitt McKean, and a son William DeWitt, Jr.[48] He was also survived by a legacy of baseball executives who continued his influence into the 21st Century.

Eleven

The DeWitt Legacy

Bill DeWitt, Sr., was one of the most unusual and interesting figures in major league baseball. He never played the game, never coached or managed a major league team, but spent nearly six decades in baseball's front offices, where he handled finances, made trades, scouted and signed ball players, and often assumed the role of head of public relations. At various times, he was an executive with six Major League teams: the St. Louis Cardinals, St. Louis Browns, New York Yankees, Detroit Tigers, Cincinnati Reds, and Chicago White Sox. He had majority ownership in only two of the six, the American League Browns and the National League Reds, but won a pennant with each of them, becoming the first general manager to accomplish that feat.

Because DeWitt Sr. so enjoyed making his living in front-office baseball, he thought his son might follow in his footsteps and began bringing him to work when the boy was quite young. Ten-year-old Bill Jr. was the team's batboy when DeWitt Sr. was an executive with the St. Louis Browns. DeWitt Jr. also recalled that as he was growing up, he was around baseball constantly—at the Browns' games in St. Louis and later in New York, Detroit, and Cincinnati, watching his teams play.

Bill DeWitt, Jr.'s, connection with baseball's various executive jobs continued as he matured. While attending Yale University in the early 1960s, he worked for the Reds in the summer. "I remember my responsibilities," said DeWitt Jr. "I worked closely with the farm department, with which I had a very good relationship. I attended the Free Agent Draft sessions, the analysis of free agents, the future development of our scouting and managerial staff, and the handling of our minor league–affiliated clubs and players."[1] Bill DeWitt, Jr., graduated from Yale in 1963 and then did graduate work at Harvard Business School, receiving his MBA in 1965.

After leaving Harvard, he sold his interest in the Reds, resigned from the team, and moved on to the more traditional business world. He

Eleven. The DeWitt Legacy

worked briefly for a Cincinnati investment firm but left when he saw an opportunity to get back into sports.

Returning on occasion to St. Louis, his native home, DeWitt Jr. saw how the expansion St. Louis Blues had become extremely popular with sellout crowds. Knowing that St. Louis and Cincinnati had similar demographics and were great sports towns, and with the National Hockey League expanding again, the time seemed right to bring Major League hockey to Cincinnati. Joining with Brian Heekin, a close friend, they formed a small group of family members and mutual friends to pursue a franchise.

The NHL required a modern indoor arena, and their application was deferred. They were successful in financing a new Cincinnati Riverfront Coliseum, but contingent upon a hockey franchise, which necessitated a switch to the newly formed World Hockey Association. They also invested in the Kentucky Colonels basketball team to be a tenant in the building. For four years, the Cincinnati Stingers gave the city enjoyable hockey with a number of young exciting players, but the team fell victim to the consolidation of four of the WHA teams into the NHL, and Major League Hockey departed Cincinnati.

DeWitt Jr. took a hiatus from sports to form the investment firm Reynolds, DeWitt and Co. with his good friend Mercer Reynolds. They were 50–50 partners and invested in a variety of enterprises, including soft drink bottling, fast food restaurants, insurance companies, waste management, and other independent businesses. In 1979 they, formed Spectrum 7 Energy Co. which they eventually merged with Bush Exploration, an independent oil company in Midland, Texas, owned and operated by George W. Bush, whose father was vice president of the United States at that time. Bush and DeWitt Jr. had much in common—both were graduates of Yale and Harvard Business School, both their fathers had invested in the oil business, and both men loved baseball.[2]

Through his baseball contacts, DeWitt Jr. heard that owner Eddie Chiles, a long-time friend of the Bush family, was looking for a buyer for his club, the Texas Rangers. Realizing he had the opportunity to return to the major leagues, DeWitt Jr. approached Bush, who was also interested in buying the Rangers.[3] They each searched out investors, and the deal came together with an impressive group led by George Bush and Rusty Rose, both highly regarded Dallas residents.

DeWitt Jr. was excited to be back in baseball, although not in an active operating role. In addition to his friendship with Bush in the oil business, he had been a classmate of Rose at Harvard Business School. Also, Mercer Reynolds, Dudley Taft, and Bob Castellini, close friends in Cincinnati, were part of the group. He certainly enjoyed his years with the Rangers during a period when he was involved full-time with the investment firm of Reynolds, DeWitt. But as time went on he became more interested in heading up a team.[4]

In late 1987, Eli Jacobs was the principal partner in a group that purchased the Baltimore Orioles from the estate of Edward Bennett Williams for $70 million, although they did not get final approval until a few weeks into the 1989 season. For four years, Jacobs was the Orioles' chairman of the board, but in 1993 he lost a great deal of money. Unable to negotiate an out-of-court settlement with his creditors, seven New York banks filed to have Jacobs placed in involuntary bankruptcy. As one of Jacobs' assets, the Orioles were to be auctioned off in court.[5]

Jacobs located a potential buyer for the Orioles, the group led by Bill DeWitt, Jr. Peter Angelos, a wealthy Baltimore attorney, was afraid that the team would be purchased by out-of-state interests. He put together a rival group of Baltimore-based investors which included novelist Tom Clancy, tennis star Pam Shriver, movie director Barry Levinson, and sportscaster Jim McKay.[6]

DeWitt Jr.'s group offered to purchase the team for $141 million, twice Jacobs' original purchase price. DeWitt admitted that he had a soft spot in his heart for the team, which his father had owned when they were the St. Louis Browns. On a more practical level, DeWitt's investment firm was already involved in a variety of businesses, and he wanted to add baseball to the portfolio. "The Orioles have a huge market area and a great new facility," he later said. "We felt it could be very successful at the right price."[7]

It turned out that three groups were ready to bid for the right to purchase the Orioles: Jeffrey Loria, a New York art dealer who owned a minor league team in Oklahoma; Jean Fugett, a Baltimore native, former pro football player, and chairman of TLC Beatrice International Holdings, Inc., the world's largest black-owned business; and an alliance of the Angelos and DeWitt groups, arranged hastily immediately prior to the auction. Angelos was to serve as the group's managing partner.[8]

After a lengthy bidding process, the Angelos-DeWitt group offered a bid of $173 million. Loria, speaking for himself, stood up, looked at Angelos, and said, "I want to congratulate the Baltimore group."[9]

Angelos had had every intention of running the Orioles, but once the sale closed, he installed his own management team, with DeWitt retaining an advisory role. In the spring of 1995, less than a year after he had purchased his shares, DeWitt sold his interest in the team to Angelos for what he had paid.[10]

Yet, DeWitt Jr. left the Orioles with only kind words for Angelos,

Eleven. The DeWitt Legacy

saying, "We didn't get into this to turn a large profit. It was a last-minute arrangement. The way things developed, I didn't have a role from a management standpoint. That was Peter's prerogative. We have an amicable relationship." As to his possible future in baseball ownership, DeWitt stated, "I don't have anything specific in mind, but certainly I have an ongoing interest."[11]

Bill DeWitt, Jr., did not have very long to wait to find the opportunity to return to major league baseball in the role he had wanted for so long. Six months after he left the Orioles, he led an investment group and negotiated with Anheuser-Busch Cos. Inc., the owners of the St. Louis Cardinals. The brewery was selling the team which the late August A. Busch, Jr., had purchased in 1953. For $150 million dollars, DeWitt Jr. and his partners purchased not only the ball club, but also parking garages and the land beneath two nearby hotels. This time, William O. DeWitt, Jr., was the principal owner in the purchase of the Cardinals.[12]

In 1996, the same year Bill DeWitt, Jr., closed the Cardinals deal, a third-generation DeWitt joined the team, becoming head of merchandising. Like his father, William O. DeWitt III had earned an undergraduate degree from Yale and an MBA from Harvard Business School. In 1998, Bill DeWitt III became the team's senior vice president of business development. He led the design and construction of the Cardinals' new ballpark, often called Busch Stadium III, which opened in 2006.

Bill DeWitt, Jr., and his son Bill DeWitt III happily display the Cardinals' 2011 World Series Trophy.

After 10 years as senior VP, in 2008 Bill DeWitt III became president of the team when his predecessor in that role–Mark Lamping—left to join the New York Jets and Giants NFL stadium effort. As president, Bill III became in charge of all aspects of the business, including sales, marketing, finance, and facility and game-day operations. He also became responsible for the team's affiliate relationships with their minor league clubs as well as their TV and radio partners.

Bill III also spearheaded the development of Ballpark Village, a large mixed-use project just beyond the outfield of Busch Stadium III which includes retail, entertainment, residential, office, and hotel properties.[13]

The St. Louis Cardinals under the DeWitts have been one of the most successful teams in professional sports. Much credit has been given to the Cardinals' present owners for running the team in a true professional manner. While the DeWitts are reluctant to talk of the success of their baseball club, they both are quick to give credit to the patriarch of the family—Bill DeWitt, Sr., for how they operate the club. Both DeWitt Jr., and DeWitt III realize that Bill DeWitt, Sr., left a legacy, both tangible and intangible. His son is quick to say, "I think, clearly, I learned my baseball knowledge from him. He was a career baseball executive and, I would say, had no other interests, no real hobbies. Baseball was really his total life. He was totally immersed in it. As a kid growing up, obviously, I was totally immersed in it as well."[14]

De Witt Sr.'s grandson, Bill DeWitt III, summarized his grandfather's life in a more personal manner. "Granddad grew up with very little money in North St. Louis—his father ran a butcher shop. Hard work and talent took him to the top. But to me and my siblings, he was just this loving guy who spent time with us, one on one, and treated us like we were the center of the universe."[15]

Chapter Notes

Chapter One

1. Biographical data, Missouri Historical Society, January 20, 1954.
2. James Neal Primm, *Lion of the Valley* (Boulder, CO: Pruett Publishing, 1981), 345.
3. *The 2018 World Almanac and Book of Facts*, 855.
4. Biographical data, Missouri Historical Society, January 20, 1954.
5. Biographical data, Missouri Historical Society, January 20, 1954.
6. Dwayne Isgrig, "Bill DeWitt," SABR Biography Project, https://sabr.org/bioproj/person/bill-dewitt/.
7. St. Louis City Directory; William Joseph DeWitt Death Certificate, Missouri State Board of Health Bureau of Vital Statistics.
8. Isgrig, "Bill DeWitt."
9. Joan M. Thomas, "Robison Field (St. Louis)," SABR Biography Project, https://sabr.org/bioproj/park/robison-field-st-louis/.
10. Burton A. Boxerman, and Benita W. Boxerman, *Ebbets to Veeck to Busch: Eight Owners Who Shaped Baseball* (Jefferson, NC: McFarland), 55, 58.
11. "St. Louis Browns Franchise History," Baseball-Reference.com, www.baseball-reference.com.; "St. Louis Browns Managers," Baseball Almanac, www.baseball-almanac.com.
12. Joan M. Thomas, "Federal League Park (St. Louis)," SABR Biography Project, https://sabr.org/bioproj/park/federal-league-park-st-louis/.
13. *The Sporting News*, February 11, 1959.
14. Arthur Mann, *Branch Rickey: American In Action* (Boston: Houghton-Mifflin, 1957), 85.
15. Lee Lowenfish, *Branch Rickey: Baseball's Ferocious Gentleman* (Lincoln: University of Nebraska Press, 2007), 84.
16. "Central Intelligence Agency," Wikipedia, www.en.wikipedia.org/wiki/Central_Intelligence_Agency.
17. Andy McCue, "Branch Rickey," SABR Biography Project, https://sabr.org/bioproj/person/branch-rickey/; Gary Gillette and Pete Palmer, *ESPN Baseball Encyclopedia,* 5th ed. (New York: Sterling, 2008), 859.
18. Mann, *Branch Rickey,* 85.
19. Robert H. Boyle, "Cincinnati's Brain Picker," *Sports Illustrated*, June 13, 1966, 4; Murray Polner, *Branch Rickey: A Biography* (New York: Atheneum, 1983), 66; Andy McCue, "Branch Rickey"; Gillette and Palmer, *ESPN Baseball Encyclopedia,* 859.
20. Steve Steinberg, "Robert Hedges," SABR Biography Project, https://sabr.org/bioproj/person/robert-hedges/; Andy McCue, "Branch Rickey."
21. Bill Borst, *Still Last in the American League: The St. Louis Browns Revisited* (West Bloomfield, NJ: Altwerger and Mandel, 1992), 37; Jonathan Fraser Light, *Cultural Encyclopedia of Baseball* (Jefferson, NC: McFarland, 1997), 633.
22. Lowenfish, *Branch Rickey,* 84.
23. "St. Louis Browns (1902–1953)," Sports Encyclopedia, www.sportsencyclopedia.com.
24. Lowenfish, *Branch Rickey,* 86.
25. Rob Rains, *The St. Louis Cardinals: The 100th Anniversary* (New York: St. Martin's Press, 1992), 19–20; Peter Golenbock, *The Spirit of St. Louis: A History of the St. Louis Cardinals and Browns* (New York: Avon, 2000), 82.

26. "Branch Rickey Now Heads Club," *Christian Science Monitor*, March 21, 1917; "How Branch Rickey Escaped Browns, Joined Cardinals," Retrosimba: Cardinals History Beyond the Box Score (website), https://retrosimba.com/2017/03/05/; Charles C. Alexander, *Rogers Hornsby: A Biography* (New York: Henry Holt, 1995), 34.
27. Golenbock, *Spirit of St. Louis*, 77; Greg Erion and Dennis Pajot, "St. Louis Browns Team Ownership History," SABR Team Ownership History Project, https://sabr.org/bioproj/topic/st-louis-browns-team-ownership-history/.

Chapter Two

1. Golenbock, *Spirit of St. Louis*, 77; Greg Erion and Dennis Pajot, "St. Louis Browns Team Ownership History."
2. Gillette and Palmer, *ESPN Baseball Encyclopedia*, 188.
3. Gillette and Palmer, *ESPN Baseball Encyclopedia*, 1696–1697.
4. Lowenfish, *Branch Rickey*, 104.
5. Lowenfish, *Branch Rickey*, 104.
6. Isgrig, "Bill DeWitt," SABR Biography Project, https://sabr.org/bioproj/person/bill-dewitt/; Golenbock, *The Spirit of St. Louis*, 320.
7. "Another National Magnate Enlists," *The Sporting News*, August 29, 1918.
8. McCue, "Branch Rickey."
9. Polner, *Branch Rickey*, 78.
10. Steinberg, *Baseball in St. Louis*, 74.
11. Gillette and Palmer, *ESPN Baseball Encyclopedia*, 184.
12. Bob Broeg, *Bob Broeg's Redbirds: A Century of Cardinals Baseball* (St. Louis: River City Publisher, 23), 1981; Polner, *Branch Rickey*, 1982.
13. Golenbock, *Spirit of St. Louis*, 83.
14. Golenbock, *Spirit of St. Louis*, 83; Rains, *St. Louis Cardinals*, 20.
15. Golenbock, *Spirit of St. Louis*, 83; Broeg, *Bob Broeg's Redbirds*, 24.
16. "Why Branch Rickey Left the Cardinals for Dodgers," Retrosimba.com., October 29, 2017; Polner, *Branch Rickey*, 79; Steinberg, *Baseball in St. Louis*, 91; Lowenfish, *Branch Rickey*, 122.
17. Carson Van Lindt, *One Championship Season: The Story of the 1944 Browns* (New York: Marabou, 1994), 8.
18. Mark Armour, "Sam Breadon," SABR Biography Project, https://sabr.org/bioproj/person/sam-breadon/.
19. Steinberg, *Baseball in St. Louis*, 91.
20. McCue, "Branch Rickey."
21. Polner, *Branch Rickey*, 79; Broeg, *Broeg's Redbirds*, 23–24.
22. Howard Megdal, *The Cardinals Way: How One Team Embraced Tradition and Moneyball at the Same Time* (New York: Thomas Dunne, 2016), 14; Golenbock, *Spirit of St. Louis*, 320.
23. Megdal, *Cardinals Way*, 5; William Marshall, "Interview with William O. 'Bill' DeWitt, Sr.," September 29, 1980, A. B. "Happy" Chandler: Desegregation of Major League Baseball Oral History Project, Louie B. Nunn Center for Oral History, University of Kentucky Libraries, https://kentuckyoralhistory.org/ark:/16417/xt7nzs2k9c74. (Hereafter designated "A. B. Chandler Oral History Project.")
24. "St. Louis Browns," Sports Encyclopedia.
25. "St. Louis Cardinals," Sports Encyclopedia, www.sportsencycopedia.com/nl/st.louiscards.
26. Charles C. Alexander, *Rogers Hornsby: A Biography* (New York: Henry Holt, 1995), 101; Armour, "Sam Breadon"; Alexander, *Our Game*, 146–147; DeWitt Files, Cincinnati Reds Baseball Club, November 1960.
27. Megdal, *Cardinals Way*, 17; Cincinnati Reds Press Release, November 1960; *The Sporting News*, March 19, 1936.
28. DeWitt Files, Cincinnati Reds; Isgrig, "Bill DeWitt."
29. Alexander, *Rogers Hornsby*, 108; Hugh Bradley, "He's Traded Three Million in Talent," *Baseball Digest*, March 1962, 63.
30. Gillette and Palmer, *Baseball Encyclopedia*, 170, 174; 1697.
31. Gillette and Palmer, *Baseball Encyclopedia*, 170.
32. Letter from William O. DeWitt to Weldon, Williams & Lick, October 15, 1926.
33. "1926 World Series," Baseball Almanac, www.baseball-almanac.com; Peter C. Bjarkman, ed, *Encyclopedia of Major League Baseball Team Histories: National League* (Westport: CT, Meckler, 1991), 522–523; John Thorn, Phil Birnbaum, Bill Deane, et al, *Total Baseball:*

The Ultimate Baseball Encyclopedia (Wilmington, DE: Sport Media Publishing, 2004), 356.
34. "St. Louis Cardinals 3, New York Yankees 2," Retrosheet.org, https://www.retrosheet.org/boxesetc/1926/B10100NYA1926.htm.
35. Megdal, *Cardinals Way*, 14.
36. Bradley, "He's Traded Three Million," 64.
37. Bjarkman, *Encyclopedia of Major League Baseball*, 525.
38. "How the Term Gas House Gang Came About," History of Cardinals.com (website), www.historyofcardinals.com.
39. "How the Term Gas House Gang Came About."
40. Bjarkman, *Encyclopedia of Major League Baseball*, 525–526.
41. Bjarkman, *Encyclopedia of Major League Baseball*, 526; Thorn et al, *Total Baseball*, 364.
42. J. Roy Stockton, *The Gashouse Gang and a Couple of Other Guys* (New York: A.S. Barnes, 1945), 35–36.
43. Mann, *Branch Rickey*, 182; Isgrig, "Bill DeWitt."
44. Vince Staten, *Ol Diz: A Biography of Dizzy Dean* (New York: HarperCollins, 1992), 157.
45. David Pietrusza, *Judge and Jury: The Life and Times of Judge Kenesaw Mountain Landis* (South Bend, IN: Diamond, 1998), 380; Frederick G. Lieb, *The St. Louis Cardinals: The Story of a Great Baseball Club* (Carbondale: Southern Illinois University Press, 2001), 184; *Hagerstown (MD) Daily Mail*, December 23, 1934; *Titusville (PA) Herald*, November 23, 1934; *St. Louis Post-Dispatch*, August 14, 1939.

Chapter Three

1. *Burlington (NC) Daily Times*, December 14, 1935.
2. Authors' Interview of Joan DeWitt McKean, May 4, 2018.
3. Interview of Joan DeWitt McKean.
4. Walter Barlow Stevens, *Centennial History of Missouri*, vol. 11 (St. Louis: S.J. Clarke, 1921): 389–390.
5. *St. Louis Post-Dispatch*, May 2, 1922.
6. *St. Louis Globe-Democrat*, May 5, 1922.
7. *St. Louis Post-Dispatch*, February 15, 1990.
8. Authors' Interview of William Francis "Bill" Holekamp, September 17, 2018; phone interview of Malcolm "Mac" Holekamp, September 21, 2018.
9. *The Sporting News*, April 9, 1936; *St. Louis Post-Dispatch*, April 1, 1936; Lowenfish, *Branch Rickey*, 270.
10. William B. Mead, *Even the Browns: Baseball During World War II* (Mineola, NY: Dover), 56.
11. Frederick G. Lieb, *The Baltimore Orioles: The History of a Colorful Team in Baltimore and St. Louis* (New York: G. P. Putnam's Sons), 202.
12. Borst, *Still Last in the American League*, 56.
13. Mead, *Even the Browns*, 56.
14. Authors' Interview of Trent Barnes Phelps, Summer 2017.
15. *The Sporting News*, August 14, 1962.
16. Borst, *Still Last in the American League*, 59.
17. Lieb, *The Baltimore Orioles*, 202, 217.
18. Borst, *Still Last in the American League*, 29; James Edward Miller, *The Baseball Business: Pursuing Pennants and Profits in Baltimore* (Chapel Hill: University of North Carolina Press, 1990); Interview of William O. DeWitt, Sr., September 29, 1980; Marshall, Interview of DeWitt, A. B. Chandler Oral History Project.
19. Mead, *Even the Browns*, 57.
20. Golenbock, *Spirit of St. Louis*, 321; Mead, *Even the Browns*, 57; Miller, *Baseball Business*, 23.
21. Donald Dewey and Nicholas Acocella, *The Ball Clubs* (New York: Harper Perennial, 1993), 519.
22. *St. Louis Post-Dispatch*, March 12, 1953.
23. *St. Louis Post-Dispatch*, November 12, 1936.
24. *St. Louis Post-Dispatch*, November 20, 1936.
25. *The Sporting News*, May 30, 1940.
26. Jim McConnell, *Bobo Newsom: Baseball's Traveling Man* (Jefferson, NC: McFarland, 2016), 53; Lieb, *Baltimore Orioles*, 203.
27. Biographical Data, Missouri Historical Society, January 20, 1954.
28. *St. Louis Post-Dispatch*, November 2, 1936; Alexander, *Rogers Hornsby*, 208;

Notes—Chapter Three

"Browns to Barnes," *Time,* November 23, 1936, 49.

29. *Zanesville (OH) Signal,* December 29, 1936; *Jefferson City (MO) Post Tribune,* December 23, 1936; *Moberly (MO) Monitor; Monroe (LA) News Star,* December 30, 1936.

30. Gillette and Palmer, *ESPN Baseball Encyclopedia,* 157.

31. "1936 St. Louis Browns," Baseball-Reference.com, baseball-reference.com/1936/teams/SLB/1936.

32. *St. Louis Post-Dispatch,* November 11, 1936; *Galveston (TX) Daily News,* November 16, 1936.

33. Miller, *Baseball Business,* 23.

34. Alexander, *Rogers Hornsby,* 209.

35. *Laredo (TX) Times,* November 24, 1936; *San Antonio (TX) Light,* December 9, 1936; *St. Louis Post-Dispatch* January 7, 1937.

36. *Hutchinson (KS) News,* December 12, 1936.

37. *St. Louis Post-Dispatch,* January 18, 1937; *St. Louis Post-Dispatch,* December 21, 1936; *St. Louis Post-Dispatch,* January 7, 1937.

38. *St. Louis Post-Dispatch,* January 18, 1937; *San Antonio (TX) Light,* January 12, 1937.

39. *St. Louis Post-Dispatch,* January 17, 1937.

40. *St. Louis Post-Dispatch,* January 17, 1937.

41. *Brookfield Lynn County (MO) Budget Gazette,* July 22, 1937.

42. *St. Louis Post-Dispatch,* January 1, 1937.

43. *St. Louis Post-Dispatch,* January 10, 1937; Gillette and Palmer, *ESPN Baseball Encyclopedia,* 1331.

44. *Jefferson City (MO) Capital News,* February 11, 1937; Gillette and Palmer, *ESPN Baseball Encyclopedia,* 1278.

45. *San Antonio (TX) Light,* December 9, 1936.

46. Dewey and Acocella, *Ball Clubs,* 519.

47. Pietrusza, *Judge and Jury,* 320.

48. *Gastonia (NC) Daily Gazette,* July 22, 1937; *St. Louis Post-Dispatch,* July 24, 1937.

49. *Monroe (LA) News,* July 10, 1938; *Lincoln (NE) State Journal,* July 10, 1938; *Helena (MT) Independent Record,* July 10, 1938.

50. "St. Louis Browns Managers (1902–1953)," Baseball Almanac.

51. *The Sporting News,* September 30, 1937.

52. Gillette and Palmer, *ESPN Baseball Encyclopedia,* 148.

53. Bill Johnson, "Jim Bottomley," SABR Biography Project, https://sabr.org/bioproj/person/jim-bottomley/.

54. Joseph Wancho, "Gabby Street," SABR Biography Project, https://sabr.org/bioproj/person/gabby-street/; *The Sporting News,* November 4, 1937; *Janesville (WI) Daily Gazette;* November 5, 1937; *St. Louis Post-Dispatch,* November 19, 1937.

55. *St. Louis Post-Dispatch,* November 23, 1937.

56. *St. Louis Post-Dispatch,* December 7, 1937.

57. *The Sporting News,* December 16, 1937.

58. *San Antonio (TX) Light,* March 6, 1938; *The Sporting News,* March 10, 1938.

59. *The Sporting News,* January 16, 1938.

60. *The Sporting News,* January 16, 1938.

61. *Laredo (TX) Times,* March 11, 1938.

62. McConnell, *Bobo Newsom,* 86.

63. *Logansport (IN) Tribune,* March 30, 1938; *Racine (WI) Journal Times,* March 30, 1938.

64. *St. Louis Post-Dispatch,* June 18, 1938.

65. Gillette and Palmer, *ESPN Baseball Encyclopedia,* 147.

66. Gillette and Palmer, *ESPN Baseball Encyclopedia,* 1701, 147.

67. *St. Louis Post-Dispatch,* October 2, 1938.

68. *The Sporting News,* October 20, 1938.

69. *St. Louis Post-Dispatch,* October 26, 1938; *New Castle (PA) News,* October 26, 1938; *Hammond (IN) Times.* October 26, 1938.

70. *St. Louis Post-Dispatch,* November 1, 1938.

71. *St. Louis Post-Dispatch,* November 2, 1938.

72. *St. Louis Post-Dispatch,* November 6, 1938.

73. McConnell, *Bobo Newsom,* 92.

74. *St. Louis Post-Dispatch,* November 10, 1938.

Notes—Chapter Three

75. *Gastonia (NC) Daily Gazette,* January 9, 1939.
76. *St. Louis Post-Dispatch,* January 13, 1939.
77. *Ironwood (MI) Daily Globe,* January 13, 1939.
78. *Lincoln (NE) State Journal,* February 3, 1939.
79. *Manetowac (MI) Herald Times,* March 8, 1939; *Hammond (IN) Times,* March 15, 1939; *Moorhead (MN) Daily News,* March 15, 1939; *San Mateo (CA) Times,* March 15, 1939.
80. *Brainard (MN) Dispatch,* March 8, 1939.
81. *New York Times,* January 7, 1939; *Jefferson City (MO) Capital News,* January 7, 1939; *Joplin (MO) Globe,* January 8, 1939; *Brainard (MN) Daily Dispatch,* January 7, 1939.
82. McConnell, *Bobo Newsom,* 93; Gillette and Palmer, *ESPN Baseball Encyclopedia,* 736.
83. McConnell, *Bobo Newsom,* 94.
84. *The Sporting News,* April 6, 1939.
85. *The Sporting News,* May 18, 1939.
86. *The Sporting News,* June 8, 1939; *St. Louis Post-Dispatch,* June 12, 1939.
87. *The Sporting News,* June 15, 1934.
88. Biographical Data, Missouri Historical Society, 1954; *The Sporting News,* June 29, 1939; Authors' interview of Joan DeWitt McKean.
89. *St. Louis Post-Dispatch,* July 13, 1939.
90. *St. Louis Post-Dispatch,* July 13, 1939; Scribbled by Scribes (department), *The Sporting News,* July 27, 1939.
91. *Appleton (WI) Crescent,* August 3, 1939; *Kingsport (TN) Times,* August 2, 1939; *North Adams (MA) Transport,* August 2, 1939.
92. "1939 St. Louis Browns Season," Sports Encyclopedia.org, www.sportsencyclopedia.org.
93. *St. Louis Post-Dispatch,* September 14, 1939.
94. *The Sporting News,* September 9, 1939.
95. *The Sporting News,* October 19, 1939.
96. *The Sporting News* November 2, 1939.
97. *The Sporting News* November 2, 1939.
98. Dewey and Acocella, *Ball Clubs,* 319.
99. *St. Louis Post-Dispatch,* January 27, 1940.
100. *St. Louis Post-Dispatch,* January 27, 1940.
101. *The Sporting News,* February 25, 1940; *The Sporting News,* November 2, 1939.
102. Gillette and Palmer, *ESPN Baseball Encyclopedia,* 630; Dewey and Acocella, *Ball Clubs,* 519; Mead, *Even the Browns,* 65–66.
103. Mead, *Even the Browns,* 65–66.
104. *The Sporting News,* February 15, 1940.
105. *The Sporting News,* February 15, 1940.
106. *The Sporting News,* May 30, 1940.
107. Dewey and Acocella, *Ball Clubs,* 519; Erion and Pajot, "St. Louis Browns Team Ownership History"; Mead, *Even the Browns,* 66.
108. *St. Louis Post-Dispatch,* March 16, 1940.
109. *St. Louis Post-Dispatch,* March 6, 1940.
110. *Beckley (WV) Register,* June 27, 1940.
111. *Joplin (MO) Herald,* July 4, 1940.
112. *Amarillo (TX) Sunday News Globe,* July 5, 1940; *Panama City (FL) News Herald,* July 6, 1940; *Helena (MT) Independent Record,* July 10, 1940.
113. Gillette and Palmer, *ESPN Baseball Encyclopedia,* 143.
114. *The Sporting News,* September 19, 1940.
115. *Brookfield (MO) Argus,* October 1, 1940.
116. *Joplin (MO) Globe,* December 4, 1940.
117. *St. Louis Post-Dispatch,* January 6, 1941; *The Sporting News,* January 9, 1941.
118. *St. Louis Post-Dispatch,* January 15, 1941.
119. *Twin Falls (ID) News,* January 19, 1941; *Joplin (MO) News Herald,* January 21, 1941.
120. *St. Louis Post-Dispatch,* January 26, 1941.
121. *St. Louis Post-Dispatch,* March 8, 1941; *The Sporting News,* March 20, 1941.
122. *St. Louis Post-Dispatch,* January 26, 1941.
123. *St. Louis Post-Dispatch,* March 14, 1941.
124. "1941 St. Louis Browns Roster,"

Baseball-Reference.com, https://www.baseball-reference.com/teams/SLB/1941-roster.shtml.
  125. *St. Louis Post-Dispatch*, May 18, 1941.
  126. Joseph Wancho, "Luke Sewell," SABR Biography Project, https://sabr.org/bioproj/person/luke-sewell/; *St. Louis Post-Dispatch*, June 5, 1941.
  127. *The Sporting News*, June 12, 1941.
  128. *The Sporting News*, August 14, 1941.
  129. Biographical Data, Missouri Historical Society; Authors' Interview of Joan DeWitt McKean.
  130. Dewey and Acocella, *Ball Clubs*, 519.
  131. Mead, *Even the Browns*, 34.
  132. Miller, *Baseball Business*, 23; Marshall, "Interview of Bill DeWitt," A. B. Chandler Oral History Project.
  133. Mead, *Even the Browns*, 33–34; Erion and Pajot, "St. Louis Browns Team Ownership History"; Dewey and Acocella, *Ball Clubs*, 519–520.
  134. Erion and Pajot, "St. Louis Browns Team Ownership History."
  135. Miller, *Baseball Business*, 23; Golenbock, *Spirit of St. Louis*, 281.

Chapter Four

  1. "World War I," Baseball-Reference.com, https://www.baseball-reference.com/bullpen/World_War_I.
  2. William B. Mead, *Even the Browns: Baseball During World War II* (Mineola, NY: Dover, 1982), 37; "President Franklin Delano Roosevelt Green Light Letter," www.baseball-almanac.com.
  3. *St. Louis Post-Dispatch*, January 27, 1942.
  4. *Post-Dispatch Ibid.*; *The Sporting News*, January 29, 1942.
  5. Carson Van Lindt, *One Championship Season* (New York: Marabou, 1944), 26; *The Sporting News*, February 19, 1942; *St. Louis Post-Dispatch*, March 4, 1942; *The Sporting News*, March 12, 1942; Greg Erion and Dennis Pajot, "St. Louis Browns Team Ownership History," SABR Team Ownership History Project,] https://sabr.org/bioproj/topic/st-louis-browns-team-ownership-history/.
  6. Authors' Interview of Margo Hieldo, January 31, 2019.
  7. *St. Louis Post-Dispatch*, March 5, 1942.
  8. *St. Louis Post-Dispatch*, March 8, 1942; *Joplin (MO) News Herald*, March 10, 1942.
  9. *St. Louis Post-Dispatch*, March 31, 1942; *The Sporting News*, April 2, 1942.
  10. *The Sporting News*, August 6, 1942.
  11. *The Sporting News*, April 14, 1942.
  12. *The Sporting News*, April 16, 1942.
  13. Dewey and Acocella, *Ball Clubs*, 319.
  14. Dewey and Acocella, *Ball Clubs*, 520.
  15. *The Sporting News*, July 30, 1942; Erion and Pajot, "St. Louis Browns Team Ownership History."
  16. *St. Louis Post-Dispatch*, August 7, 1942; *The Sporting News*, August 20, 1942.
  17. *The Sporting News*, October 8, 1942.
  18. *The Sporting News*, October 22, 1942.
  19. *The Sporting News*, October 15, 1942.
  20. *The Sporting News*, November 5, 1942; *Salt Lake Tribune*, November 26, 1942; *New York Times*, November 26, 1926.
  21. *The Sporting News*, November 26, 1942.
  22. *The Sporting News*, January 8, 1943.
  23. *The Sporting News*, January 14, 1943.
  24. Lieb, *Baltimore Orioles*, 205.
  25. Lowenfish, *Branch Rickey*, 318.
  26. *St. Louis Post-Dispatch*, February 28, 1953.
  27. *St. Louis Post-Dispatch*, December 8, 1942.
  28. Gillette and Palmer, *ESPN Baseball Encyclopedia*, 655.
  29. Erion and Pajot, "St. Louis Browns Team Ownership History."
  30. *Lubbock (TX) Morning Avalanche*, February 2, 1943; *Twin Falls (ID) Times News*, February 2, 1943.
  31. *Salt Lake City Tribune*, March 17, 1943.
  32. *Lincoln (NE) State Journal*, March 29, 1943.
  33. Bill Gilbert, *They Also Served: Baseball and the Home Front, 1941–1945* (New York: Crown, 1992), 116.
  34. *Moberly (MO) Monitor and Democrat*, June 2, 1943.

Notes—Chapter Four

35. *Brainerd (MN) Dispatch,* June 15, 1943.
36. Gillette and Palmer, *ESPN Baseball Encyclopedia,* 1171; *New Castle (PA) News,* June 18, 1943.
37. *St. Louis Post-Dispatch,* June 29, 1943.
38. *St. Louis Post-Dispatch,* July 20, 1943.
39. *St. Louis Post-Dispatch,* August 19, 1943.
40. Gillette and Palmer, *ESPN Baseball Encyclopedia,* 1425; *St. Louis Post-Dispatch,* August 31, 1943; *New Castle (PA) News,* September 1, 1943; Jim McConnell, *Bobo Newsom: Baseball's Traveling Man* (Jefferson, NC: McFarland, 2016), 157–159.
41. *St. Louis Post-Dispatch,* October 31, 1943.
42. *St. Louis Post-Dispatch,* December 4, 1943.
43. *The Sporting News,* December 9, 1943.
44. *The Sporting News,* December 23, 1943.
45. *The Sporting News,* December 23, 1943.
46. *The Sporting News,* December 23, 1943.
47. *The Sporting News,* December 30, 1943.
48. *St. Louis Post-Dispatch,* January 23, 1944; Gilbert, *They Also Served,* 126.
49. Gilbert, *They Also Served,* 126.
50. Gilbert, *They Also Served.*
51. Richard Goldstein, *Spartan Season: How Baseball Survived the Second World War* (New York: Macmillan, 1980), 186.
52. Gilbert, *They Also Served,* 137.
53. Lieb, *Baltimore Orioles,* 206.
54. John Heidenry and Brett Topel, *The Boys Who Were Left Behind* (Lincoln: University of Nebraska Press, 2006), 43.
55. Heidenry and Topel, *Boys Who Were Left Behind,* 43.
56. *St. Louis Post-Dispatch,* February 9, 1944.
57. *St. Louis Post-Dispatch* February 9, 1944.
58. Heidenry and Topel, *Boys Who Were Left Behind,* 43.
59. *St. Louis Post-Dispatch,* March 1, 1944.
60. *The Sporting News,* March 2, 1944.
61. Borst, *Still Last in the American League,* 68.
62. Gillette and Palmer, *ESPN Baseball Encyclopedia,* 942–943; Borst, *Still Last in the American League,* 69–70; *The Sporting News,* June 8, 1944.
63. *St. Louis Post-Dispatch,* August 18, 1944.
64. Bill Borst, *The Best of Seasons: The 1944 St. Louis Cardinals and St. Louis Browns* (Jefferson, NC: McFarland,1995), 116.
65. Borst, *The Best of Seasons,* 135–136.
66. *St. Louis Post-Dispatch,* October 15, 1944.
67. Lieb, *Baltimore Orioles,* 206–207; Joseph Wancho, "Luke Sewell."; Dewey and Acocella, *Ball Clubs,* 520; Miller, *Baseball Business,* 23.
68. Miller, *Baseball Business,* 23.
69. Gillette and Palmer, *ESPN Baseball Encyclopedia,* 134.
70. Borst, *Still Last in the American League,* 73–74.
71. John Thorn, et al, *Total Baseball,* 374.
72. Borst, *Still Last in the American League,* 74.
73. Thorn et al, *Total Baseball,* 374.
74. Thorn et al, *Total Baseball,* 374.
75. William Marshall, *Baseball's Pivotal Era 1945–1951* (Lexington: University of Kentucky Press, 1999), 16.
76. *St. Louis Post-Dispatch,* December 27, 1944.
77. *The Sporting News,* December 28, 1944.
78. *Bluefield (WV) Daily Telegraph,* July 6, 1944; *Biloxi (MS) Daily Herald,* July 6, 1944.
79. *Lincoln (NE) State Journal,* January 8, 1945.
80. *Lincoln (NE) State Journal,* January 8, 1945.; *Salt Lake Tribune,* January 8, 1945; *Kingsport (TN) News,* January 8, 1945.
81. *St. Louis Post-Dispatch,* January 17, 1945.
82. *St. Louis Post-Dispatch,* February 25, 1945.
83. William C. Kashatus, *One-Armed Wonder: Pete Gray, Wartime Baseball, and the American Dream* (Jefferson, NC: McFarland, 1995), 90–91.
84. *Joplin (MO) Globe,* March 9, 1945.

85. *Jefferson City (MO) Sunday News & Tribune*, March 18, 1945; *St. Louis Post-Dispatch*, March 21, 1945; *Jefferson City (MO) Daily Capital News*, March 22, 1945.
86. *St. Louis Post-Dispatch*, March 14, 1945.
87. *Moorhead (MN) Daily News*, April 13, 1945.
88. Baseball-Reference, baseball-reference.com/players.
89. *St. Louis Post-Dispatch*, March 14, 1945, 16.
90. Kashatus, *One-Armed Wonder*, 90–91.
91. Kashatus, *One-Armed Wonder*, 116.
92. *St. Louis Post-Dispatch*, August 10, 1945; Marshall, DeWitt, Sr., interview, A.B. "Happy" Chandler Oral History Collection.
93. Kashatus, *One-Armed Wonder*, 115.

Chapter Five

1. Lieb, *Baltimore Orioles*, 209; Marshall, DeWitt, Sr., interview, A.B. "Happy" Chandler Oral History Collection.
2. Borst, *Still Last in the American League*, 79.
3. *St. Louis Post-Dispatch*, August 10, 1945.
4. Kashatus, *One-Armed Wonder*, 116.
5. "1945 St. Louis Browns Season," Baseball Almanac, https://www.baseball-almanac.com/teamstats/schedule.php?y=1945&t=SLA.
6. *St. Louis Post-Dispatch*, August 10, 1945.
7. *Zanesville (OH) Signal*, September 8, 1945.
8. *New York Times*, October 17, 1945; *Kingsport (TN) News*, October 17, 1945.
9. *Nevada State Journal (Reno)*, October 28, 1945.
10. *Moberly (MO) Monitor Index*, November 20, 1945; *Joplin (MO) Globe*, November 21, 1945; *The Sporting News*, November 22, 1945; Kashatus, *One-Armed Wonder*, 122.
11. Lowenfish, *Branch Rickey*, 385.
12. Lowenfish, *Branch Rickey*, 386.
13. Lowenfish, *Branch Rickey*, 386–387.
14. *The Sporting News*, December 28, 1945.
15. *New York Times*, January 6, 1946; *Montana Standard (Butte)*, January 6, 1946; *Lincoln (NE) State Journal*, January 6, 1956; *Kingsport (TN) News*, January 6, 1946.
16. *Jefferson City (MO) Daily News*, January 22, 1946.
17. *The Sporting News*, February 14, 1946.
18. *New York Times*, January 31, 1946.
19. *New York Times*, February 11, 1946.
20. *St. Louis Post-Dispatch*, February 9, 1946; *Jefferson City (MO) News and Tribune*, February 14, 1946.
21. *The Sporting News*, February 14, 1946.
22. *Lincoln (NE) State Journal*, February 10, 1946.
23. *St. Louis Post-Dispatch*, February 25, 1946.
24. *St. Louis Post-Dispatch*, March 6, 1946.
25. *Ironwood (MI) Daily Globe*, March 12, 1946.
26. *St. Louis Post-Dispatch*, March 27, 1946.
27. *St. Louis Post-Dispatch*, March 30, 1946; *Kalispell (MT) Inter Lake*, March 30, 1946.
28. *Jefferson City (M0) News and Tribune*, March 31, 1946.
29. *San Antonio (TX) Light*, April 1, 1946.
30. *Thomasville (GA) Times Enterprise*, April 6, 1946; *New York Times*, April 6, 1946.
31. *Billings (MT) Gazette*, April 7, 1946.
32. *St. Louis Post-Dispatch*, March 5, 1946.
33. *St. Louis Post-Dispatch*, March 19, 1946.
34. *St. Louis Post-Dispatch*, March 19, 1946.
35. *Jefferson City (MO) News and Tribune*, March 31, 1946.
36. *Charleston (WV) Daily March*, March 31, 1946; *New York Times*, April 1, 1946.
37. *Nevada State Journal (Reno,)* April 20, 1946.
38. *St. Louis Post-Dispatch*, April 1, 1946.
39. *St. Louis Post-Dispatch*, April 13, 1946.
40. *The Sporting News*, June 12, 1946.
41. *The Sporting News*, June 26, 1946.
42. *The Sporting News*, July 1, 1946.

43. *St. Louis Post-Dispatch*, July 1, 1946.
44. "St. Louis Browns Managers (1902–1953)."
45. *The Sporting News*, September 11, 1946.
46. Borst, *Still Last in the American League*, 81.
47. Lieb, *Baltimore Orioles*, 209.
48. *The Sporting News*, September 11, 1946.
49. *The Sporting News*, September 11, 1946.
50. *New York Times*, September 22, 1946; *St. Louis Star Times*, September 21, 1946.
51. "St. Louis Browns Managers (1902–1953)."
52. *St. Louis Post-Dispatch*, October 9, 1946; *San Antonio Light*, October 9, 1946; *The Sporting News*, October 16, 1946, October 30, 1946.
53. Sid Keener, "Park Improvements Here and San Antonio Pinched Club by Far Exceeding Budget Costs," *St. Louis Star and Times*, November 21, 1947, 34, quoted in Denis Pajot and Greg Erion, "St. Louis Browns Team Ownership History."
54. *Hagerstown (MD) Daily Mail*, December 10, 1947; *The Sporting News*, November 21, 1947; *St. Louis Post-Dispatch*, November 3, 1946.
55. *St. Louis Post-Dispatch*, January 19, 1947.
56. *St. Louis Post-Dispatch*, January 16, 1947; *Portland (ME) Press Herald*, January 16, 1947.
57. *St. Louis Post-Dispatch*, January 14, 1947, January 27, 1947.
58. *St. Louis Post-Dispatch*, February 2, 1947.
59. *The Sporting News*, April 16, 1947; *Joplin (MO) Globe*, February 16, 1947.
60. *The Sporting News*, February 5, 1947; *St. Louis Post-Dispatch*, January 28, 1947.
61. *The Sporting News*, February 5, 1947.
62. *Moberly (MO) Monitor Index*, March 24, 1947; *Joplin News Herald*, March 24, 1947; *Zanesville (OH) Signature*, March 24, 1947.
63. *St. Louis Post-Dispatch*, March 24, 1947.
64. *St. Louis Post-Dispatch*, March 24, 1947.
65. *Butte (MT) Standard*, May 31, 1947.
66. *St. Louis Post-Dispatch*, May 31, 1947.
67. Lowenfish, *Branch Rickey*, 433.
68. Arnold Rampersad, *Jackie Robinson* (New York: Alfred A. Knopf, 1997), 183.
69. Colin McBride, "The Kansas City Monarchs (1920–1965)," Black Past (website), www.blackpast.org/african-american-history/kansas-city-monarchs.
70. Marshall, *Baseball's Pivotal Era*, 147.
71. Lowenfish, *Branch Rickey*, 64; Gillette and Palmer, *ESPN Baseball Encyclopedia*, 354; Jonathan Fraser Light, *Cultural Encyclopedia of Baseball* (Jefferson, NC: McFarland, 1997), 378.
72. Rick Swaine, *The Integration of Major League Baseball* (Jefferson, NC: McFarland, 2009), 65.
73. Swaine, *The Integration of Major League Baseball*, 65.
74. *Billings (MT) Gazette*, July 26, 1947.
75. *The Sporting News*, July 30, 1947.
76. *The Sporting News*, August 6, 1947.
77. *The Sporting News*, August 27, 1947.
78. "St. Louis Browns Managers (1902–1953)."
79. Gillette and Palmer, *ESPN Baseball Encyclopedia*, 129.
80. Borst, *Still Last In the American League*, 81–82.
81. *St. Louis Star and Times*, November 5, 1947; *The Sporting News*, November 4, 1947.
82. *New York Times*, November 6, 1957.
83. *The Sporting News*, November 12, 1947.
84. *New Castle (PA) News*, November 12, 1947.
85. Sid C. Keener, "Ex-Vendors Show Millionaires How to Operate," *The Sporting News*, September 5, 1951, 15.
86. *Monroe (LA), Morning World*, November 18, 1947; *Charleston (WV); New York Times*, November 18, 1947; Dewey and Acocella, *Ball Clubs*, 521; and Retrosheet.org, https://www.retrosheet.org/boxesetc/1947/11171947.htm.
87. *New York Times*, November 18, 1947.
88. *The Sporting News*, November 26, 1947; *St. Louis Post-Dispatch*, November 18, 1947.
89. *The Sporting News*, December 10, 1947.

90. With the exception of the Heath sale, the details of which come from page 15 of the September 5, 1951, issue of *The Sporting News*, all trade details from Retrosheet.org.
91. Lieb, *Baltimore Orioles*, 211; Borst, *Still Last in the American League*, 82; Ray Gillespie, "Rickey Office Boy Out-Harums Old Boss," *The Sporting News*, December 22, 1948, 6.
92. *New York Times*, December 2, 1947.
93. *St. Louis Post-Dispatch,* January 8, 1948.
94. *St. Louis Post-Dispatch,* January 20, 1948.
95. *The Sporting News,* January 21, 1948.
96. *The Sporting News,* February 11, 1948.
97. *The Sporting News,* February 11, 1948.
98. *The Sporting News,* February 11, 1948.
99. *St. Louis Post-Dispatch,* March 25, 1948.
100. *San Antonio (TX) Light,* March 31, 1948.
101. *The Sporting News,* April 7, 1948.
102. *St. Louis Post-Dispatch,* May 19, 1948.
103. *San Mateo (CA) Times,* June 25, 1948; *Lawton (OK) Constitution,* June 25, 1948.
104. *St. Louis Star-Times,* June 24, 1948.
105. *St. Louis Star-Times,* June 25, 1948.
106. *St. Louis Post-Dispatch,* June 27, 1948.
107. *The Sporting News,* July 7, 1948.
108. *The Sporting News,* July 7, 1948.
109. *The Sporting News,* August 11, 1948.
110. *Walla Walla (WA) Union Bulletin,* September 17, 1948.
111. *St. Louis Post-Dispatch,* September 19, 1948.
112. Isgrig, "Bill DeWitt."
113. *St. Louis Post-Dispatch,* December 13, 1948.
114. *New York Times,* December 14, 1948; *St. Louis Post-Dispatch,* December 14, 1948.
115. *St. Louis Post-Dispatch,* December 14, 1948.

Chapter Six

1. Borst, *Still Last in the American League*, 84.
2. *New York Times,* February 3, 1949; *The Sporting News,* February 9, 1949.
3. *St. Louis Star-Times,* April 19, 1949.
4. *San Antonio (TX) Express,* February 19, 1950; *Lowell (MA) Sun,* February 19, 1950.
5. "About Us," DeWitt Insurance, www.dewittins.com/about-us/index.html.
6. Borst, *Still Last in the American League*, 85.
7. *St. Louis Post-Dispatch,* February 17, 1949.
8. Robert A. Godin, *The 1922 St. Louis Browns: Best of the American League's Worst* (Jefferson: NC: McFarland, 1991), 205.
9. Godin, *1922 St. Louis Browns,* March 2, 1949.
10. "A Salute to William 'Bill' DeWitt," Knights of the Cauliflower Ear program, April 18, 1949.
11. "Zarilla Goes to Red Sox," *Kansas City Times,* May 6, 1949; *San Antonio (TX) Light,* May 6, 1949.
12. "Zarilla, Taylor Disagree on Reasons Browns Flop," *Boston Globe,* May 12, 1949.
13. *The Sporting News,* August 17, 1949, 14.
14. Bob Broeg and William J. Miller, Jr., *Baseball from a Different Angle* (South Bend, IN: Diamond Communications, 1949), 97; *The Sporting News,* August 19, 1949.
15. *St. Louis Post-Dispatch,* August 14, 1949.
16. *St. Louis Post-Dispatch,* August 14, 1949.
17. *St. Louis Post-Dispatch,* August 22, 1949; *Portland (ME) Press Herald,* August 23, 1949.
18. *St. Louis Post-Dispatch,* August 24, 1949.
19. *The Sporting News,* August 31, 1949.
20. Gillette and Palmer, *ESPN Baseball Encyclopedia,* 125.
21. "1949 St. Louis Browns," Baseball-Reference.com, https://www.baseball-reference.com/teams/SLB/1949.shtml.
22. *The World Almanac and Book of Facts 2020,* World Almanac Books, 925.
23. Gillette and Palmer, *ESPN Baseball Encyclopedia,* 305.
24. Borst, *Still Last in the American League*, 88.

25. DeWitt to Norman Handel, July 29, 1949.
26. DeWitt to Handel, October 21, 1959.
27. *New York Times*, October 28, 1949; *Jacksonville (IL) Courier*, October 28, 1949; *Neosho (MO) Daily Democrat*, October 28, 1949; *Moberly (MO) Index*, October 28, 1949.
28. *Joplin (MO) Globe*, November 16, 1949; *Centralia (IL) Evening Sentinel*, November 16, 1949; *Bismarck (ND) Tribune*, November 16, 1949.
29. *New York Times*, December 14, 1949; *St. Louis Post-Dispatch*, December 14, 1949.
30. *Nashua (NH) Telegraph*, December 14, 1949; *Wichita (TX) Daily Times*, December 14, 1949; *Lowell (MA) Sun*, December 14, 1949.
31. *New York Times*, December 15, 1949.
32. *New York Times*, December 15, 1949.
33. *The Sporting News*, December 21, 1949; Miller, *The Baseball Business*, 24.
34. Mitchell Nathanson, *A People's History of Baseball* (Urbana: University of Illinois Press, 2012), 130–131.
35. Borst, *Still Last in the American League*, 89–90.
36. *The Sporting News*, January 11, 1950.
37. *Newport (RI) News*, February 14, 1950.
38. *St. Louis Post-Dispatch*, February 17, 1950.
39. *San Antonio (TX) Express*, February 19, 1950; *Lowell (MA) Sun*, February 19, 1950.
40. *St. Louis Post-Dispatch*, February 21, 1950.
41. *Ada (OK) Evening News*, March 13, 1950; *Lowell (MA) Sun*, March 13, 1950.
42. *St. Louis Post-Dispatch*, March 17, 1950.
43. *St. Louis Post-Dispatch*, March 17, 1950.
44. *St. Louis Post-Dispatch*, April 14, 1950.
45. *Hutchinson (KS) News*, April 16, 1950; *New York Times*, April 16, 1950.
46. *Montana Standard (Butte)*, December 20, 1949.
47. *Albert Lea (MN) Evening Tribune*, December 20, 1949; *Moberly (MO) Monitor Index*, December 19, 1949.
48. *The Sporting News*, January 18, 1950.
49. Borst, *Still Last in the American League*, 99; Donald Quentin Voigt, *From Postwar Expansion to the Electronic Age*, Volume III (University Park: Pennsylvania State University Press, 1983), 78; *Charleston (WV) Gazette*, May 30, 1950.
50. *Nevada State Journal (Reno)*, May 11, 1950.
51. *St. Louis Post-Dispatch*, May 12, 1950.
52. *St. Louis Post-Dispatch*, June 2, 1950.
53. *Panama City (FL) News Herald*, June 16, 1950; *Kokomo (IN) Tribune*, June 16, 1960.
54. *Walla Walla (WA) Union Bulletin*, June 22, 1950; *New Castle (PA) News*, June 22, 1950.
55. Borst, *Still Last in the American League*, 90.
56. *Panama City (FL) News Herald*, July 7, 1950; *Montana Standard (Butte)*, July 7, 1950.
57. *Austin (MN) Herald*, October 10, 1950; *San Antonio (TX) Express*, October 10, 1950; *Lowell (MA) Sun*, October 10, 1950.
58. *Corpus Christi Times*, October 11, 1950; *Alton (IL) Telegraph*, October 11, 1950; *Maryville (MO)*, October 11, 1950.
59. Gillette and Palmer, *ESPN Baseball Encyclopedia*, 123; "St. Louis Browns Managers (1902–1953)."
60. Borst, *Still Last in the American League*, 91.
61. *Pittsfield (MA) Berkshire Evening*, October 25, 1950; *St. Louis Post-Dispatch*, October 25, 1950.
62. *St. Louis Post-Dispatch*, October 27, 1950; *Thomasville (GA)* October 28, 1950; *Maryville (MO) Daily Forum*, October 28, 1950; *Portland (ME) Press Herald*, October 30, 1950.
63. *Ironwood (MI) Daily Globe*, December 5, 1950; *Dixon (IL) Evening Telegraph*, December 5, 1950.
64. *Panama City (FL) News*, December 17, 1950.
65. *The Sporting News*, December 27, 1950.
66. *The Sporting News*, January 10, 1951.
67. *San Antonio Express*, January 28, 1951; *Monroe (LA) Morning World*, January 18, 1951.

68. *St. Louis Post-Dispatch,* February 27, 1971; *San Mateo (CA) Times,* February 28, 1951.
69. *San Antonio (TX) Express,* March 10, 1951; "1950 St. Louis Browns Statistics, "Baseball-Reference.com, https://www.baseball-reference.com/teams/SLB/1950.shtml.
70. *New York Times,* March 15, 1951; *Harlingen (TX) Valley Morning Star,* March 15, 1951; *Portland (ME) Press Herald,* March 15, 1951.
71. *Ironwood (MI) Globe,* April 4, 1951; *Wichita Falls (TX) Daily Times,* April 4, 1951.
72. *The Sporting News,* April 11, 1951.
73. *Traverse City (MI) Record Eagle,* April 14, 1951; *Portland (ME) Press,* April 14, 1951; *Baytown (TX) Sun,* April 18, 1951.
74. Dick Peebles, "Browns' Saucier Hits the Top as 'Minor Leaguer of the Year,'" *The Sporting News,* January 3, 1951, 2.
75. Peebles, "Browns' Saucier Hits the Top."
76. *El Paso (TX) Herald Post,* May 10, 1951.
77. *New York Times,* May 11, 1951.
78. Paul Dickson, *Bill Veeck: Baseball's Greatest Maverick* (New York: Walker, 2012), 63–64.
79. Erion and Pajor, "St. Louis Browns Team Ownership History."
80. *Maryville (MO) Daily Forum,* May 16, 1951; *Rocky Mount (NC) Evening Tribune,* March 16, 1951.
81. Lieb, *The Baltimore Orioles,* 214; *The Sporting News,* May 23, 1951.
82. *San Antonio Light,* May 15, 1951; *The Sporting News,* May 23, 1951.
83. *St. Louis Post-Dispatch,* June 4, 1941.
84. *St. Louis Post-Dispatch,* June 5, 1951.
85. *Charlotte (WV) Gazette,* June 1, 1951; *Winona (MN) Republic Herald,* June 9, 1951.
86. *Bridgeport (CT) Telegram,* June 9, 1951.
87. *New York Times,* June 9, 1951.
88. *Winona (MN) Republican Herald,* June 13, 1951.
89. *San Antonio Press,* June 14, 1951; *Alton (IL) Evening Telegraph,* June 14, 1951; *Greeley (CO) Daily Tribune,* June 14, 1951.
90. *San Antonio Light,* June 21, 1951.
91. *New York Times,* June 22, 1951.
92. *Kingsport (TN) News,* June 22, 1951; *Rocky Mount (NC) Evening Telegram,* June 22, 1951.
93. *Sporting News,* June 27, 1951.
94. *San Antonio (TX) Express,* July 4, 1951.
95. *Thomasville (GA) Times Enterprise,* July 6, 1951; *Kokomo (IN) Tribune,* July 6, 1951; *Rocky Mount (NC) Evening Telegram,* July 6, 1951.
96. Borst, *Still Last in the American League,* 101.
97. Borst, *Still Last in the American League,* 101.
98. *Oklahoma City Oklahoman,* July 6, 1951; *Ada (OK) Evening News,* July 6, 1951; *St. Louis Post-Dispatch,* July 6, 1951.
99. *The Sporting News,* July 11, 1971.
100. *The Sporting News,* July 11, 1971.

Chapter Seven

1. Golenbock, *Spirit of St. Louis,* 326.
2. Dickson, *Bill Veeck,* 186.
3. Miller, *Baseball Business,* 26.
4. Golenbock, *Spirit of St. Louis,* 328.
5. *Statesville (NC) Record,* August 20, 1951.
6. Borst, *Still Last in the American League,* 108; Donald Honig, *Baseball in the 50's: A Decade of Transition* (New York: Cron, 1987); 33; Light, *Cultural Encyclopedia,* 451; Dewey and Acocella, *Ball Clubs,* 522.
7. Borst, *Still Last in the American League,* 108, 111–112.
8. Gillette and Palmer, *ESPN Baseball Encyclopedia,* 121.
9. *The Sporting News,* December 5, 1951.
10. *Pittsfield (MA) Berkshire Evening Eagles,* December 12, 1951; *San Antonio (TX) Light,* December 5, 1951.
11. *Rocky Mount (NC) Evening Telegram,* February 14, 1952.
12. *Lubbock (TX) Evening Journal,* March 4, 1952.
13. Dewey and Acocella, *Ball Clubs,* 521.
14. *St. Louis Post-Dispatch,* March 9, 1952; *Nevada (Reno) State Journal,* March 12, 1952.
15. *San Antonio (TX) Express,* March 27, 1952.

16. Henry Robinson Luce, "Hard-Boiled Hornsby Starts in on Browns," *Life*, March 31, 1952, 84.
17. *Nevada (Reno) State Journal*, March 30, 1952.
18. *Salt Lake (UT) Tribune*, May 12, 1952.
19. Borst, *Still Last in the American League*, 114; *Joplin (MO) Globe*, June 10, 1952.
20. "St. Louis Browns Managers (1902–1953)."
21. "St. Louis Browns Managers (1902–1953)."
22. Dewey and Acocella, *Ball Clubs*, 522.
23. *St. Louis Post-Dispatch*, March 13, 1953; Gerald Eskenazi, *Bill Veeck: A Baseball Legend* (New York: McGraw-Hill, 1988), 105.
24. Dewey and Acocella, *Ball Clubs*, 522.
25. Miller, *Baseball Business*, 27.
26. *The Sporting News*, February 4, 1953; *New York Times*, January 2, 2000.
27. Dickson, *Bill Veeck*, 208; Boxerman and Boxerman, *Ebbets to Veeck to Busch*, 139, 180–181.
28. Dickson, *Bill Veeck*, 208.
29. Boxerman and Boxerman, *Ebbets to Veeck to Busch*, 139.
30. Leonard Koppett, *Koppett's Concise History of Major League Baseball* (New York: Carroll & Graf, 1988), 234.
31. Dewey and Acocella, *Ball Clubs*, 523.
32. Erion and Pajot, "St. Louis Browns Team Ownership History."
33. Erion and Pajot, "St. Louis Browns Team Ownership History."
34. Authors' Interview of Joan DeWitt McKean, May 14, 2018; Authors' Interview of Bill DeWitt, Jr., August 17, 2018.
35. *St. Louis Post-Dispatch*, March 14, 1953.
36. Borst, *Still Last in the American League*, 116.
37. *Kingsport (TN) News*, March 17, 1953.
38. Dewey and Acocella, *The Ball Clubs*, 523.
39. *St. Louis Post-Dispatch*, March 18, 1953.
40. *St. Louis Post-Dispatch*, March 18, 1953.
41. *The Sporting News*, March 18, 1953.
42. *The Sporting News*, March 25, 1953.
43. *The Sporting News*, March 25, 1953.
44. *The Sporting News*, May 27, 1953.
45. *The Sporting News*, July 1, 1953.
46. *St. Louis Post-Dispatch*, April 23, 1953.
47. *The Sporting News*, August 12, 1953.
48. "St. Louis Browns Managers (1902–1953)."
49. Dewey and Acocella, *Ball Clubs*, 523; *The Sporting News*, October 7, 1953.
50. Erion and Pajot, "St. Louis Browns Team Ownership History."
51. Boxerman and Boxerman, *Ebbets to Veeck to Busch*, 140.

Chapter Eight

1. *Nevada State Journal*, September 30, 1953.
2. *St. Louis Globe-Democrat*, September 30, 1953; *St. Louis Post-Dispatch*, September 30, 1953.
3. *Kokomo (IN) Tribune*; *Dixon (IL) Evening Telegraph*, October 14, 1953.
4. *Fergus Falls (MN) Daily Journal*, October 27, 1953; *Alton (IL) Evening Telegraph*, October 17, 1953.
5. *New York Times*, October 27, 1953; *Hagerstown (MD) Morning Herald*, October 27, 1953.
6. Gillette and Palmer, *ESPN Baseball Encyclopedia*, 1694, 1702, 1694.
7. *The Sporting News*, November 4, 1953.
8. *New York Times*, April 28, 1954; *Panama City (FL) News*, April 28, 1954; *St. Louis Globe-Democrat*, April 28, 1954.
9. *The Sporting News*, May 12, 1954.
10. *Lubbock (TX) Morning Avalanche*, April 29, 1954.
11. *Panama City (FL) News*, April 29, 1954.
12. *St. Louis Post-Dispatch*, November 19, 1954; Gillette and Palmer, *ESPN Baseball Encyclopedia*, 1575; *St. Louis Post-Dispatch*, May 7, 1954.
13. Gillette and Palmer, *ESPN Baseball Encyclopedia*, 115.
14. Gillette and Palmer, *ESPN Baseball Encyclopedia*, 1739.
15. *The Sporting News*, November 10, 1954.
16. *St. Louis Post-Dispatch*, November 16, 1954.

17. Publicity Sheet Cincinnati Baseball Club, November, 1960.
18. *The Sporting News*, December 1, 1954.
19. *The Sporting News*, December 8, 1954.
20. *The Sporting News*, December 8, 1954.
21. *St. Louis Post-Dispatch*, February 16, 1955; *San Mateo (CA) Times*, February 16, 1955.
22. *The Sporting News*, February 16, 1955.
23. *St. Louis Post-Dispatch*, March 13, 1955.
24. *St. Louis Post-Dispatch*, March 13, 1955.
25. *St. Louis Post-Dispatch*, March 13, 1955.
26. Bill Madden, *Pride of October: What it Was to Be Young and a Yankee* (New York: Warner Books, 2003), 173–174.
27. Gillette and Palmer, *ESPN Baseball Encyclopedia*, 112–113.
28. Thorn et al, *Total Baseball*, 188, 384–385.
29. *New York Times*, October 8, 1965; *The Sporting News*, October 12, 1955.
30. *Lowell (MA) Sun*, October 25, 1955.
31. *Hagerstown (MD) Morning Herald*, October 27, 1955.
32. *Marshall (MI) Evening Chronicle*, November 8, 1955; *Newcastle (PA) News*, November 8, 1955.
33. *St. Louis Post-Dispatch*, November 8, 1955.
34. *St. Louis Post-Dispatch*, November 9, 1955.
35. *The Sporting News*, December 14, 1955, 21.
36. Telegram from Bill DeWitt to Rufus Clement, January 20, 1956, Branch Rickey Papers, Box 9, Library of Congress.
37. Telegram from Branch Rickey to Bill DeWitt, January 27, 1956, Branch Rickey Papers, Box 9, Library of Congress.
38. *The Sporting News*, January 25, 1956.
39. *The Sporting News*, January 25, 1956.
40. *The Sporting News*, January 25, 1956.
41. *The Sporting News*, February 8, 1956.
42. *St. Louis Post-Dispatch*, February 9, 1956.
43. *Monroe (LA) News Star*, February 9, 1956.
44. *New York Times*, February 29, 1956.
45. *Montana Standard (Butte)*, March 2, 1956.
46. *New York Times*, March 4, 1956.
47. *The Sporting News*, March 28, 1956.
48. *Lawton (OK) Constitution*, April 6, 1956.
49. *The Sporting News*, June 20, 1956.
50. *Holland (MI) Evening Sentinel*, July 16, 1956.
51. Gillette and Palmer, *ESPN Baseball Encyclopedia*, 111–113.
52. "1956 New York Yankees," Baseball-Reference.com, https://www.baseball-reference.com/teams/NYY/1956.shtml.
53. "1956 New York Yankees."
54. Thorn et al, *Total Baseball*, 386.
55. Robert Obojski, *Bush League: A History of Minor League Baseball* (New York: Macmillan, 1975), 28–29.
56. Obojski, *Bush League*, 28–29.
57. *St. Louis Post-Dispatch*, December 4, 1956; *Lowell (MA) Sun*, December 4, 1956; *Chicago Daily Tribune*, December 4, 1956.
58. Authors' Interview of Bill DeWitt, Jr., August 17, 2018.
59. *St. Louis Post-Dispatch*, December 4, 1956; *Lowell (MA) Sun*, December 4, 1956; *Chicago Daily Tribune*, December 4, 1956.
60. Obojski, *Bush League*, 28–29.
61. *New York Times*, December 4, 1956; *St. Louis Globe-Democrat*, December 4, 1956.
62. *St. Louis Globe-Democrat*, December 4, 1956; Dean A. Sullivan, *Late Innings: A Documentary History of Baseball, 1945–1972* (Lincoln: University of Nebraska Press, 2002), 102.
63. Robert Creamer, "The Sick Man of Baseball," *Sports Illustrated*, December 21, 1956, 48–50.
64. *St. Louis Post-Dispatch*, December 28, 1956; *The Sporting News*, January 2, 1957.
65. *Salina (KS) Journal*, May 3, 1957.
66. *Salina (KS) Journal*, May 15, 1957.
67. *Salina (KS) Journal*, May 22, 1957.
68. *Chicago Defender*, October 17, 1957; *Centralia (WA) Daily Chronicle*, October 17, 1957; *Lowell (MA) Sun*, Octo-

ber 17, 1957; *The Sporting News*, October 23, 1957.
69. *The Sporting News*, October 23, 1957.
70. *Newport (RI) Daily News*, October 31, 1957.
71. *St. Louis Post-Dispatch*, November 12, 1957.
72. *Centralia (IL) Sentinel*, November 6, 1957.
73. Golenbock, *Spirit of St. Louis*, 417–418.
74. *The Sporting News*, January 15, 1958.
75. *St. Louis Post-Dispatch*, January 26, 1958.
76. *The Sporting News*, March 5, 1958.
77. *The Sporting News*, March 12, 1958.
78. *Monroe (LA) News Star*; November 5, 1958; *Ironwood (MI) Daily Globe*, November 5, 1958.
79. *Arizona Republic (Phoenix)*, November 7, 1958; *Reno Evening Gazette*, November 7, 1958.
80. *Joplin (MO) Globe*, November 1, 1958.
81. *The Sporting News*, November 26, 1958.
82. *New York Times*, October 1, 1959.
83. Obojski, *Bush League*, 29.
84. *Benton Harbor (MI) News Palladium*, October 11, 1959.
85. *Arizona Daly Sun*, October 1, 1959; *Salt Lake Tribune*, October 1, 1959.
86. *Charleston (WV) Gazette*, October 1, 1959; *Charleston (WV), Daily Mail*, October 1, 1959.
87. *The Sporting News*, November 25, 1959.
88. *The Sporting News*, October 29, 1959.
89. *The Sporting News*, November 18, 1959.
90. *The Sporting News*, December 9, 1959.
91. *The Sporting News*, December 9, 1959.
92. *Benton Harbor (MI) News Palladium*, January 12, 1960.
93. *Benton Harbor (MI) News Palladium*, January 12, 1960.
94. *New York Times*, October 1, 1959; *Ironwood (MI) Daily Globe*, March 9, 1960; *Adrian (MI)* March 9, 1960.
95. *Adrian (MI) Daily Globe*, April 6, 1960; *Kingsport (TN) News*, April 6, 1960; *St. Louis Post-Dispatch*, April 6, 1960.
96. *Charleston (WV) Gazette*, April 7, 1960; *Monroe (LA) News Star*, April 7, 1960.
97. *Benton Harbor (MI) News Palladium*, April 7, 1960; *St. Louis Post-Dispatch*, April 7, 1960.
98. Boxerman, Burton A, and Benita W. Boxerman, *George Weiss: Architect of the Golden Age Yankees* (Jefferson: NC: McFarland, 2016), 158.
99. "Continental League," Baseball-Reference.com Bullpen, https://www.baseball-reference.com/bullpen/Continental_League.
100. Lowenfish, *Branch Rickey*, 567.
101. Gillette and Palmer, *ESPN Baseball Encyclopedia*, 445.
102. Dewey and Acocella, *Ball Clubs*, 247; Gillette and Palmer, *ESPN Baseball Encyclopedia*, 381.
103. Dewey and Acocella, *Ball Clubs*, 247; Gillette and Palmer, *ESPN Baseball Encyclopedia*, 401, 657; Thorn et al, *Total Baseball*, 1113, 1369; *Lincoln (NE) Evening Journal*, April 18, 1960; *New York Times*, April 18, 1960.
104. *The Sporting News*, April 27, 1960.
105. Letter from Ty Cobb to Bill DeWitt, May 4, 1960, printed copy in possession of authors.
106. Letter from Bill DeWitt to Ty Cobb, June 29, 1960, typed copy in possession of authors.
107. Peter C. Bjarkman, ed, *Encyclopedia of Major League Baseball Team Histories* (Westport: CT: Meckler, 1991), 166; Dewey and Acocella, *Ball Clubs*, 247; Peter Morris, *A Game of Inches: The Stories Behind the Innovations That Shaped Baseball* (Chicago: Ivan R. Dee, 2006), 304.
108. Patrick J. Harrigan, *The Detroit Tigers: Club and Community, 1945–1995* (Toronto: University of Toronto Press, 1997), 70.
109. *Flagstaff (AZ) Sun*, August 4, 1960; *Reno Evening Gazette*, August 4, 1960.
110. *Lowell (MA) Sun*, August 4, 1960; *Salt Lake City Tribune*, August 4, 1960; *St. Louis Post-Dispatch*, August 4, 1960.
111. *The Sporting News*, September 14, 1960.
112. *The Sporting News*, September 14, 1960.
113. *Ada (Ok) Evening News*, October 4, 1960; *Walla Walla (WA)* October 4, 1960.

114. *St. Louis Post-Dispatch*, October 8, 1960.
115. *The Sporting News*, October 19, 1960; *Kingsport (TN) News*, October 12, 1960; *Phoenix Republic*, October 20, 1960.
116. *Holland (MI) Evening Sentinel*, October 20, 1960; *Joplin (MO) News*, October 20, 1960; *Ironwood (MI) Daily Globe*, October 20, 1960; *New York Times*, October 21, 1960.
117. *The Sporting News*, October 26, 1960.

Chapter Nine

1. *St. Louis Post-Dispatch*, November 3, 1960; Leonard Koppett, *Koppett's Concise History*, 286; Floyd Connor and John Snyder, *Day By Day in Cincinnati Reds History* (New York: Leisure Press, 1983), 120.
2. Snyder, *Day By Day*, 120; *Holland (MI) Evening Sentinel*, November 3, 1960.
3. *The Sporting News*, June 28, 1961. Authors 'interview with Joan McKeon, May 4, 2018.
4. *Cincinnati Sentinel*, November 3, 1960.
5. *The Sporting News*, November 9, 1960.
6. *St. Louis Post-Dispatch*, November 3, 1960.
7. Gillette and Palmer, *ESPN Baseball Encyclopedia*, 102.
8. Greg Rhodes and John Snyder, *Redleg Journal: Year by Year and Day by Day with the Cincinnati Reds Since 1866* (Cincinnati: Road West, 2000), 414.
9. *Salt Lake Tribune*, November 11, 1960.
10. *The Sporting News*, November 16, 1960.
11. *The Sporting News*, November 23, 1960.
12. Bill Pennington, *Billy Martin: Baseball's Flawed Genius* (Boston: Houghton Mifflin Harcourt, 2015), 148; *St. Louis Post-Dispatch*, December 4, 1960.
13. *The Sporting News*, December 14, 1960.
14. *St. Louis Post-Dispatch*, December 16, 1960; Richard Lindberg, *Who's on Third?* (South Bend: Icarus Press, 1983), 197; Donald Honig, *The Cincinnati Reds: An Illustrated History* (New York: Simon & Schuster, 1992), 169.
15. *Zanesville (OH) Times Recorder*, December 16, 1960; *Phoenix (AZ) Republic*, December 16, 1960; Gillette and Palmer, *ESPN Baseball Encyclopedia*, 502.
16. *The Sporting News*, January 18, 1961; *Charleston (WV) Daily Mail*, January 20, 1961; *The Sporting News*, February 1, 1961.
17. *The Sporting News*, January 25, 1961.
18. Robert H. Boyle, "Cincinnati's Brain-Picker," *Sports Illustrated*, June 13, 1966, 47; *Lincoln (NC) Evening Journal*, March 29, 1961; *Kingsport (TN) Times*, March 31, 1961; *Phoenix (AZ) Republic*, March 29, 1961; *Marshall (MI) Chronicle*, March 31, 1961; *New York Times*, March 31, 1961.
19. *The Sporting News*, April 3, 1961.
20. *Ibid.*, April 19, 1961.
21. *Corpus Christie Times*, April 24, 1961.
22. *Middlesboro (KY) Daily News*, April 28, 1961; *Charleston (WV) Gazette*, April 28, 1961.
23. *St. Louis Post-Dispatch*, May 12, 1961.
24. *The Sporting News*, May 3, 1961.
25. "1961 Reds Season Schedule," Baseball-Reference.com, https://www.baseball-reference.com/teams/CIN/1961-schedule-scores.shtml; Peter C. Bjarkman, ed, *Encyclopedia of Major League Baseball Team Histories: National League* (Westport: CT: Meckler, 1991), 209.
26. Dewey and Acocella, *The Ball Clubs*, 192.
27. "Cincinnati Reds History," Baseball Almanac, www.baseballalmanac.com; *San Mateo (CA) Times*, June 1, 1961; *Columbus (NE) Daily Telegram*, June 1, 1961; *The Sporting News*, June 21, 1961; *Lawton (OK) Constitution*, June 27, 1961.
28. "Cincinnati Reds History."
29. *The Sporting News*, June 28, 1961.
30. *St. Louis Post-Dispatch*, September 27, 1961; *Ironwood (MI) Daily Globe*, October 4, 1961.
31. *Charleston (WV) Daily Mail*, August 29, 1961; *St. Louis Post-Dispatch*, August 28, 1961; *The Sporting News*, September 6, 1961; *New York Times*, August 29, 1961.
32. Dewey and Acocella, *The Ball Clubs*, 192; Bjarkman, *Encyclopedia of Major League Baseball Team Histories: National League*, 209.

Notes—Chapter Nine

33. Doug Wilson, *Fred Hutchinson and the 1964 Cincinnati Reds* (Jefferson, NC: McFarland, 2010), 47.
34. Eric Enders, *100 Years of the World Series* (New York: Barnes & Noble, 2003), 154.
35. Enders, *100 Years of the World Series*, 154.
36. Thorn et al, *Total Baseball*, 391.
37. Enders, *100 Years of the World Series*, 156.
38. *Cincinnati Post and Times Star*, October, 23, 1961; *St. Louis Post-Dispatch*, October 22, 1961.
39. *The Sporting News*, December 6, 1961.
40. *St. Louis Post-Dispatch*, December 17, 1961; *The Sporting News*, December 27, 1961.
41. *The Sporting News*, December 18, 1961.
42. January 14, 1962; *St. Louis Post-Dispatch*, January 14, 1962; *The Sporting News*, January 24, 1962; "Cincy Signs Robinson for $55,000," *Washington Post*, January 14, 1962.
43. *The Sporting News*, January 17, 1962; *Bridgeport (CT) Telegram*, February 15, 1962.
44. *Marshall (MI) Evening Chronicle*, February 16, 1962.
45. *Bridgeportn (CT) Post*, February 28, 1962.
46. *Alton (IL) Evening Telegraph*, March 1, 1962; *Joplin (MO) Globe*, March 7, 1962; *Winona (MN) Daily News*, March 7, 1962.
47. *The Sporting News*, March 14, 1962.
48. *Zanesville (OH) Times*, January 25, 1962; *The Sporting News*, February 28, 1962.
49. Connor and Snyder, *Day By Day in Cincinnati Reds History*, 15.
50. *Bridgeport (CT) Post*, March 24, 1962.
51. *The Sporting News*, March 28, 1962.
52. *The Sporting News*, April 11, 1962.
53. *The Sporting News*, April 11, 1962.
54. *The Sporting News*, April 25, 1962.
55. *St. Louis Post-Dispatch*, May 29, 1962; *The Sporting News*, April 26, 1962.
56. *St. Louis Post-Dispatch*, June 4, 1962; *Albert Lea (MN) Evening Tribune*, June 4, 1962; *Newport (RI) News*, June 4, 1962.
57. *Petersburg (VA) Progress Index*, June 6, 1962.
58. *The Sporting News*, June 23, 1962.
59. *The Sporting News* June 9, 16, 1962.
60. *The Sporting News* June 22, 1962.
61. "1962 Reds Statistics," Baseball-Reference.com, https://www.baseball-reference.com/teams/CIN/1962.shtml; "1962 Cincinnati Reds Schedule" Baseball-Reference.com, https://www.baseball-reference.com/teams/CIN/1962-schedule-scores.shtml.
62. Brad Snyder, *A Well-Paid Slave* (New York: Viking, 2006), 169; Danny Peary, *We Played the Game: 65 Players Remember Baseball's Greatest Era: 1947–1964* (New York: Hyperion, 1994), 511.
63. Dewey and Acocella, *Ball Clubs*, 192.
64. *New York Times*, July 21, 1962.
65. The *New York Times* estimated that Robinson's 1962 salary was instead $42,000, and the paper reported that he was hopeful of a $23,000 raise for 1963. See "Robinson Changes His Stand on Retirement," *New York Times*, October 2, 1962, 49.
66. *Joplin (MO) Globe*, September 30, 1962; *Florence (SC) Morning News*, September 30, 1962.
67. *The Sporting News*, November 17, 1972.
68. Connor and Snyder, *Day By Day in Cincinnati Reds History*, 128; "Reds Safe At Home," *Sports Illustrated*, January 14, 1963, 8.
69. *Marshall (MI) Evening Chronicle*, January 14, 1963; *Petersburg (VA) Progress Index*, January 13, 1963.
70. *Phoenix (AZ) Republic*, February 19, 1963; *Bridgeport (CT) Telegram*, February 19, 1963.
71. *Phoenix (AZ) Republic*, February 19, 1963.
72. *The Sporting News*, February 2, 1963.
73. *Kingston (TN) News*, February 7, 1963; *Scottsdale (AZ) Daily Progress*, February 7, 1963; *Hagerstown (MD) Morning Herald*, February 7, 1963.
74. *The Sporting News*, February 2, 1963.
75. *Benton Harbor (MI) News Palladium*, February 21, 1963.
76. *Ruston (LA) Daily Leader*, June 11, 1963; *Kalispell (MT) Daily Interlake*, June 11, 1963.
77. Mark Armour, "Jim Brosnan," SABR

Biography Project, https://sabr.org/bioproj/person/jim-bouton/.
78. *The Sporting News,* April 6, 1963.
79. *The Sporting News,* April 13, 1963.
80. *New York Times,* May 8, 1963; *The Sporting News,* May 18, 1963.
81. Gillette and Palmer, *ESPN Baseball Encyclopedia,* 1109.
82. Mark Armour, "Jim Brosnan."
83. *The Sporting News,* June 22, 1963; August 10, 1963.
84. *The Sporting News,,* July 27, 1963.
85. *Escanaba (MI) Daily Press,* August 2, 1963; *The Sporting News,* August 3, 1963.
86. *The Sporting News,* August 31, 1963.
87. *The Sporting News,* October 5, 1963.
88. *Joplin (MO) News Herald,* October 10, 1963; *The Sporting News,* October 19, 1963; Gillette and Palmer, *ESPN Baseball Encyclopedia,* 804, 916, 1575.
89. *The Sporting News,* November 2, 1963.
90. *Scottsdale (AZ) Progress,* January 4, 1964; *Billings (MT) Gazette,* January 4, 1964.
91. *Phoenix (AZ) Republican,* January 8, 1964.
92. *The Sporting News,* January 11, 1964.
93. Gillette and Palmer, *ESPN Baseball Encyclopedia,* 1301.
94. *St. Louis Post-Dispatch,* March 13, 1964; *Austin (MN) Daily Herald,* March 14, 1964.
95. *Scottsdale (AZ) Progress,* May 5, 1916; *Zanesville (OH) Times Recorder,* May 16, 1964.
96. Gillette and Palmer, *ESPN Baseball Encyclopedia,* 1301.
97. *Austin (MN) Daily Herald,* July 1, 1964.
98. *Joplin (MO) Globe,* July 8, 1964.
99. *Statesville (NC) Record and Landmail,* August 5, 1964; *The Sporting News,* August 8, 1964.
100. *Joplin (MO) Globe,* August 14, 1964.
101. *The Sporting News,* August 29, 1964.
102. *The Sporting News,* September 19, 1964.
103. *The Sporting News,* September 19, 1964.
104. *The Sporting News,* September 26, 1964.
105. Bjarkman, *Encyclopedia of Major League Baseball Team Histories: National League,* 210.
106. "Bill Henry," Baseball-Reference.com, https://www.baseball-reference.com/players/h/henrybi01.shtml.
107. *St. Louis Post-Dispatch,* November 13, 1964.
108. *Salt Lake (UT) Tribune,* November 13, 1964.
109. *Centralia (IL) Sentinel,* January 13, 1965; *Austin (MO) Daily Herald,* January 13, 1965.
110. *The Sporting News,* November 14, 1964.
111. *The Sporting News,* December 12, 1964; *Twin Falls (ID) Times News,* November 26, 1964.
112. *The Sporting News,* March 27, 1965.
113. *The Sporting News,* December 26, 1964.
114. *The Sporting News,* March 6, 1965.
115. *Gastonia (NC) Gazette,* April 18, 1965.
116. *San Mateo (CA) Times,* June 16, 1965; *Holland (MI) Evening Sentinel,* June 16, 1965.
117. *Jacksonville Daily Journal,* August 22, 1965; *New York Times,* August 22, 1965; Bjarkman, *Encyclopedia of Major League Baseball Team Histories,* 211.
118. *Salt Lake (UT) Tribune,* October 6, 1965.
119. *St. Louis Post-Dispatch,* September 23, 1965; *Charleston (WV) Gazette,* September 23, 1965.
120. Conner and Snyder, *Day By Day,* 113.
121. *Billings (MT) Gazette,* October 5, 1965.
122. *Billings (MT) Gazette,* October 5, 1965.
123. John P. Carmichael, "There's No Substitute for Defense," *Baseball Digest,* March, 1966, 29.
124. *Petersburg (VA) Progress,* March 21, 1965; *Benton Harbor (MI) News Palladium,* March 21, 1965.
125. *Salisbury (MD) Daily Times,* September 21, 1965.
126. Don Heffner—Wikipedia en. Wikipedia.org/wiki/.
127. *Escanaba (MI) Daily Press,* October 27, 1965; *Newport (RI) News,* October 27, 1965; *The Sporting News,* November 6, 1965.

128. *The Sporting News*, December 4, 1965.
129. *The Sporting News*, December 4, 1965.
130. *San Mateo (CA) Times*, December 9, 1965; *Annapolis (MD) Capital*, December 10, 1965.
131. *St. Louis Post-Dispatch*, December 10, 1965; *New York Times*, December 10, 1965; James Enright, "Why Reds Traded Robinson," *Baseball Digest*, February, 1966, 19–20.
132. Tommy Fitzgerald, "Robinson Learns Why He's an Oriole," *Miami News*, April 3, 1966, 25. DeWitt made his comment on April 2, before a Reds loss in Miami. Robinson understood DeWitt to say that he was an "old thirty," which is how the quotation is often remembered. There may be a difference between "old" and "not young"—but, in light of the fact that DeWitt was defending his decision to move one of the game's premier sluggers, probably not one of any significance.
133. Robert H. Boyle, "Cincinnati's Brain Picker," 50.
134. "Reds' Robinson Fined $250 on Gun Charge," *Washington Post*, March 21, 1961, A1; James Enright, "Why Reds Traded Robinson," *Baseball Digest*, February, 1966.
135. Donald Honig, *The Cincinnati Reds: An Illustrated History* (New York: Simon & Schuster, 1992), 183.
136. John Eisenberg, *From 33rd Street to Camden Yards: An Oral History of the Baltimore Orioles* (New York: Contemporary Books, 2001), 150.
137. *The Sporting News*, December 25, 1965.
138. *Billings (MT) Gazette*, December 11, 1965; *Ada (OK) Constitution*, December 14, 1965.
139. *The Sporting News*, January 29, 1966.
140. *Cincinnati Enquirer*, February 5, 1966.
141. *The Sporting News*, March 5, 1966.
142. *Pittsburgh (VA) Progress*, March 19, 1966.
143. *The Sporting News*, March 26, 1966.
144. *Charleston (WV) Daily Mail*, April 4, 1966; *Hagerston (MD) Morning Herald*, April 4, 1966; *The Sporting News*, April 19, 1966.
145. *Middlesboro (KY) Daily News*, April 23, 1966; *Kingsport (TN) News*, April 23, 1966.
146. *The Sporting News*, June 25, 1966.
147. Connor and Snyder, *Day By Day*, 68.
148. *St. Louis Post-Dispatch*, July 14, 1966; *Austin (MN) Daily Herald*, July 14, 1966.
149. *St. Louis Post-Dispatch*, July 14, 1966.
150. *San Mateo (CA) Times*, July 16, 1966.
151. Gillette and Palmer, *ESPN Baseball Encyclopedia*, 90–91.
152. Gillette and Palmer, *ESPN Baseball Encyclopedia*, 739.
153. *New York Times*, September 27, 1966.
154. *New York Times*, September 27, 1966; *Bridgeport (CT) Telegram*, September 27, 1966.
155. *St. Louis Post-Dispatch*, September 25, 1966; *The Sporting News*, October 8, 1966.
156. *The Sporting News*, October 29, 1966.
157. *The Sporting News*, October 29, 1966.
158. Conner and Snyder, *Day By Day In Cincinnati Reds History*, 124; Leonard Koppett, *Koppett's Concise History*, 298; *Atlantic Journal*, December 6, 1966; *Hartford (CT) Courant*, December 6, 1966.
159. *Bridgeport (CT) Telegram*, December 6, 1966.
160. *Nashua (NH) Telegraph*, December 6, 1966.
161. *Joplin (MO) Globe*, December 31, 1966.
162. *Las Vegas Sun*, December 7, 1967.
163. Bill DeWitt, Jr., to authors, August 7, 2020.
164. *Bridgeport (CT) Telegram*, January 23, 1967; *Zanesville (OH) Times Recorder*, January 27, 1967; *New York Times*, January 23, 1967; *Pittsfield (MA) Berkshire Eagle*, January 23, 1967.
165. *The Sporting News*, December 31, 1966.
166. *Marshall (MI) Evening Chronicle*, December 6, 1966.
167. *New York Times*, April 13, 1967, 43.
168. Joseph P. Preston, *Major League Baseball in the 1970s: A Modern Game*

Emerges (Jefferson, NC: McFarland, 2004), 136–137.

Chapter Ten

1. *The Sporting News,* February 11, 1967.
2. *The Sporting News,* March 4, 1967.
3. *The Sporting News,* January 27, 1968.
4. *The Sporting News,* March 16, 1968.
5. Shirley Povich, "Senators Are Sold To Short: Lemon Retains Minor Interest In Franchise Short Wins Bidding for Senators Team Won't Move Short Owned Lakers Undaunted by Losses," *Washington Post,* December 4, 1968; *Pittsfield (MA) Berkshire Eagle,* December 4, 1968; "Washington Senators Team Ownership History," SABR Team Ownership History Project, https://sabr.org/bioproj/topic/washington-senators-i-team-ownership-history/.
6. *St. Louis Post-Dispatch,* May 29, 1969.
7. *St. Louis Post-Dispatch,* February 3, 1970.
8. *New York Times,* February 13, 1970.
9. "Pilots' Move to Milwaukee Is Cleared by Court," *New York Times,* April 1, 1970; "1970 Milwaukee Brewers," Baseball Reference.com, https://www.baseball-reference.com/teams/MIL/1970-schedule-scores.shtml.
10. *Middletown (NY) Times Herald Record,* August 18, 1971.
11. *Woodland (CA) Daily Democrat,* March 14, 1972.
12. *Joplin (MO) Globe,* May 25, 1972.
13. *St. Louis Post-Dispatch,* May 25, 1972, June 28, 1973.
14. *St. Louis Post-Dispatch,* November 2, 1975.
15. *The Sporting News,* November 25, 1975.
16. *The Sporting News,* November 25, 1975.
17. *The Sporting News,* November 25, 1975.
18. *St. Louis Post-Dispatch,* November 25, 1975.
19. *New York Times,* November 26, 1975.
20. *Independence (MO) Examiner,* November 28, 1975.
21. *Edwardsville (IL) Intelligencer,* November 6, 1875.
22. *Fremont (CA) Argus,* November 27, 1975.
23. *Blytheville (AK) Courier News,* December 4, 1975; *Monroe (LA) News Star,* December 4, 1975.
24. *Morgantown (WV) Post,* December 12, 1975; *Bemidji (MN) Pioneer,* December 12, 1975.
25. *Ada (OK) Evening News,* December 11, 1975.
26. *The Sporting News,* December 27, 1975.
27. "Busch Fears 'The War Is Lost,'" *St. Louis Post-Dispatch,* July 15, 1976.
28. *Monroe (LA) News Star,* January 19, 1977.
29. *Monroe (LA) News Star,* January 19, 1977.
30. *The Sporting News,* December 23, 1978.
31. Undated letter, Edward Stack to authors.
32. *Jacksonville (IL) Courier,* October 12, 1977.
33. *The Sporting News.* October 6, 1979.
34. Don Zminda, Don. *The Legendary Harry Caray: Baseball's Greatest Salesman.* (Lanham, MD: Rowman & Littlefield, 2019), 155.
35. *The Sporting News,* September 6, 1980; Paul Dickson, *Bill Veeck: Baseball's Greatest Maverick* (New York: Walker & Company, 2012), 321.
36. Dickson, *Bill Veeck,* 322.
37. Dickson, *Bill Veeck,* 324.
38. *The Sporting News,* December 21, 1980.
39. Gerald Eskenazi, *Bill Veeck: A Baseball Legend* (New York: McGraw-Hill, 1988), 177.
40. *Lowell (MA) Sun,* March 4, 1982.
41. *St. Louis Globe-Democrat,* March 4, 1982.
42. *St. Louis Globe-Democrat,* March 4, 1982.
43. Bartholomay interview by authors, December 13, 2017.
44. Bartholomay interview.
45. Bartholomay interview.
46. Joan McKean interview by authors, May 4, 2018; *St. Louis Post-Dispatch,* March 4, 1982.
47. *St. Louis Post-Dispatch,* March 3, 1982.
48. *St. Louis Post-Dispatch,* March 4, 1982.

Chapter Eleven

1. Megdal, *The Cardinals* Way, 46.
2. Bruce Rushton, "The Midas Touch," *Riverfront Times* online, February 7, 2001, www.riverfronttimes.com; authors' interview of William O. DeWitt, Jr. August 17, 2020.
3. *New York Times,* March 19, 1989; Mark L. Armour and Daniel R. Levitt, *In Pursuit of Pennants* (Lincoln: University of Nebraska Press, 2015), 392.
4. Authors' interview of William O. DeWitt, Jr; *Ladue News (St. Louis),* October 18, 2011.
5. "Eli Jacobs," Baseball-Reference.com, https://baseball-reference.com/bullpen/Eli_Jacobs.
6. Eisenberg, *From 33rd Street to Camden Yards,* 432.
7. John Helyar, *Lords of the Realm,* 534–535.
8. Eisenberg, *From Third Street to Camden Yards,* 433.
9. Helyar, *Lords of the Realm,* 537.
10. Rushton, "The Midas Touch."
11. *Washington Post,* May 24, 1995.
12. *St. Louis Post-Dispatch,* December 22, 1995; *Riverfront Times,* February 7, 2001; Golenbock, *Spirit of St. Louis,* 582–583.
13. *Ladue News (St. Louis),* July 25, 2013; Front Office Directory, www.mlb.com/cardinals/team/front-office; William DeWitt III, stlouis.Cardinals.mlb.com/stl/team/front office.
14. Rushton, "The Midas Touch."
15. "Baseball's in His Blood: Bill DeWitt," *Town & Style,* April 2, 2014.

Bibliography

Books

Alexander, Charles C. *Breaking the Slump.* Champaign: University of Illinois Press, 1986.
_____. *Our Game: An American Baseball History.* New York: Henry Holt, 1991.
_____. *Rogers Hornsby: A Biography.* New York: Henry Holt, 1995.
Allen, Lee. *The World Series, the Story of Baseball's Annual Championship.* New York: G. P. Putnam's Sons, 1969.
Appel, Marty. *Pinstripe Empire: The New York Yankees from Before the Babe to After the Boss.* New York: Bloomsbury, 2012.
Armour, Mark L., and Daniel R. Levitt. *In Pursuit of Pennants: Baseball Operations from Deadball to Money Ball.* Lincoln: University of Nebraska Press, 2015.
_____. *Paths to Glory: How Great Baseball Teams Got That Way.* Washington, D.C.: Brassey's, 2003.
Bjarkman, Peter, ed. *Encyclopedia of Major League Baseball Team Histories: American League.* Westport, CT: Meckler, 1991.
_____. *Encyclopedia of Major League Baseball Team Histories: National League.* Westport, CT: Meckler, 1991.
Borst, Bill. *The Best of Seasons: The 1944 St. Louis Cardinals and St. Louis Browns.* Jefferson, NC: McFarland, 1995.
_____. *Still Last in the American League: The St. Louis Browns Revisited.* West Bloomfield, MI: A&M, 1992.
Borst, Bill, Bill Rogers, and Ed Wheatley. *St. Louis Browns: The Story of a Beloved Team.* St. Louis: Reedy Press. 2017.
Boxerman, Burton A., and Benita W. Boxerman. *Ebbets to Veeck to Busch: Eight Owners Who Shaped Baseball.* Jefferson, NC: McFarland, 2003.
_____, and _____. *George Weiss: Architect of the Golden Age Yankees.* Jefferson, NC: McFarland, 2016.
Bready, James H. *Baseball in Baltimore: The First 100 Years.* Baltimore: Johns Hopkins University Press, 1998.
Broeg, Bob. *Redbirds: A Century of Cardinals' Baseball.* St. Louis: River City Publishers, 1981.
Broeg, Bob, and William J. Miller, Jr. *Baseball from a Different Angle,* South Bend: Diamond Communications, 1988.
Brosnan, Jim. *The Long Season.* New York: Harper & Brothers, 1960.
_____. *Pennant Race.* New York: Harper & Brothers, 1962.
Bullock, Steven R. *Playing for Their Nation: Baseball and the American Military During World War II.* Lincoln: University of Nebraska Press, 2004.
Burk, Robert F. *Much More Than a Game: Players, Owners & American Baseball, 1921.* Chapel Hill: University of North Carolina Press, 2001.
Chadwick, Bruce. *The Cincinnati Reds: Memories and Memorabilia of the Big Red Machine.* New York: Abbeville, 1994.
Conner, Floyd, and John Snyder. *Day by Day in Cincinnati Reds History.* New York: Leisure, 1983.
Cook, William A. *Pete Rose: Baseball's All-Time Hit King.* Jefferson, NC: McFarland, 2004.
Danzig, Allison, and Joe Reichler. *The History of Baseball: The Great Players, Teams and Managers.* Englewood Cliffs, NJ: Prentice Hall, 1959.

Dewey, Donald, and Nicholas Acocella. *The Ball Clubs.* New York: Harper Perennial, 1996.

____, and ____. *Biographical History of Baseball.* New York: Carroll and Graf, 1995.

Dickey, Glen. *The History of National League Baseball Since 1876.* New York: Stein and Day, 1979.

Dickson, Paul. *Bill Veeck: Baseball's Greatest Maverick.* New York: Walker & Company, 2012.

Durso, Joseph. *Baseball and the American Dream.* St. Louis: Sporting News, 1986.

Dworkin, James. *Owner Versus Players: Baseball and Collective Bargaining.* Boston: Auburn House, 1981.

Dykes, Jimmy, and Charles O. Dexter. *You Can't Steal 1st Base.* New York: J. B. Lippincott, 1967.

Eisenberg, John. *From Thirty-Third Street to Camden Yards: An Oral History of the Baltimore Orioles.* New York: Contemporary, 2001.

Enders, Eric. *100 Years of the World Series.* New York: Barnes & Noble, 2003.

Eskenazi, Gerald. *Bill Veeck: A Baseball Legend.* New York: McGraw-Hill, 1988.

Falkner, David. *Great Time Coming: The Life of Jackie Robinson from Baseball to Birmingham.* New York: Simon & Schuster, 1995.

Falls, Jack. *The Detroit Tigers: An Illustrated History.* New York: Walker & Company, 1989.

Fehler, Gene. *Tales from Baseball's Golden Age.* Champaign, IL: Sports, 2000.

Feldmann, Doug. *Dizzy and the Gas House Gang: The 1934 St. Louis Cardinals and Depression-Era Baseball.* Jefferson, NC: McFarland, 2004.

Frick, Ford. *Games, Asterisks, and People: Memoirs of a Lucky Fan.* New York: Crown, 1962.

Frisch, Frank. *The Fordham Flash: As Told to J. Roy Stockton.* Garden City, NY: Doubleday, 1962.

Frommer, Harvey. *Big Red Machine.* Englewood Cliffs, NJ: Prentice-Hall/Rutledge, 1976.

Gay, Timothy M. *Satch, Dizzy & Rapid Robert: The Wild Saga of Interracial Baseball Before Jackie Robinson.* New York: Simon & Schuster, 2010.

Gilbert, Bill. *They Also Served: Baseball and the Home Front, 1941–1945.* New York: Crown Publishers, 1992.

Gillette, Gary, and Peter Palmer. *ESPN Baseball Encyclopedia.* New York: Sterling, 2008.

Gitlin, Marty. *The Cincinnati Reds.* Edina, MN: ABDO, 2011.

Godin, Robert A. *The 1922 St. Louis Browns: Best of the American League's Worst.* Jefferson, NC: McFarland, 1991.

Goldstein, Richard. *Spartan Seasons: How Baseball Survived the Second World War.* New York: Macmillan, 1980.

Golenbock, Peter. *The Spirit of St. Louis: The History of the St. Louis Cardinals and Browns.* New York: Avon, 2000.

Green, G. Michael, and Roger D. Launius. *Charles Finley: The Outrageous Story of Baseball's Super Showman.* New York: Walker & Company, 2010.

Gregory, Robert. *Dizzy Dean and Baseball During the Great Depression.* New York: Viking, 1992.

Gutman, Dan. *Baseball Babylon: From the Black Sox to Pete Rose: The Real Stories Behind the Scandals That Rocked the Game.* New York: Penguin, 1992.

Harrigan, Patrick. *The Detroit Tigers: Club and Community 1945–1995.* Toronto: University of Toronto Press, 1997.

Harwell, Ernie. *Tuned to Baseball.* South Bend: Diamond Communications, 1985.

Heidenry, John. *The Gashouse Gang: How Dizzy Dean, Branch Rickey, Pepper Martin and Their Colorful, Come-From-Behind Ball Club Won the World Series and America's Heart During the Great Depression.* New York: Public Affairs, 2007.

Heidenry, John, and Brent Topel. *The Boys Who Were Left Behind: The 1944 World Series Between the Hapless St. Louis Browns and the Legendary St. Louis Cardinals.* Lincoln: University of Nebraska Press, 2006.

Helyar, John. *Lords of the Realm: The Real History of Baseball.* New York: Villard, 1994.

Honig, Donald. *Baseball Between the Lines: Baseball In the '40s and '50s As Told by the Men Who Played It.* New York: Coward, McCann & Geoghegan, 1976.

____. *Baseball in the '50s: A Decade of Transition.* New York: Crown Publishers, 1987.

_____. *The Cincinnati Reds: An Illustrated History.* New York: Simon & Schuster: 1992.

Hood, Robert. *The Gashouse Gang,* New York: William Morrow, 1976.

Hornsby, Rogers, and Bill Serface. *My War with Baseball,* New York: Coward-McCann, 1962.

Huhn, Rick. *The Sizzler: George Sisler, Baseball's Forgotten Great.* Columbia: University of Missouri Press, 2004.

Johnson, Lloyd, and Mike Wolff, eds. *The Encyclopedia of Minor League Baseball.* Durham, NC: Baseball America, 1997.

Kashatus, William C. *One-Armed Wonder: Pete Gray, Wartime Baseball, and the American Dream.* Jefferson, N.C: McFarland, 1995.

Kelley, Brent. *Baseball's Biggest Blunder: The Bonus Rule of 1953–1957.* Lanham, MD: Scarecrow, 1997.

_____. *Voices from the Negro Leagues: Conversations with 54 Baseball Standouts of the Period 1924–1960.* Jefferson, NC: McFarland, 1998.

Kennedy, Kostya. *Pete Rose: An American Dilemna.* New York: Sports Illustrated, 2014.

Kerrane, Kevin. *Dollar Sign on the Muscle.* New York: Beaufort, 1984.

Koppett, Leonard. *Koppett's Concise History of Major League Baseball.* New York: Carroll & Graf, 1998.

_____. *Man in the Dugout: Baseball's Top Managers and How They Got That Way.* Philadelphia: Temple University Press, 2000.

Kuhn, Bowie. *Hardball: The Education of a Baseball Commissioner.* New York: Times, 1987.

Lamb, Chris. *Black Out: The Untold Story of Jackie Robinson's First Spring Training.* Lincoln: University of Nebraska Press, 2004.

Lanctot, Neil. *Negro League Baseball: The Rise and Ruin of a Black Institution.* Philadelphia: University of Pennsylvania Press, 2004.

Launius, Roger D. *Seasons in the Sun: The Story of Big League Baseball in Missouri.* Columbia: University of Missouri Press, 2002.

Leavy, Jane. *The Big Fella: Babe Ruth and the World He Created.* New York: HarperCollins. 2018.

Leitner, Irving A. *Baseball: Diamond in the Rough.* New York: Criterion, 1972.

Lieb, Frederick G. *The Baltimore Orioles: The History of a Colorful Team in Baltimore and St. Louis.* New York: G. P. Putnam's Sons, 1955.

_____. *The St. Louis Cardinals: The Story of a Great Baseball Club.* New York: G. P. Putnam's Sons, 1955.

_____. *The Story of the World Series: An Informal History.* New York: G. P. Putnam's Sons, 1949.

Light, Jonathan Fraser. *Cultural Encyclopedia of Baseball.* Jefferson, NC: McFarland, 1997.

Lindberg, Richard. *Who's on 3rd? The Chicago White Sox Story.* South Bend, IN: Icarus, 1983.

Lipman, David. *Mr. Baseball: The Story of Branch Rickey.* New York: G. P. Putnam's Sons, 1966.

Lowenfish, Lee. *Branch Rickey: Baseball's Ferocious Gentleman.* Lincoln: University of Nebraska Press, 2007.

Lowenfish, Lee, and Tony Lupien. *The Imperfect Diamond: The Story of Baseball's Reserve System and the Men Who Fought to Change It.* New York: Stein and Day, 1990.

Madden, Bill. *Pride of October: What It Was to Be Young and a Yankee.* New York: Warner, 2003.

Mann, Arthur. *Branch Rickey: American in Action.* Boston: Houghton Mifflin, 1957.

Marshall, William. *Baseball's Pivotal Era 1945–1951.* Lexington: University Press of Kentucky. 1999.

McCollister, John. *Tigers and Their Den: Official Story of the Detroit Tigers.* Lenexa, KS: Addox, 1999.

McConnell, Jim. *Bobo Newsom: Baseball Traveling Man.* Jefferson, NC: McFarland, 2016.

McGregor, Robert Kuhn. *A Calculus of Color: The Integration of Baseball's American League.* Jefferson, NC: McFarland, 2015.

Mead, William B. *Even the Browns: Baseball During World War II.* Mineola, NY: Dover, 1982.

Meany, Tom. *Baseball's Greatest Teams.* New York: A. S. Barnes, 1949.

Megdal, Howard. *The Cardinals Way: How One Team Embraced Tradition and Moneyball at the Same Time.* New York: Thomas Dunne, 2016.

Mileur, Jerome M. *High-Flying Birds: The 1942 St. Louis Cardinals.* Columbia: University of Missouri Press, 2009.

Miller, James Edward. *The Baseball Business: Pursuing Pennants & Profits in Baltimore.* Chapel Hill: University of North Carolina Press, 1990.

Moffi, Larry, and Jonathan Kronstadt. *Crossing the Line: Black Major Leaguers, 1947–1959.* Iowa City: University of Iowa Press, 1994.

Morris, Peter. *A Game of Inches: The Stories Behind the Innovations That Shaped Baseball.* Chicago: Ivan R. Dee, 2006.

Nathanson, Mitchell. *A People's History of Baseball.* Urbana: University of Illinois Press, 2012.

Neal, Bill. *The International League 1884–1991.* Austin, TX: Eakin, 1991.

_____. *The Southern League: Baseball in Dixie 1885–1994.* Austin, TX: Eakin, 1994.

Neyer, Rob, and Eddie Epstein. *Baseball Dynasties: The Greatest Teams of All Time.* New York: W. W. Norton, 2000.

Oakley, J. Ronald. *Baseball's Last Golden Age, 1946–1960.* Jefferson, NC: McFarland, 1994.

Obojski, Robert. *Bush League: A History of Minor League Baseball.* New York: Macmillan, 1975.

Okrent, Daniel, and Steve Wulf. *Baseball Anecdotes.* New York: Oxford University Press, 1989.

Peary, Danny. *We Played the Game: Memories of Baseball's Greatest Era.* New York: Black Dog & Leventhal, 2002.

_____. *We Played the Game: 65 Players Remember Baseball's Greatest Era, 1947–1964.* New York: Hyperion, 1994.

Pennington, Bill. *Billy Martin: Baseball's Flawed Genius.* Boston: Houghton Mifflin Harcourt, 2015.

Pietrusza, David. *Judge and Jury: The Life and Times of Judge Kenesaw Mountain Landis.* South Bend: Diamond Communications, 1998.

Polner, Murray. *Branch Rickey: A Biography.* New York: Atheneum, 1982.

Preston, Joseph G. *Major League Baseball in the 1970s: A Modern Game Emerges.* Jefferson, NC: McFarland, 2004.

Primm, James Neal. *Lion of the Valley: St. Louis, Missouri.* Boulder, CO: Pruett, 1981.

Rader, Benjamin. *Baseball: A History of the American Game.* Urbana: University of Illinois Press, 2002.

Rains, Rob. *The St. Louis Cardinals: the 100th Anniversary History.* New York: St. Martin's, 1992.

Rampersad, Arnold. *Jackie Robinson: A Biography.* New York: Alfred A. Knopf, 1997.

Rhodes, Greg, and John Snyder. *Redleg Journal: Year by Year and Day by Day with the Cincinnati Reds Since 1866.* Cincinnati: Road West, 2000.

Ritter, Lawrence, and Donald Honig. *The Image of Their Greatness: An Illustrated History of Baseball 1900 to the Present.* New York: Crown Publishers, 1984.

Robinson, Frank, with Al Silverman. *My Life in Baseball.* Garden City, NY: Doubleday, 1968.

Seymour, Harold, and Dorothy Seymour Mills. *Baseball: The Golden Age, Vol. 2.* New York: Oxford University Press, 1971.

Shannon, Mike, and Scott Hanning. *Hutch: Baseball's Fred Hutchinson and a Legacy of Courage.* Jefferson NC: McFarland, 2011.

Smith, Robert. *Baseball in the Afternoon.* New York: Simon & Schuster, 1993.

Snyder, Brad. *A Well-Paid Slave: Curt Flood's Fight for Free Agency in Professional Sports.* New York: Viking, 2006.

Solomon, Burt. *Baseball Time Line.* New York: Avon, 1997.

Spink, J. G. Taylor. *Judge Landis and Twenty-Five Years of Baseball.* New York: Thomas Y. Crowell, 1947.

Staten, Vince. *Ol' Diz: A Biography of Dizzy Dean.* New York: HarperCollins, 1992.

Staudohar, Paul D. *Diamond Mines: Baseball & Labor.* Syracuse: Syracuse University Press, 2000.

Steinberg, Steve. *Baseball in St. Louis: 1900–1925.* Charleston, SC: Arcadia. 2004.

Stevens, Walter Barlow. *Centennial History of Missouri, Volume XI.* Chicago: S. J. Clarke, 1921.

Sullivan, Dean A., ed. *Late Innings: A Documentary History of Baseball, 1945–1972,* Lincoln: University of Nebraska Press, 2002.

Swaine, Rick. *The Integration of Major League Baseball: A Team by Team History.* Jefferson, NC: McFarland, 2009.

Thomas, Joan M. *Baseball's First Lady: Helene Hathaway Robison Britton and the St. Louis Cardinals*. St. Louis: Reedy Press. 2010.
Thorn, John, Phil Birnbaum, Bill Deane, et al., eds. *Total Baseball: The Ultimate Baseball Encyclopedia*. Wilmington, DE: Sport Media, 2004.
Tracy, David F. *The Psychologist at Bat*. New York: Sterling, 1951.
Tygiel, Jules. *Baseball's Great Experiment: Jackie Robinson and His Legacy*. New York: Oxford University Press, 1983.
Van Lindt, Carson. *One Championship Season: The Story of the 1944 Browns*. New York: Marabon, 1994.
Vescey, George. *History of America's Favorite Game*. New York: Modern Library, 2000.
Voigt, David Quentin. *American Baseball, Volume III: From Postwar Expansion to the Electronic Age*. University Park: Pennsylvania State University Press, 1983.
Wallop, Douglas. *Baseball: An Informal History*. New York: W. W. Norton, 1969.
Weeks, Jonathan. *Baseball's Dynasties and the Players Who Built Them*. Lanham, MD: Rowman & Littlefield, 2016.
Wheeler, Lonnie, and John Baskin. *The Cincinnati Game*. Wilmington, OH: Orange Frazer, 1988.
Wilson, Doug. *Fred Hutchinson and the Cincinnati Reds*. Jefferson, NC: McFarland, 2010.
Zminda, Don. *The Legendary Harry Caray: Baseball's Greatest Salesman*. Lanham, MD: Rowman & Littlefield, 2019.

Magazine Articles

"Angels and the Hot Foot." *Time*, February 14, 1949, 72.
"Ballcasts Curb?" *Broadcasting*, December 4, 1950, 27, 112.
Boyle, Robert H. "Cincinnati's Brain-Picker." *Sports Illustrated*, June 13, 1966, 41–42, 47–48, 50.
Bradley, Hugh. "He's Traded Three Million in Talent." *Baseball Digest*, March 1962, 63–66.
Brosnan, Jim. "Boom Go the Big Red Bats." *Sports Illustrated*, August 16, 1965, 12–13, 52–53.
_____. "Businessmen Are Wrecking Baseball." *Saturday Evening Post*, May 30, 1964, 8.
"The Brothers DeWitt." *Newsweek*, February 14, 1949, 71–72.
"Browns to Barnes." *Time*, November 23, 1936, 40.
Burnes, Robert L. "Damper on Interleague Deals." *Baseball Digest*, February 13, 1967, 13–14.
Carmichael, John P. "There's No Substitute for Defense." *Baseball Digest*, March 1966, 29–30.
Cope, Myron. "Frank Robinson: The Facts Behind His Discontent." *Sport*, June 1963, 57–60, 63–65.
_____. "The Shadow Hanging Over the Cincinnati Reds." *Sport*, June 1962, 40–43, 90.
Creamer, Robert. "The Sick Man of Baseball." *Sports Illustrated*, December 17, 1956, 48–49.
Crichton, Kyle. "The Unbelievable Browns." *Collier's*, September 2, 1944, 14, 40.
"Died. William DeWitt." *Time*, March 15, 1982, 92.
Donnelly, Joe. "Frank Robinson's Crusade." *Sport*, August 1966, 20, 22–23, 73.
Enright, James. "Why Reds Traded Robinson." *Baseball Digest*, February 1966, 19–20.
Fay, Bill. "Inside Sports." *Collier's*, March 26, 1949, 79.
"He Should Have Signed the Co-Pilot." *Baseball Digest* September 1965, 108.
"Homers by Hypnosis." *American Magazine*, April 1950, 101.
Hornsby, Rogers, and Kyle Crichton. "Here's What I Mean." *Collier's*, February 16, 1938, 20, 52–53.
Izenberg, Jerry. "Frank Robinson: Pressures on the Triple-Crown Winner." *Sport*, August 1967, 65–70.
Leggett, William. "The Men Who Fired Managers." *Sports Illustrated*, September 12, 1966, 44–45.
Leo, John. "Baseball's Happy Hustler." *Time*, January 13, 1986, 86.
Luce, Henry Robinson. "Hard-Boiled Hornsby Starts in on Browns." *Life*, March 31, 1952, 84.
Macht, Norman. "Roy Sievers: A Forgotten Power Hitter of the 1950s." *Baseball Digest*, February 1990, 56–58.
McHugh, Roy. "Joey Jay in Control of Himself." *Sport*, August 1963, 49–52, 55–57.

McIver, Stuart. "Will Baltimore Be Another Milwaukee?" *Sport,* March 1954, 20–21, 82–85.
Miller, Hub. "The Mahatma's Magic." *Baseball Magazine* 76 (DATE MISSING), 299–300, 320, 322.
"Reds Safe at Home." *Sports Illustrated,* January 14, 1963, 8.
"A Respectable Sideline." *Sports Illustrated,* February 14, 1956, 11–12.
Robinson, Frank, and Roy Blount, Jr. "I'll Always Be Outspoken." *Sports Illustrated,* October 20, 1974, 31–37.
Shecter, Leonard. "Deron Johnson: The Man and the Challenge." *Sport,* February 1966, 53, 55–58.
Sports Collectors Digest, September 3, 2010, 8–9.
"Thanks, Bill." *Time,* September 30, 1966, 69.
"Tinker to Evers to Freud." *Collier's,* March 11, 1950, 74.
Twombly, Wells. "Taps for an Era." *Baseball Digest,* February 1966, 63–64.
Veech, Ellis J. "The DeWitt Brothers and the Browns." *Baseball Magazine,* May 1949, 417–418.
_____. "Horatio Alger Success in Baseball." *Baseball Magazine,* February 1949, 301–302.
Veeck, Bill, and Ed Linn. "Back Where I Belong." *Sports Illustrated,* March 15, 1976, 73, 81–82.
Young, Dick. "The Big Leagues' Iron Curtain." *Sport,* September 1963, 18, 73).

SABR BioProject Profiles

Armour, Mark. "Jim Brosnan."
___. "Sam Breadon."
Ferkovich, Scott. "Sportsmen's Park (St. Louis)."
Isgrig, Dwayne. "Bill DeWitt."
Johnson, Bill. "Jim Bottomley."
McCue, Andy. "Branch Rickey."
Steinberg, Steve. "Robert Hedges."
Thomas, Joan M. "Federal League Park (St. Louis)."
___. "Robison Field (St. Louis)."
Wancho, Joseph. "Gabby Street."
___. "Luke Sewell."

Newspapers

Ada (OK) *Evening News*
Adrian (MI) *Daily Globe*
Albert Lea (MN) *Union Tribune*
Alton (IL) *Telegraph*
Amarillo Sunday News Globe
Annapolis (MD) *Capital*
Appleton (WI) *Crescent*
Arizona Republic
Austin (MN) *Herald*
Baytown (TX) *Sun*
Beckley (WV) *Post Herald & Register*
Benton Harbor (MI) *News-Palladian*
Billings (MT) *Gazette*
Biloxi (MS) *Daily Herald*
Bismarck (ND) *Tribune*
Bluefield (WV) *Daily Telegraph*
Blytheville (AK) *Courier News*
Brainard (MN) *Dispatch*
Bridgeport (CT) *Post*
Bridgeport (CT) *Telegram*
Brookfield (MO) *Argus*
Brookfield Lynn County (MO) *Budget Gazette*
Burlington (NC) *Daily Times*
Butte (MT) *Gazette*
Butte Montana Standard
Centralia (IL) *Evening Sentinel*
Charleston (WV) *Daily Mail*
Chicago Daily Tribune
Chicago Defender
Cincinnati Enquirer
Columbus (NE) *Daily Telegram*
Corpus Christi Times
Edwardsville (IL) *Intelligencer*
El Paso (TX) *Herald Post*
Escanaba (MI) *Daily Press*
Fergus Falls (MN) *Daily Journal*
Flagstaff (AZ) *Sun*
Florence (SC) *Morning News*
Galveston (TX) *Daily News*
Gastonia (NC) *Daily Gazette*
Greeley (CO) *Tribune*
Hagerstown (MD) *Daily Mail*
Hammond (IN) *Times*
Harlingen (TX) *Valley Morning Star*
Helena (MT) *Independent Record*
Holland (MI) *Evening Sentinel*
Hutchinson (KS) *News*
Independence (MO) *Examiner*
Ironwood (MI) *Daily Globe*
Jacksonville (IL) *Courier*
Janesville (WI) *Daily Gazette*
Jefferson City (MO) *Capitol News*
Jefferson City (MO) *Post Tribune*
Joplin (MO) *Argus*
Joplin (MO) *Herald*
Kalispell (MT) *Inter Lake*
Kingston (TN) *Times*

Bibliography

Kokomo (IN) *Tribune*
Ladue News *(St. Louis)*
Las Vegas (NV) *Sun*
Lawton (OK) *Constitution*
Lincoln (NE) *State Journal*
Logansport (IN) *Tribune*
Loredo (TX) *Times*
Lowell (MA) *Sun*
Lubbock (TX) *Morning Avalanche*
Manetowac (MI) *Herald Times*
Marshall (MN) *Evening Chronicle*
Maryville (MO) *Daily Forum*
Miami News
Middlesboro (KY) *Daily News*
Middletown (NY) *Times Herald Record*
Moberly (MO) *Monitor*
Monroe (LA) *News Star*
Moorhead (MN) *Daily News*
Morgantown (WV) *Post*
Nashua (NH) *Telegram*
Neosho (MO) *Daily Democrat*
New Castle (PA) *News*
New York Times
North Adams (MA) *Transport*
Panama City (FL) *News Herald*
Petersburg (VA) *Progress Index*
Phoenix Daily Republican
Pittsfield (MA) *Berkshire Eagle*
Portland (ME) *Press Herald*
Racine (WI) *Journal Times*
Rocky Mount (NC) *Evening Forum*
Ruston (LA) *Daily Leader*
St. Louis Globe-Democrat
St. Louis Post-Dispatch
St. Louis Star Times
Saline (KS) *Journal*
Salisbury (MD) *Daily Times*
Salt Lake City Tribune
San Antonio Light
San Mateo (CA) *Times*
Scottsdale (AZ) *Daily Progress*
The Sporting News
Statesville (NC) *Record*
Thomasville (GA) *Times Enterprise*
Traverse City (MI) *Record Eagle*
Twin Falls (ID) *News*
Walla Walla (WA) *Union Bulletin*
Wichita (TX) *Daily Times*
Woodland (CA) *Daily Democrat*
Zanesville (OH) *Signal*
Zanesville (OH) *Times Reporter*

INTERVIEWS AND ORAL HISTORIES

Bartholomay, William (Bill). Telephone interview by authors, December 13, 2017.
DeWitt, William O., Jr. Interview by authors, August 17, 2018.
DeWitt, William O. (Bill), Sr. Interview by William J. Marshall, September 29, 1980. A. B. "Happy" Chandler: Desegregation of Major League Baseball Oral History Project. Louie B. Nunn Center for Oral History. University of Kentucky Libraries.
Herzog, Whitey. Telephone interview by authors, March 13, 2018.
Holekamp, Malcolm (Mac). Telephone interview by authors, September 21, 2018.
Holekamp, Stark. Interview by authors May 4, 2018.
Holekamp, William Francis (Bill). Interview by authors, September 17, 2018.
Lambert, DeDe. Telephone interviews by authors, April 4, 2018 and August 8, 2018.
Lowenfish, Lee. Telephone interview by authors, April 10, 2019.
McKean, Joan DeWitt. Interview by authors, May 4, 2018.
Phelps, Trent Barnes. Interview by authors, July 2017.
Stack, Edward W. Telephone interview by authors, June 11, 2018.

ON-LINE RESOURCES

Baseball-almanac.com
Baseball-reference.com
DizzyDean.com
Findagrave.com/memorial
Hansen Marketing Services.com
HistoryofCardinals.com
Razzball.com
Retrosheet.org
SABR.org

Index

Numbers in ***bold italics*** indicate pages with illustrations

Aaron, Hank 170
Airey, Guy 39
Alexander, Grover Cleveland 18, 19
All American Professional Football Conference 82
All-Star Game 169
Allen, Johnny 42, 43
Alpha Sigma Nu 17
American Association 29, 68, 76, 102, 113, 120; Denver 137
American Investment Company 27
American League 28–30, 34, 37, 40, 44, 45, 49, 55, 56, 57, 60, 63, 66, 69, 73, 78, 85, 89, 94, 97, 99, 101, 102, 104, 107, 108, 110–111, 113–114, 116, 121, 124–125, 134–136, 143, 146–147, 166, 169, 174, 178–180
Anaheim, CA 70
Anderson, Andy 91
Angelos, Peter 184
Anheuser-Busch Brewery 111, 185
Aparicio, Luis 134
Appling, Luke 134
Appreciation Night 93
Arft, Hank 96
Arthur, Harry 45
Aspromonte, Bob 161
Atlanta Braves 159
Auker, Eldon 40, 41, 43, 44, 49, 51
Auto Security Company (Springfield, IL) 27
Autry, Gene 177

Bailey, Ed 144–145
Baldschun, Jack 165, 167
Ball, Philip DeCatesby 9–10, 27 75
Ballpark Village (St. Louis) 186
Baltimore Colts 82
Baltimore Orioles 45, 95, 112, 116–118, 125, 165–166, 168–170, 185
Bannister, Alan 178

Barnes, Anita (Donald's daughter) 27
Barnes, Donald 27, ***28***–29, 31–***32***, 33, 34, 35, 37–38, 39, 40, 41, 42, 43, 45, 47, 48, 49, 52, 53, 54, 55, 59, ***61***, 64, 65–66, 92, 104, 112, 118. 150, 153
Barrett, Charles 12, 16, 19
Bartholomay, Billl 181
Baseball Coordinator (Minor Leagues) 126–128, 130–131, 132
Baseball Writers' Association of America 93
Baseball's Executive Council, 1977 179
Batts, Matt 108
Bauer, Hank 123
Bean, Bill 37
Bearden, Gene 108, 110
Bell, Gus 142, 145
Bell, Lester 4
Bell, William Randolph (grandson DeWitt, Sr.) 144
Bench, Johnny 172
Benswanger, Bill 54
Berardino, John 36, 37, 39, 40, 42, 48, 49, 68, 73, ***74***, 76, 95, 100
Berberet, Lou 120
Berra, Yogi 120, 124–125, 147
Big Red Machine 172
Birmingham Black Barons 80
Blades, Ray 19
Blasingame, Don 144–145
Blyzka, Mike 114
Bonds, Barry 7
Bonds, Bobby 7
Boone, Aaron 7
Boone, Bob 7
Boone, Bret 7
Boone, Ray 7
Boston Bees 43
Boston Braves 13, 111, 113

217

Boston Red Sox 27, 33, 40, 41, 42, 59, 67, 73, 74, 84, 85, 91, 95–96, 115, 118, 123, 126, 150
Bottomley, Jim 19, 32–33. 178
BPO Elks #9 119
Bradley, Alva 44
Bradley, George 70, 73
Breadon, Sam 15, 16, 18, 40, 45, 55, 63, 112
Brecheen, Harry "The Cat" 60, 109
Briggs, Walter O. 133
Briggs Stadium 133, 136–137, 139
Bristol, Dave 168–169, 171
Britton, Helene Robison 11, 15
Broeg, Bob 138
Brooklyn Dodgers 35, 52, 54, 69, 75, 78, 109, 122, 125, 135
Brosnan, Jim 146, 153, 155–156
Brown, Kenyon 136
Brown, Willard 78, 79, *80*
Brownie Brigade 14, 72
Browns Boys and Girls Brigade 41
Browns Hall of Fame 181
Brucker, Earle 94, 100
Buffalo, New York 173
Burbank, CA 84, 90, 96
Burnett, Dick 99
Busch, August A., Jr. 111, 175, 178, 185
Busch Stadium III 185–186
Bush, George W. 183
Bush Exploration 183
Buskey, Mike 178
Butler, Willis 59
Byrnes, Milt 69

Cahill, Ray 39
Cain, Bob 108, 110
California Angels 177
Campbell, Jimmy 134
Cape Girardeau, MO 50, 53, 54, 64, 68
Caray, Harry 76
Cardenos, Leo 157, 164
Carleton, Tex 20, 64
Carpenter, Bob 126–127
Carroll, Parke 119
Carruthersville, MO 50
Cash, Norman 135
Castellini, Bob 183
Caster, George 42, 43, 68
Catholic Archdiocese of St. Louis 90
Chandler, "Happy" 68, 71, 72, 99
Chartak, Mike 49, 52
Chase Manhattan Bank 175
Chicago American 165
Chicago Cardinals (NFL) 52
Chicago Cubs 24, 45, 50, 102, 120, 145, 150
Chicago White Sox 7, 34, 50, 51, 87, 115, 117, 122, 142, 155–156, 158, 176, 178–180, 182

Chiles, Eddie 183
Christman, Mark 37, 57, 60, 67, 70–71
Cincinnati Board of Trustees 151
Cincinnati Chamber of Commerce 167
Cincinnati Enquirer 142, 167, 171
Cincinnati Municipal Baseball Advisory Council 162
Cincinnati Reds 7, 18, 29, 140–*141*, 142–145, 147–148, 150–156, 157–160, 163, 165–167, 169–170, 172, 182
Cincinnati Riverfront Coliseum 183
Cincinnati Shriners Hospital Crippled Children 161
Cincinnati Stingers 175, 183
Cincinnati Traffic Club 151
City Ice and Fuel 48, 67, 90
Clancy, Tom 184
Clary, Ellis 53
Clement, Dr. Rufus Early 123
Cleveland Indians 31, 35, 40, 44, 48, 57, 73, 76, 78, 103, 119, 120–121, 129–130, 135–136, 166, 174
Cleveland Ohio Plain Dealer 100
Clift, Harlond 36, 39, 40, 42, 53
Coates, Jim 147
Cobb, Ty 136–137
Colavito, Rocky 136–137
Cole, Ed 40
Coleman, Gordon 145, 157, 164, 167
Coleman, Jerry 122, 125, 134
Coleman, Ray 94
Collins, "Ripper" 20
Columbus Red Birds 54, 68
Comb, Earle 82
Comiskey Park 176
Continental League 135
Conzelman, Jimmy 52
Cook, Cliff 150
Cooper, Mort 60, 61, 77
Corpus Christi Times 144
Courtney, Clint 110
Cox, Bill 36
Craig, Roger 155, 162
Creamer, Robert 127–128
Crosley, Powel, Jr. 140, 142–143, 148, 150, 152
Crosley Field 159, 161–163
Crosley Foundation 150–152
Cullenbine, Roy 43

Daily, Arthur 107
D'Alesandre, Thomas 98, 117
Daley, Bill 174
Dallas Eagles (Texas League) 99
Dalton, Harry 164
Daniel, Dan 92
Darst, Joseph 113

Index

Davis, Marvin 179
Davis, Piper 80
Dean, Jay Hannah "Dizzy" 20–*21*, 22–*23*, 24, 76, 77, 109
Dean, Paul 20, *23*, 51, 52
DeBartolo, Edward J., Sr. 179–180
Defense Transportation Coordinator 50
DeLancey, Bill 20
Delsing, Jim 98
DeMars, Billy 94
Demeter, Steve 135
Democratic Party 90
Denver Bears 121
Detroit Tigers 7, 35, 37, 40, 41, 51, 55, 58, 60, 68, 85, 94, 108, 131–132, 135–139, 164, 177, 182
Detroit Times 134–135
Devine, Bing 138, 171
DeWitt, Charles Wakefield (brother) 8, 33–34, 39, 43, 75, *79*, 81, 84, 88–*90*, 92, 96, 97, 98, 100, 101, 104–106, 131, 172
DeWitt, Donna Dorothy "DeeDee" (daughter) 37, 121, 144, 181
DeWitt, Joan Margaret (daughter) 29, 112, 181
DeWitt, LuLu May (mother) 8, 131
DeWitt, Margaret Holekamp (wife) 25, *26*, 29, 43, 112, 132, 140, 154, 174, 176, 181
DeWitt, William Joseph (father) 8
DeWitt, William, Jr. (son) 44, *89*, 107, 112, 156, 162, 171, 175, 182, 184, *185*
DeWitt, William O., Sr. *13*, *23*, *26*, *32*, *75*, *79*, *80*, *90*, *93*, *105*, *109*, *118*, *129*, *141*, *158*, *161*, *177*, 186
DeWitt, William O. III *177*, *185*
DeWitt Brothers 8, 89, 114
DeWitt Insurance Agency 89
Dickey, Bill 35
Dillhoefer, "Pickles" 14
Dillinger, Bob 50, 70, *80*, 88, 91, 93, 94, 95
DiMaggio, Joe 73
Doby, Larry 78
Donnelly, Blix 60
Douthit, Taylor 19
Drabowski, Mo 150
Dunn, Jack III 113
Duren, Ryne 116
Durney, William 96
Durocher, Leo "Lipppy" 20, 35
Dyer, Eddie 19
Dykes, Jimmy 108, 133, 135–137

Eastern League 96, 108, 120
Edwards, John 157, 159–161, 164
Ehlers, Arthur 116–117
Einhorn, Eddie 180
Eliot, Bob 113

Ellis, Sammy 150, 159–161, 164, 167
Elmira, NY 82
Elmira, NY (Eastern League) 57, 82
Embree, Red 88
Enright, James 165
Epps, Harold 54
Erie County Legislature 173
Erie County, New York 173
Estallela, Bobby 43
Executive of Year: (1944) 62; (1961) 147

Falls, Joe 134
Falstaff Brewery 107
Fan Manager for a Day 108
Fanchot and Marco 45
Fannin, Cliff 88
Federal League 9–10
Feller, Bob 73
Ferrell, Rick 43, 52, 133–135, 138
Ferrick, Tom 98
Fetzer, John 132, 135, 139, 177
Finch, Robert 74
Finley, Charles 177–178
Finney, Lou 69, 70, 73
Florida State League 30
Ford, Whitey 122, 125, 146
Fort Smith AR Class C Farm Club (Cardinals) 19
Fournier, Jack 30, 34, 54, 75, 95
Fox, Nellie 134
Freese, Gene 142, 145–146
Frick, Ford 111, 124, 152, 160, 163
Frisch, Frank 20
Fritsh, Walter 27
Fuggeth, Jean 184
Fullis, Chuck 20
Fulton County Stadium 181
Funston, Keith G. 163

Gaedel, Eddie 107–108
Galehouse, Dennis 42, 43, 49, 52, 60, 73
Gallagher, Joe 39, 56
Garver, Ned 99, 100, 101, 110
Gas House Gang 19–20
Gehrig, Lous 125
Giles, Warren 29, 113, 140, 143, 150, 166
Gill, George 37
Gilliland, G.E. "Eddie" 30, 128, 130
Glenn, Joe 34, 35, 3, .39, 40
Gordon, Joe 94, 134, 136–138
Grace, Joe 39, 42, 43, 69, 73
Graham, Jack 96
Grand, Charles 96
Grapefruit League 109–110
Gray, James 25
Gray, Pete 63, *66*, 68
Gray & Holekamp 25

Index

Green Light Letter 47
Greenberg, Hank 73, 77, 129–130, 176
Griffey, Ken, Jr. 7
Griffey, Ken, Sr. 7
Griffith, Clark 47
Grim, Bob 122, 124
Grimes, Burleigh 34, 35
Grimm, Charlie 101–103
Groat, Dick 134
Gryska, Sig 36
Gustine, Frank 94, 96
Gutteridge, Don 47, 67, 70

Hafey, Chick 19
Haines, Jesse 18, 20
Hallahan, Bill 20
Hamey, Roy 117
Handel, Norman 93, 174
Haney, Fred 35, 37, 38, 41, 43, 44
Hannegan, Robert 47
Hannibal, MO 50
Hansen, Harvey 136
Harper, Tommy 150, 155, 161, 164, 167
Harridge, William 40, 41, 71, 73, 108, 117, 125
Harris, Bob 37, 42
Harris, Bucky 178
Harrist, Earl 110
Harshanny, Sam 37, 39
Harvard Business School (MBA) 182, 185
Hayworth, Myron 64
Heath, Jeff 73, 76
Hedges, Robert 10
Heeken, Brian 183
Heffner, Don 33, 36, 39, 52, 164, 167–168
Held, Woodie 121
Helms, Tommy 155, 162
Henry, Bill 145, 155, 160
Herman, Billy 178
Hildebrand, Oral 31, 34, 35
Hillenkoetter, Roscoe 10
Hillman, Dave 150
Hitchcock, Billy 137–138
Hoag, Myril 34, 35, 37, 39
Hodges, Gil 122
Hoffberger, Jerry 111, 115
Hofmann, Freddy 65, 81, 94
Holekamp, Fred (Margaret's father) 26, 56, 173
Holekamp, Richard (Margaret's uncle) 26
Holekamp, Robert Augustus (Margaret's grandfather) 25
Holekamp Lumber Company (Webster Groves, MO) 25, 173
Hollingsworth, Al "Boots," 47, 49, 67
Hollomon, BoBo 115

Holm, Wattie 19
Hook, Jay 145
Hope, Bob 174
Hopp, Johnny 77
Hornsby, Rogers "Rajah" 16, *17*, 18, 27, 29–*32*, *109*
Houghton, Percy 13
Houk, Ralph 121, 146
Houston Astros 161
Houston Colt .45s 140, 142, 145
Howard, Elston 120, 147
Howsam, Bob 171–173
Hoyt, Waite 18
Hubbard, Cal 178
Huggins, Millard 11
Hunter, Billy 122
Hurley, Ed 107
Hurth, Charles 135
Hutchinson, Fred 137, *141*, 145, 149, 155–*158*, 159, 161, 167–168
Hyland, Robert 147

inaugural Browns night game 40
integration, racial 54, 57, 78
International League 33, 95, 99, 116
International Shoe Company 28
Ippolitto, Rocco 94, 114

Jacobs, Eli 184
Jakucki, Sig 60, 67
Jay, Joey 142, 145, 148–149, 153–159, 161, 164, 167
Johnson, Arnold 119, 126
Johnson, Darrell 121
Johnson, Deron 164, 167, 170
Johnson, Ernest Duncan 116
Johnston, James 173
Jones, Fielder 11
Jones, James 11, 14
Jones, Willie 142
Judnich, Walter 40, 43, 48, 51, 69

Kaat, Jim 178
Kaline, Al 137
Kansas City Athletics 167
Kansas City Blues 94, 119
Kansas City Monarchs 78, 116
Karst, Eugene 22
Kearney, James R. 39
Keeley, James J. 123
Keener, Sid. 38, 82, 86
Kell, George 110
Kennedy, Vernon 37, 41, 43
Kentucky Colonials 183
Keough, Marty 155
Kess, Mrs. Stanley E. (Crosley's daughter) 143, 151

Index   221

Kess, Stanley E. (Crosley's son-in-law) 143, 148
Killibrew, Harmon 136
Kinder, Ellis 64, 72
Kiner, Ralph 77, 120
Klein, Chuck 178
Klippstein, Johnny 150, 155
Knights of the Cauliflower Ear 91, 147
Knothole Gang (St. Louis Cardinals) 14, 72
Kokos, Dick 96, 114
Konstanty, Jim 122, 124
Koupal, Louis 31
Kramer, Jack 54, 57, 63, 64, 70, 73, 82, 118
Kraus, Pete 39
Kreevich, Mike 57, 68
Kress, Red 33, 36, 37
Kryhoski, Dick 108, 110
KSD-TV 77
Kubek, Tony 121
Kucks, Johnny 125
Kuenn, Harvey 136
Kuhn, Bowie 176. 179
Kwak, Karol 116

Laabs, Chet 37, 39, 43, 49, 52, 55, *61*, 67, 69
LaMacchia, Al 73
Lamping, Mark 186
Landis, Commissioner Kenesaw Mountain 16, 23, 43, 47, 54, 61
Lane, Frank 130, 135–137
Lanier, Max 60
Lardner, John 107
Larsen, Don 114, 120–122, 125–126
Lavan, Jimmy 14
Lawson, Roxie 37
Layden, Pete 82
Lazzeri, Tony 19
Lehner, Paul 94, 103
LeMay, Curtis E. 163
Lemon, Bob 99
Lemon, James H., Sr. 174
Lenhardt, Don 101, 103
Leonard, Dutch 60
Levinson, Barry 184
Lewis, Johnny 162
Lieb, Frederick G. 62
Lindstrum, Fred 178
Linke, Ed 33
Littlefield, Dick 108
Litwhiler, Danny 60, 61
Lollar, Sherman 88
Long Season 155
Lopat, Eddie 121
Lopez, Al 178
Loria, Jeffrey 184

Los Angeles, CA 45–46, 100
Los Angeles Dodgers 144, 156–157, 163, 169, 179
Los Angeles Times 107
Lucadello, Johnny 39, 42
Lutz, Barney 58, 70
Lynch, Jerry 146, 148, 151, 155

MacDougal, Gil 125
Mack, Connie 57, 68, 72, 117, 119, 124
MacPhail, Andy 7
MacPhail, Larry 7, 51, 143
MacPhail, Lee 7, 176
Maloney, Jim 145, 154, 161–164, 167
Manager of Year, 1944 62
Mancuso, Gus 50, 63
Mantle, Mickey 120, 124–125, 146
Mapes, Cliff 108
Marion, Marty 61, 109, 110, 114, 117
Maris, Roger 146
Marshall, Clarence 114, 117
Martin, Babe (Martinovich, Boris Michael) 65, 70, 72
Martin, Billy 124–125, 142
Martin, Pepper 20, *22*
Maxwell, Charlie 134
May, Lee 162
Mazeroski, Bill 134
McCarthy, Joe 82
McCool, Billy 161, 164, 167
McDermott, Maury 124
McElroy, Mark (Ohio attorney general) 151–153
McEvoy, Lew C. 27
McGraw, John 163
McHale, John 133
McKane, Archie 54
McKay, Jim 184
McLaughlin, Jim 173
McLish, Cal 142
McManus, Marty 43
McMillan, Roy 142, 155
McQuillen, Glenn 39, 51
McQuinn, George "Red" 33, 36, 37, 39, 40, 42, 51, 55, 57, 60, 67, 68, 69, 72
Medwick, Joseph "Ducky" 20
Melillo, Oscar 27, 33, 34, 35
Memorial Stadium (Baltimore) 113
Mercer Reynolds 183
Merrill Lynch, Inc. 175
Mexican baseball 71, 76
Miles, Clarence (Baltimore Orioles chairman) 115–117, 122–123
Miller, Fred 100, 101, 113
Mills, Buster 33, 34, 35
Mills, John 53
Milner, Al 58

Milwaukee Braves 100, 101, 115, 122, 142, 145, 159, 181
Milwaukee Brewers 174
Minar, Al 73
Minnesota Twins 169
Mission Stadium (San Antonio) 101
Missouri South East University (Cape Girardeau) 55
Mize, Johnny 178
Monahan, Pat 39
Moncrief, Bob 57
Mooney, Jim 20
Moore, Gene 64, 69–70
Moore, Ray 125
Mora, George 95
Mora, Mrs. George 95
Morgan, Tom 122
Moss, Les 76, 95
Muckerman, Richard "Dick" 75, 78–80, 81–82, 86, 88, 89, 103, 114, 118
Muckerman Death 90
Mueller, Heine 19
Muncrief, Bob 67
Murray, Jim 107
Musial, Stan 60, 160, 181

National Association Professional Baseball Leagues 127
National Baseball Hall of Fame Veterans Committee 178
National Brewing Company 111
National Defense League 55
National Hockey League 175, 183
National League 34, 59, 111, 113, 119, 122, 136, 140, 142–143, 151. 153, 158, 160, 163, 165–166, 168, 170–173, 175, 180; Most Valuable Player (1961) 148
National League Pennant 145, 149–150
Negro American League 80, 116
Negro National League 78, 79
Nerinx High School 27
New York Giants 58, 79, 119, 135; NFL stadium effort 186
New York Jets 186
New York Mets 143, 155, 164, 168
New York-Pennsylvania League 169
New York Times 107, 172
New York Yankees 7, 16, 18, 30, 32, 33, 34, 40, 50, 53, 55, 59, 60, 67, 72, 73. 85, 92, 94, 95, 98, 99, 109, 117–125, 138, 146–147, 164, 179, 182
Newark Eagles 78
Newsom, Bobo 27, 33, 36, 37, 53–54
Nieman, Bob 110
Niggling, Johnny 43
night baseball 28–29, 53, 71–72, 85, 111
Noerdman, Bill 10

Noren, Irv 124
Nunn, Howie 145
Nuxall, Joe 142, 154, 164, 167

Oak Grove Cemetery (St. Louis) 181
Oakland A's 177
Oceak, Frank 161
Office of Defense Transportation 59
O'Hara, Johnny 76
Ohio State Bar Association 171
Ohio State League 68
O'Malley, Walter 126
Orsatti, Ernie 20
Osley, Bill 39
Ostermueller, Fritz 42, 43, 54
Ostrowski, Joe 82, 98
Otero, Reggie 157, 161
O'Toole, Jim 145–148, 153–155, 160, 167

Pacific Coast League 31, 45, 72, 164
Pappas, Milt 165–167
Partee, Roy 88
Pasquel Brothers 71
Paul, Gabe 126, 140, 145. 163, 166
Pavletich, Don 150, 159, 164
Pellagrini, Eddy 82
Pennant Race 153, 155
Pennock, Herb 18
Perez, Tony 159, 162, 164, 172
Perini, Lou 111–112, 181
Perkins, Vachal 116
Perry, Emory C. 80
Philadelphia Athletics 57, 58, 67, 68, 72, 86, 94, 103, 108, 112, 115, 117, 119, 164
Philadelphia Phillies 117, 142, 159, 178
Pierce, Billy 122
Pilgrim, Bill 100
Pillette, Duane 98, 101
Pinkerton (Agency) 31
Pinson, Vada 145, 155, 161, 164, 167
Pittsburgh Pirates 40, 50, 54, 84, 100, 120, 135, 137, 141, 144–145
Pizzaro, Juan 142
Plews, Herb 124
Podres, Johnny 122
Polar Wave Ice & Fuel 48
Poplar Bluff, MO 50
Porter, Roy 82
Porterfield, Bob 123
Post, Jim 116
Post, Wally 145, 147, 155
Potter, Nelson 60, 73
Povich, Shirley 117
Power, Wallace (Cincinnati Public Utilities) 162
Price, Jackie 137

Priddy, Jerry 84, 91, 93, 94
Purkey, Bob 145, 153–155, 157, 162

Quinn, John 126

Reinsdorf, Jerry 180
Reynolds, Allie 119
Reynolds, DeWitt & Co. 183
Rhem, Flint 19
Richards, Paul 117, 122, 125, 125, 176
Richardson, Bob 121, 125
Richman, Milton 169
Rickey, Branch 9–12, 14, 16, **22**, 26–27, 29–30, 35, 50, 51, 57, 69, 78, **79**, 99, 100, 119, 123, 135, 147, 166, 174, 180–181
Rickey, Branch, Jr. 51, 69
Rippe, Joseph, Jr. 151–152
Riverfront Stadium (Cincinnti) 175
Rizzuto, Phil 94, 134
Robert Hyland Award 147
Robeson, Paul 54
Robinson, Eddie 122
Robinson, Frank 142, 145–148, **149**, 153–154. 157, 161, 164–166, 168–171
Robinson, Herky 173
Robinson, Jackie 78
Robison Field 9, 11, 15
Rodenberger, Bob 82
Rojas, Cookie 150
Rolfe, Red 108
Roosevelt, Frankin Delano 47, 62
Rose, Pete 155, 161, 164, 172
Rose, Rusty 183
Roseboro, John 157
Rothrock, Jack 20
Ruel, Harold "Muddy" 34–35, 74, **75**, 81–82, 146
Ruiz, Chico 150, 159
Ruth, Babe 18–19, 35, 87, **89**
Ruthven, Dick 178

Saigh, Fred M., Jr. 91, 92, 100, 102, 108, 111–112
Sain, Johnny 119
St. Louis Advertising Club 98
St. Louis Baseball Writers 147
St. Louis Blues 183
St. Louis Browns 7, 9–10, 12, 14–16. 24–25, 27–40, 44, 45, 48, 49, 50, 51, 52, 53, 54, 55, **56**, 57, 58, 59, 60, 61, **63**, 67, 67, 70, 71, 72, 73, 74, 77, 78, 79, 80, 81, 84, 91, 92, 95, 97, 98, 100–103, 106, 111–114, 116–118, 120, 164, 171, 182; booster club 7; farm system 93–94; pitching squad 62; pitching statistics, 1947 81; statistics, 1948 87
St. Louis Cardinals 7, 9–10, 12, 18–19, 29–30, 47, 51, 55, 60–61, 69–70, 72, 77, 82, 91–92, 100, 102, 106, 108, 111–113, 115, 125, 135, 140, 142, 147, 160, 162, 171, 175–176, 178–179, 182
St. Louis Chamber of Commerce 95
St. Louis Maternity Hospital 144
St. Louis Post-Dispatch 30, 92, 137, 175
St. Louis *Star Times* 38
St. Louis Terriers 9–10
St. Louis University 17, 96
San Antonio Missions 30, 31, 41, 43, 44, 50, 68, 74, 75, 82, 90, 114
San Diego Padres (Pacific Coast League) 169
San Francisco Giants 144, 152–153, 169, 179
Sanders, Ray 60–61
Sanford, Fred 50, 117
Sanford, Jack 54
Sarasota, FL 158
Saucier, Frank 101, 102, 107
Save the Minor Leagues Committee 126
Sawyer, Charles 152
Sax, Sam **23**
Schacht, Al 137
Schacht, Sidney 96
Schaffer, Rudie 105, 113, 115, 175
Schalk, Ray 34, 35
Schmees, George 110
Schmidt, Bob 144
Schoendiest, Red 147
Schulte, Leonard 65, 71
Sears, Kenny 72
Seattle Pilots 174–175
Sedalia, MO 50
Seghi, Phil 158, 166
Sewell, Joe 178
Sewell, Luke 43, 44, 48, 49, 50, 53, 54, 56, 58, 59, 65, 67–70, 73, 74
Shaughnessy, Frank 99
Shea, William 135
Shea Stadium 168
Sherdel, Bill 18
Shirley, Tex 58
Shore, Ray 161
Short, Ed 156
Short, Red 174
Shotton, Burt 14
Shriver, Pam 184
Siebert, Dick 68
Siebert, Norman "Sunny" 72
Sievers, Roy 92–**93**, 96, 98
Silvera, Charley 120
Simpson, Dick 165
Sisler, Dave 7, 150, 155
Sisler, Dick 7, 157, 160–**161**, 162–163
Sisler, George 7, 16
Sisson, Harry M. 136

224 Index

Skowran, Bill 125, 147
Slapnicka, C.C. 48
Smith, Lou 142
Solomon, Sid, Jr. 104–105
Soriano, Dewey 174
Soriano, Max 174
Southern Association 64
Spahn, Warren 148
Spectrum 7 Energy Co. 183
Spence, Stan 60, 91
Spindel, Harold 37
The Sporting News 29, 39, 50, 61, 69, 77, 102, 113, 132, 136, 141, 143, 145, 147, 149–150, 155, 160, 175
Sportsman's Park 9, 11, 15, 28–29, 35, 40, 41, 44, 50, 52, 57, 58, *63*, 66, 67, 75, 82, 86, 95, 101, 108, *129*, 172
spring training: (1942) 50; (1943) 51–52, *53*; (1945) 63; (1946) 70; (1947) 75; (1964) 158
Springfield IL 55, 59
Staab, Charles 167
Stack, Ed 178–179
Stadium Steering Committee 167
Starr, Dick 88, 96
Stein Bros. & Boyce 117
Steinberg, Mark 103
Stengel,Casey 118, 122. 124, 146
Stephens, Vernon 42, 43, 49, 51, 55, 57, 59, 61, 67, 70–72, 76, 82, 118
Stevens, Chuck 43
Stia, Charley 39
Stifel, Otto 9
Stirnweiss, George "Snuffy" 98, 101
Stock, Milton 14
Stocksick, Bill 9
Stocksick's Stadium 175
Stockton, J. Roy 21, 30–31, 35, 38, 42, 51, 86, 92, 97, 98, 114
Stoneham, Horace 126
Strange, Alan 39
Street, Gabby 33, 34, 76
Sturdivant, Tom 122, 125
Sullivan, Billy 36
Sundra, Steve 73
Swift, Bob 39, 42, 43

Taft, Dudley 183
Taylor, Vernon 96
Taylor, Zack 74, 82, 84, 86, 87, 89, 91, 94, 97, 98, 99, 100, 101, 105, 107, 109
Tebbetts, Birdie 145
television 111
Temple, Johnny 155
Terry, Ralph 121
Tettlebach, Dick 124
Texas League 30, 68, 102

Texas Rangers 7, 183
Thevonow, Tommy 19
Thomas, Leo 98, 110
Thomas, Roy 178
Thompson, Henry "Hank" 78–*80*
Three-I League 30, 68
Throneberry, Marv 121
TLC Beatrice International Holdings, Inc. 184
Tobin, John 90, 94, 100
Tolan, Bobby 172
Tolson, Harold 37
Toledo Mud Hens 35, 52, 54, 55, 59, 73, 74, 76, 84
Toomey, James M. 92
Toporcer, George 19
Topping, Dan 117–*118*
Tracy, Dr. David, pschologist 97, 98
Trautman, George 29, 127–128, 133
Tri-State League 116
Trucks, Virgil 113
Turley, Bob 114, 118, 120
Turner, Jim 157, 161

uniform player contract 153
United Press International (UPI) 147, 167
University of Missouri Journalism School 95

Van Weise, Louis B. 27
Veeck, Bill 100, 102, 104–*105*, 106–108, 110–116, 150, 176–177, 179–180
Vitt, Oscar 44

Wagner, Mayor Robert 135
Wahl, Kermit 103
Walker, Bill 20
Walkup, Jim 37
Walsingham, Bill 112
Walthe, Herbert W. 105
Washington Post 117
Washington Senators 27, 29, 44, 47, 51, 53–54, 59, 60, 68, 71, 87, 92, 108, 112, 123, 150, 173
Washington University (St. Louis) 13, 17
Webb, Del *118*, 119
Weiss, George *118*–119, 121–122, 124, 143, 180
Western League 30, 116
White, Albert "Fuzz" 69
Wiesler, Bob 124
Wilks, Ted 61
Williams, Edward Bennett 184
Williams, Joe 20
Williams, Ted 73
Willier, Robert A. and Associates 95
Wilson, Hack 178
Wilson, Jimmy 34, 82, 125

Index

Wilson, Johnny 125
Winegarner, Ralph 82, 94, 100
Witchita, KS 116
Witte, Jerry 76
Wood, Ken 108
World Hockey Association 175, 183
World Series: 1926 18; (1934) 20; (1942) 50; (1944) 60–61; (1955) 122; (1956) 125–126; (1961) 146–147; (1966) 169; (2011) *185*
World War I 12

World War II 65
Wright, Tom 108
Wrigley, Philip K. 45

Yale University 182, 185
Yankee Stadium 19, 97
Young, Bobby 110

Zarilla, Al 52, 57, 91, 95
Zoldak, Sam 70
Zuckert, Eugene M. 163

www.ingramcontent.com/pod-product-compliance
Ingram Content Group UK Ltd.
Pitfield, Milton Keynes, MK11 3LW, UK
UKHW041950140426
5217IPUK00014B/737